Origins of psychopathology

Origins of psychopathology

Problems in research and public policy

Edited by

DAVID F. RICKS
University of Cincinnati

BARBARA S. DOHRENWEND
Columbia University

CAMBRIDGE UNIVERSITY PRESS
Cambridge
London   New York   New Rochelle
Melbourne   Sydney

Published by the Press Syndicate of the University of Cambridge
The Pitt Building, Trumpington Street, Cambridge CB2 1RP
32 East 57th Street, New York, NY 10022, USA
296 Beaconsfield Parade, Middle Park, Melbourne 3206, Australia

First published in 1983

Printed in the United States of America

Library of Congress Cataloging in Publication Data

Main entry under title:

Origins of psychopathology.

Includes index.

1. Mental illness – Etiology. 2. Psychiatric research.
2. Mental health policy. I. Ricks, David F.
II. Dohrenwend, Barbara Snell. [DNLM: 1. Confidentiality – Congresses. 2. Longitudinal studies – Congresses. 3. Mental disorders – Etiology – Congresses.
4. Psychopathology – Congresses. 5. Public policy – Congresses. WM 100 0696 1983]
RC454.4.074 1983 616.89′071 82–14638
ISBN 0 521 25298 9

Contents

Contributors

Stanley J. Aronoff
Ohio State Senate

Haroutun M. Babigian
Department of Psychiatry
University of Rochester School of Medicine and Dentistry

John M. de Figueiredo
Department of Psychiatry
Yale University

Joyce B. DeVoge
Social Skills Development Program
Department of Health
City of Cincinnati

Barbara S. Dohrenwend
Division of Sociomedical Sciences
School of Public Health
Columbia University

Bruce P. Dohrenwend
Social Psychiatry Research Unit
Columbia University

Margaret E. Ensminger
Department of Psychiatry
Pritzker School of Medicine
University of Chicago

L. Erlenmeyer-Kimling
New York State Psychiatric Institute

Joanne C. Gersten
Division of Behavioral Health Services
Arizona Department of Health Services

Goldine C. Gleser
Department of Psychiatry
College of Medicine
University of Cincinnati

Bonnie L. Green
Department of Psychiatry
College of Medicine
University of Cincinnati

Sheppard G. Kellam
Department of Psychiatry
Pritzker School of Medicine
University of Chicago

Daniel S. Kirschenbaum
Department of Psychology
University of Wisconsin

Raymond A. Knight
Department of Psychology
Brandeis University

Maria Kovacs
Department of Psychiatry
University of Pittsburgh School of Medicine

Thomas S. Langner
Division of Epidemiology
School of Public Health
Columbia University

JoAnne L. Pedro-Carroll
Department of Psychology
University of Rochester

David F. Ricks
Department of Psychology
University of Cincinnati

Lee N. Robins
Department of Psychiatry
School of Medicine
Washington University, St. Louis

James D. Roff
Department of Psychology
Eastern Michigan University

Carmi Schooler
Laboratory of Socio-Environmental Studies
National Institute of Mental Health

Ora Simcha-Fagan
Division of Epidemiology
School of Public Health
Columbia University

Marlene B. Simon
Department of Psychiatry
University of Chicago

Thomas A. Wills
Division of Epidemiology
School of Public Health
Columbia University

Lyman C. Wynne
Department of Psychiatry
University of Rochester School of Medicine and Dentistry

Preface

Scientists have often chosen to work quietly on problems of surpassing interest to themselves and a few colleagues, only to find that their discoveries have embroiled them in public controversy and legal confrontation. Life history researchers in psychopathology have been working for several years on the genetic, childhood, and social roots of such disorders as depression, alcoholism, and schizophrenia. At times in the past they wondered why their work, which had very powerful implications for early identification of children likely to have trouble, and often for prevention of this trouble, was so frequently ignored by practicing clinicians and by the public that paid for the research. In the last 5 or 6 years, life history research has had a new visibility. But its newfound prominence is not without problems. Accordingly, this book, and the conference that preceded it, were planned around some issues of public policy as well as questions of research strategy, data analysis, and clinical applications of our findings.

Versions of all of the chapters in the book were given as papers at the seventh (1978) conference of the Society for Life History Research in Psychopathology, a group whose acronym, SHLRP, suggests a certain catholicity about accepting any and all information that may come its way. The society is composed of psychiatrists, sociologists, psychologists, and others brought together by a common interest in longitudinal research into the origins and course of psychopathology. As Robert Cancro said at an earlier meeting of this group, longitudinal research is not the only way to decipher human psychopathology, but among several valid approaches, it is "the most powerful and appropriate way to study, conceptualize, and influence" the course of disturbed development. The group meets together because all of its members have a commitment to accepting the challenges of longitudinal research. Among these are search for early vulnerabilities that may not be fully manifested for many years, an attempt to find order within the complexities of real lives in everyday environments, and the need to develop conceptual, research design, and statistical models adequate to describe people who are both influenced by the world around them and able to make choices and influence that world in turn. This book deals with all of these issues as well as our new problems of social impact.

Public interest in life history research might be dated, if it were not for the unfortunate letters involved, BS and AS, Before Sheehy and After Sheehy. When Gail Sheehy published *Passages*, based largely on work that Daniel Levinson and George Vaillant had earlier reported to SHLRP, over a million readers became aware of life span development, and "male midlife crisis" became enough a part of everyday life to find instant recognition in cartoons and stories. The later publications of more scholarly works, such as *Seasons of a Man's Life*, by Levinson and others, and Vaillant's *Adaptation to Life*, gave more substance to this popularity. We can now assume some public understanding and acceptance of the ideas of life span development. Newer textbooks in psychopathology, such as Allman and Jaffe's *Psychopathology in the Life Cycle*, Neale and Oltmann's *Schizophrenia*, and especially White and Watt's *The Abnormal Personality*, have a life span orientation.

While life history research was developing, but largely independent from it, a movement dedicated to early intervention in the family, school, and community came into being. When Gerald Klerman, a major contributor to the earlier meetings of this group, became the administrator of the National Institute of Mental Health, he made prevention a major focus of the work of that agency, raising it to the level of the old trinity of service, research, and education. As a result, at least some NIMH guidelines for research and training now recognize the importance of development over the course of life, and funding groups are not so worried as they once were when asked to support longitudinal research. The recent NIMH publication *Primary Prevention: An Idea Whose Time Has Come* provides many examples of the practical implementation of ideas that originated in life history oriented research.

The first section of the book is devoted to the core topic in life history research in psychopathology, the search for early antecedents of later difficulty. In the first chapter, Nikki Erlenmeyer-Kimling, working with a sample of children who are at high risk for schizophrenia because one or both of their parents are schizophrenic, describes methods for early assessment of vulnerability to schizophrenia. Then Sheppard Kellam and his colleagues show how adolescent drug use can be predicted from characteristics of the child and his family that are evident by first grade. Research in psychopathology often makes an unexamined assumption similar to the assumption that researchers in race relations have called the "deficit model," that is, that the child who will later be hospitalized or jailed or have some other undesirable outcome has some sort of deficit. A particularly compelling aspect of the research reported in this chapter is that the children who show the most maturity and intellectual promise are those *most* likely later to use certain drugs in the particular community studied, near the University of Chicago. In the next chapter Thomas Langner and his team probe methods for separating the relative power of the early environment and the child's own early behavior as predictors of later behavior.

Life history research has by now largely discredited the old assumption that adult psychopathology could be traced to particular traumatic events in infancy and childhood. In the paper that was particularly influential in demolishing these models, Herbert Birch described methods for assessing degrees of response to the trauma of starvation, as well as methods for measuring recovery, and he argued that because we can measure recovery, we have to get away from simplistic event models and work on more complex but more useful developmental models. In this book we include two chapters that make this attempt. In the first, Green and Gleser describe a traumatic event, but also take into account the social matrix disrupted by this event, differential effects on men and women over time, and the effects of having a coping role or a passive role. The research had real life consequences – the settlement of a large legal case partly on the basis of psychological damage. In the second chapter in this section, Dohrenwend and de Figueiredo describe how early life events may establish a specific vulnerability to similar events in adult life.

The third section of the book is the most technical and difficult. It may be the most important for the future of life history research, because its chapters deal with crucial new developments in the measurement of psychopathology and in analysis of data gathered in complex systems over long periods of time. In the first chapter here, Maria Kovacs describes a new discovery in psychopathology in the last few years, one in which she has had a major role. This is simply that depression is not an adult monopoly, that substantial numbers of children are depressed, and that the degree to which they are depressed can be measured by methods that she has developed.

In the second chapter of this part, Knight and Roff use cross-lagged panel analysis and path analysis to examine childhood and young adult predictors of long-term schizophrenic outcomes. Many people had believed, partly because of an extensive review article on antecedents of schizophrenia for which one of the authors of this book (David F. Ricks) must bear some responsibility, that emotional characteristics of children were not very useful predictors of long-term outcomes. Now, with better measurement methods and with more sophisticated handling of the data, Knight and Roff show that early emotional characteristics are indeed good predictors. The third chapter of this section, the most complex in the volume, is Schooler's methodological exploration of the long-term reciprocal effects of work on personality and of personality on work. Jerome Myers and others have shown many of the ways in which work is important for the study of psychopathology – for instance, that ability to get and hold a job is the best predictor that an ex-patient can avoid rehospitalization. So work is of interest in its own right, as is personality. But the most important lesson of this chapter for research in psychopathology is the demonstration that interactions over time, between persons and environments, can be measured precisely and can be made the basis for powerful predictions.

If life history researchers were not having any impact, and if nobody knew what we were doing, there might be no pressing need to examine legal or ethical issues raised by our work. One can promote cannibalism among planaria without raising a legislative eyebrow. But we are concerned with schizophrenia, depression, drug usage, and so on. For our data to have value they have to be gathered at different points in the life cycle, and usually the more detailed and comprehensive the data are, the more value they have. So we poke into private lives, and we put the results into files and computers. What are we to do when a governmental agency comes to us and demands our information about a fellow citizen? Issues of confidentiality, privacy, and computer security can become as crucial to us as to a Swiss banker. Accordingly, the fourth section of the book is devoted to issues of confidentiality in medical and other records, in research that deals with extremely sensitive data and stores records of private relationships and personal tragedies for long periods of time. Lee Robins, a sociologist who has worked with public records and private interviews of people with histories of drug addiction, in addition to studying childhood histories and adult outcomes of deviant children, examines the implications for research of recent recommendations for the protection of citizen privacy. Haroutun Babigian, a psychiatrist who developed the nation's most comprehensive and systematic psychiatric data register, describes the protections for individuals built into that system. Finally, Stanley Aronoff, a lawyer and legislator with special expertise in the law of privacy, examines issues of confidentiality, access, and public policy relevant to life history research.

The last section of the book is devoted to outcomes of life history research, the question of what we learn from all of this work and what we can do with what we have learned. In the first chapter here, Lyman Wynne offers some reflections based on a lifetime of research on families and psychopathology, reflections that lead to some troubling thoughts about the emotional involvements and emotional projections of the investigators. In the other chapter of this part, Daniel Kirschenbaum and colleagues describe a successful attempt to apply what we now know about the promotion of social and academic skills to development of an early intervention program in the schools.

Donald Langsley played a major role in planning this book and the conference that preceded it. We are also grateful to the conference coordinator, Carolyn Rafales, to Daniel Ransahoff, and to James Brush and the other graduate students who helped us with registration, scheduling, and recording of our proceedings. This book is theirs as well as ours.

May 1982

D. F. R.
B. S. D.

On June 28, 1982, Barbara Dohrenwend died. She had been involved in every phase of this book from initial plans to final editing. The book is part of what Barbara left the world.

D. F. R.

Part I

Early predictors of later health and psychopathology

1 A prelude to preventive intervention: early assessment of vulnerability to schizophrenia

L. Erlenmeyer-Kimling

Primary prevention is becoming one of the focal points of the field of mental health. Prevention, rather than treatment and repair, is likely to be the chief mental health objective of the 1980s. Unfortunately, it is a thrust that may be doomed to failure unless sharp distinctions are made at the outset between the efforts that are needed to improve mental health in a general way and those that are needed to prevent specific disorders. There are many laudable and frequently mentioned steps that can be taken toward improving public physical and mental health. Some of them can be taken right away, and many of them require little or no research. But global correctives to social woes will not prevent schizophrenia, certain forms of affective disorder, or many other disabling conditions. These require the slow piecing together of puzzles and the provision of specific remedies that relate to the etiology of the disorder.

High-risk research in schizophrenia or in other mental disorders serves as at least one kind of prelude to preventive intervention, because such research addresses itself to the three basic questions that must be answered before intervention is possible – what to prevent, how to prevent it, and in whom to try to do so. Until the answers are forthcoming, primary prevention of the mental illnesses will remain a dream.

Background to high-risk research

Pearson and Kley (1957) first outlined the general model for high-risk research in an article in the *Psychological Bulletin*. They proposed that individuals who are at high statistical risk for schizophrenia should be

This work was supported in part by grant MH 19560 from the U.S. Public Health Service and by the Department of Mental Hygiene of the state of New York. The author wishes to acknowledge, with appreciation, the large group of collaborators, consultants, and research staff who have made the study possible. Thanks are due also to the directors and staff of the psychiatric facilities that have assisted in the research.

studied prospectively, preferably from infancy. The high-risk approach was urged because it had become clear that retrospective studies of people who had already had a schizophrenic episode could not yield uncontaminated data on variables that were thought to be of etiological significance. Furthermore, it had become obvious that studies of schizophrenic patients do not allow the separation of disturbances in functioning into those that are the result of the illness and those that are basic to and antecedent to the development of disordered behavior.

Pearson and Kley suggested that the children of schizophrenic parents, especially those with two affected parents, were the population of choice for high-risk investigations, as earlier genetic studies had shown high empirical risks in such children (about 12% when one parent is schizophrenic, about 36%–40% when both parents are schizophrenic). Whether the empirical risks were interpreted as an indication that genetic factors were involved or as the outcome of a schizophrenogenic environment, there could be no quarrel with the fact that the children of schizophrenic parents represented a population at unusually high statistical risk. Of course, the later adoption studies by Heston (1966) and by Kety, Rosenthal, Wender, and colleagues (Kety et al., 1968; Rosenthal et al., 1968; Wender et al., 1974) have lent strong support to the hypothesis that genetic components are important in schizophrenia and that the offspring of schizophrenic parents are at high risk even when they are reared away from their schizophrenic parents or other biological relatives. These studies, along with other evidence that has accumulated since Pearson and Kley's article appeared, have solidified the concept of genetic and environmental interaction as the basis for schizophrenia.

At first thought, it might be supposed that the findings pointing to genetic involvement in schizophrenia are counterindications for high-risk research. After all, it would be unreasonable to make a point of identifying vulnerable children unless there existed a possibility of ultimately being able to prevent the development of the disorder. One of the most common misconceptions about disorders with a heritable basis, however, is that they cannot be prevented from manifesting themselves in predisposed individuals. The tendency is to equate genetic theories about physical or mental conditions, or about other aspects of behavior, with the once-popular belief that the entire course of a human life was preordained by fate. Thus either genetic hypotheses and the findings of genetic research have had to be defensively rejected or their acceptance has been thought to signal the prediction of inevitable doom. Such a choice is unnecessary, however. A number of acknowledgedly hereditary conditions can be treated, or their symptom manifestations prevented. The list is growing and can be expected to be augmented appreciably through future research (Erlenmeyer-Kimling, 1977). High-risk studies may help to add schizophrenia to the list of preventable disorders with genetic roots.

The New York study

Description

High-risk research on schizophrenia has burgeoned since the model was proposed in 1957 and especially since 1971, when our study was started in the New York City metropolitan area. The New York study is concerned with developmental characteristics of high-risk children and calls for longitudinal assessments of these children and of low-risk comparison subjects over a period of several years. A first sample (Sample A) of high-risk and comparison subjects has been followed continuously since 1971, and a second sample (Sample B) is now being collected. This report will deal with Sample A only. The study was described in greater detail in Erlenmeyer-Kimling (1975).

Sample A consists of 205 "study-children" who were between the ages of 7 and 12 years at the time of first examination and who are now between the ages of 14 and 19. They are 80 high-risk children and 125 low-risk children. Of the high-risk children, 44 have a schizophrenic mother, 23 have a schizophrenic father, and 13 have two schizophrenic parents. (Group labels are S-1 for a single schizophrenic parent and S-2 for two schizophrenic parents.) The low-risk comparison subjects are 25 children with a parent who has another psychiatric disorder (group C-P) and 100 children whose parents had never received psychiatric treatment at least up to the time of intake into the study (group C-N). In addition to the extensive data collected on the study-children, developmental data and follow-up histories have been gathered for their 122 older and younger siblings.

In both samples, all families are white and English-speaking, with both parents present at the time of intake so that both biological parents can be examined. An attempt has been made to recruit families with at least two children in the target age range of 7–12 years to make possible a number of comparisons between siblings with respect to behavioral and biological variables, as well as micro-environmental variables. Thus it may be possible to determine the characteristics that distinguish children who break down later on from their siblings who are raised in the same home but remain healthy.

Families with a mentally ill parent or parents were ascertained for both samples by screening all consecutive admissions at several state psychiatric centers in the New York metropolitan area. Patients with diagnoses of chronic alcoholism, drug addiction, brain trauma, or psychoses of toxic origin were excluded. As an initial diagnostic evaluation, records of patients who passed the screening criteria were reviewed independently by two psychiatrists in our group (John D. Rainer and Michael Stone) after all references to hospital diagnoses and medications had been removed from the records. Each of the reviewers assigned a diagnosis based on the record materials, completed a symptom checklist, and scored the 100-point Global Assessment Scale (Endicott et al., 1976) assessing the severity of functional impairment. Only those cases in which there was full diagnostic agreement were retained for the study. This procedure has been applied in Sample A and is being applied in Sample B.

A second diagnostic evaluation is being obtained by interviews with the patients using the SADS-L (Spitzer & Endicott, 1978). Further evaluations will take into account all of the accumulated material on each patient, including the Minnesota Multiphasic Personality Inventory (MMPI), which is administered during a home visit.

In Sample A, the normal comparison (C-N) group was obtained with the cooperation of two large school systems that agreed to send our letter asking for participants to families that met the screening criteria described (i.e., white, English-speaking, intact family, two or more 7–12-year-old children). The obvious disadvantage was that the C-N group was a strictly volunteer group. For Sample B, the latter problem has been avoided by enlisting a population sampling firm to conduct a survey for the purpose of obtaining demographic information on a large number of families, a group that forms a pool from which matches to our Sample B high-risk subjects can be drawn; matching is based on the family's socioeconomic level and the age and sex of the children. In both Samples A and B, families were excluded from the C-N group if either parent was found to have had psychiatric treatment.

Procedures

Sample A was reexamined approximately 2 years after the first examination and is now being seen for a third time. Over the course of the study, telephone contacts have been maintained at 3- to 6-month intervals to permit us to keep up-to-date about the children, the family, and events in their lives. School record data and teachers' evaluations of the Sample A subjects are collected in a collaborative study with Norman Watt of the University of Denver.

Table 1.1. *Laboratory procedures administered to Sample A in the first round of testing (1971–1972)*

Anthropometric measures and photographs
Cognitive and attentional measures
Wechsler Intelligence Scale for Children
Continuous Performance Test
(playing card, projector version)
Attention Span Task
Neurological and motoric measures
Neurological examination
Lincoln Oseretsky Test of Motor Impairment
Psychophysiology
Conditioning paradigm, skin conductance responses
Clinical and social measures
Structured videotaped interview

Each round of examinations consists of a home visit and a full day of testing the children in our laboratory. In the home visit, a structured interview is administered to the well parent (or the more intact of the two parents if both are schizophrenic, or a randomly chosen parent in the C-N group). The initial interview covered family histories on both parents and developmental histories (including pregnancy and birth histories, early developmental milestones, physical health, school and peer relationships, and behavior) on each child in the family. Subsequent interviews are concerned with changes in the family and with the further development of the children. The parent who is not given the structured interview receives a shorter interview concerning his or her perceptions of the children. In addition, each parent is administered the MMPI and a clinical interview that can be rated for global psychopathology, using the 100-point Global Assessment Scale (Endicott et al., 1976). An interview is also conducted with each study-child separately, and various psychological tests, including the Bender-Gestalt and a figure-drawing test, are administered.

Some of the laboratory measures have been changed over the course of the study, some have been dropped, and others have been added, as it was discovered that certain procedures were not informative or that new and potentially more promising measures were available. Table 1.1 shows the measures that were administered in the first laboratory visit

Table 1.2. *Current laboratory procedures for Sample A, third round, and Sample B, first round*

	Administered to
Anthropometric measures and photographs	All ages
Cognitive and attentional measures	
Wechsler Intelligence Scale for Children – Revised	Ages 7–16
Wechsler Intelligence Scale for Adults	Ages 16+
Wisconsin Card Sorting Test	Ages 13+
Short-term memory lag test	Ages 13+
Goldman-Fristoe-Woodcock Auditory Distraction Test	All ages
Neurological, motoric, and laterality measures	
Neurological examination	Ages 7–12
Lincoln Oseretsky Test of Motor Impairment	Ages 7–12
Purdue Pegboard	Ages 7–12
Dichotic Listening Test	All ages
Psychophysiology	
Auditory event–related potentials	Ages 10+
Visual event–related potentials	Ages 10+
Vigilance Task	All ages
Continuous Performance Test (digit, computerized version)	All ages
Stimulus Level Intensity Gradients	Ages 10+
Skin conductance and heart rate	Ages 10+
Auditory absolute threshold	Ages 10+
Auditory aversion threshold	Ages 10+
Clinical and social measures	
Psychiatric interview (videotaped)	All ages
Friendship and intimacy interview	All ages

Note: Ages of Sample A in the third round are 13+ years; ages of Sample B are 7–12 years.

of Sample A and that form the basis for most of this report. Table 1.2 lists the measures that are currently being administered to Sample A, in the third round of testing, and to Sample B. Important additions are the expansion of the cognitive and information-processing measures; a videotaped psychiatric interview that was developed for this project by Clarice Kestenbaum (St. Luke's Hospital) and Hector Bird (Babies Hospital, Columbia Presbyterian); the much increased psychophysiology battery, which now includes a number of measures of cortical evoked-response potentials; and a friendship and intimacy interview adapted for the project by Dolores Kreisman (New York State Psychiatric Institute) from her earlier retrospective study of adolescent friendship patterns reported by adult schizophrenics.

Most of the current battery will be administered again to Sample A in its fourth and final visit and to Sample B in its second visit.

Some early laboratory results

The results of a Continuous Performance Test (CPT) were among the most interesting for the first round of testing. The CPT was modified from a task used by Kornetsky and Mirsky (1966) to differentiate schizophrenic patients from normals and from patients with other psychiatric disorders. The modification of the CPT in the first round of testing used slides of playing cards as stimuli, presented by a carousel projector at the rate of 1.4 cycles/sec. The subject was instructed to press a key as rapidly as possible when a slide was identical, in playing card number and suit, to the one immediately preceding it. (See Cornblatt, 1978; Erlenmeyer-Kimling, 1975; Rutschmann, Cornblatt, & Erlenmeyer-Kimling, 1977, for complete descriptions and data analyses.) Four blocks of 80 slides each were presented without distraction, and four blocks of 80 slides each were presented with distraction, which consisted of a tape-recorded female voice reciting digits at varying rates of presentation. The distraction tape was played into the subject's earphones, which were worn throughout the CPT session.

There were 40 opportunities to make a correct response, or "hit," in each condition (distraction and no distraction). High-risk subjects made significantly fewer hits and significantly more irrelevant responses in each condition than did the comparison subjects. A signal-detection analysis (Rutschmann et al., 1977) showed a significantly smaller *d'* for the high-risk subjects, indicating that they have less sensitivity or less ability to discriminate the stimuli than do the comparison subjects. Moreover, distraction had a greater effect on the high-risk subjects, leading to a larger decline in performance from the distraction to the no-distraction condition than was experienced by the comparison subjects. Reaction time (the latency of the keypress response) did not differ between the high-risk and low-risk subjects – a surprising discovery in view of the rather consistent finding that schizophrenic patients show slower reaction times than normal adults – and we are therefore studying our subjects' reaction times in some other, possibly more pressured, situations.

Except for the failure to show differences in reaction time, the CPT data are in accord with our expectations: High-risk subjects do less well on a task that demands sustained attention, they are especially unable to ignore irrelevant stimuli, and they are more disturbed by external distraction than are the comparison subjects.

Another attentional measure administered in the first round of testing was an auditory attention-span task modified from a procedure reported by Hawks and Robinson (1971) in a study of schizophrenic patients. In the adaptation for our project, sequences of either three or five letters were recited at either a fast or a slow rate of presentation (1 letter/sec or 1 letter/1.5 sec) in a tape recording played into the subject's earphones. The subject was instructed to recall each sequence immediately following its presentation. Twenty-four trials, counterbalanced for rate of presentation and sequence length, were presented without distraction, and another 24 trials, similarly counterbalanced, were presented with distraction. Distraction consisted of a male voice reciting letters in the intervals between the target letters, which were presented in a female voice. Subjects were instructed to ignore the male voice.

The attention-span task was generally less effective than the CPT in discriminating between high-risk and comparison subjects (Erlenmeyer-Kimling & Cornblatt, 1978). Only on the five-letter sequences presented at the fast rate did the high-risk children perform significantly more poorly than the comparison subjects, and then only in the no-distraction condition. Distraction disorganized performance in both groups to about the same degree.

Analyses combining the CPT and the attention-span task used eight performance indexes from the two measures (viz., in the CPT, errors of omission, "false alarms," other irrelevant errors – each of these recorded separately for the no-distraction and the distraction conditions – and in the attention-span task, trials missed on the five-letter sequences in both the no-distraction and the distraction conditions). Standardized scores, controlling for age, were obtained for the C-N groups on each of the indexes, and the 5% of C-N subjects who performed most poorly on a given index were identified. Subjects in the high-risk group whose standardized scores were at least as extreme (in the direction of poor performance) were then located. Whereas about 72% of the C-N subjects did not fall into the extreme 5% of the distribution for their group on any index, this was true for only about 40% of the high-risk subjects. In the C-N group, 4% of the subjects had extreme scores on three indexes, and none were extreme scorers on more than three indexes. By contrast, 19% of the high-risk subjects had extreme scores on three or more indexes. Thus the two attentional measures together flag a significant number of the high-risk children as showing a degree of performance impairment not seen in the normal comparison subjects.

Strong differences between high-risk and comparison subjects also appeared on several other measures in the first battery of tests. One of these is the Bender-Gestalt test scored as a test of neuropsychological development (Koppitz, 1963). A second is the Draw-a-Person test, which is scored to yield both a developmental score and a score for special signs of deviation. Both the Bender-Gestalt and the Draw-a-Person tests suggested a developmental lag in the high-risk subjects, reminiscent of Lauretta Bender's observations of schizophrenic children (Bender & Freedman, 1952) and Barbara Fish's reports on children of schizophrenic mothers (Fish, 1975). Another measure, the Lincoln-Oseretsky Test of Motor Impairment, appeared at first analysis to discriminate very well between the high-risk and the comparison subjects. The test taps gross and fine motor coordination, and the motor coordination of the high-risk subjects appeared to be much poorer than that of the comparison subjects. However, when a forced stepwise multiple regression analysis was applied to control for age, sex, and IQ effects on each of the tests, the group difference on the Lincoln-Oseretsky disappeared, whereas the group differences on the other measures remained. At present, therefore, we have to reserve judgment about the usefulness of the motor-coordination tasks in discriminating between high-risk and low-risk subjects.

Although group differences are interesting, a major goal of the study is to determine whether it is possible to identify individual subjects who are deviant on several of these measures. Therefore, a linear discriminant function analysis was performed using five indexes – the Bender-Gestalt developmental score, the developmental and special scores from the Draw-a-Person test, the number of irrelevant responses on the CPT, and the difference between the number of correct responses under distraction and the number under no distraction on the CPT. These indexes were selected because differences between the S-1 group and C-N group subjects on them remained after age, sex, and IQ effects were partialed out. The purpose of the linear discriminant function analysis is, first, to show how the groups differ on the several indexes taken all together and, second, to identify those subjects who have deviant composite scores.

Figure 1.1 shows the distributions of the discriminant scores for the S-1 subjects and the C-N subjects; the other two groups are too small to plot effectively. The negative discriminant scores indicate good performance on the composite of the five indexes, and positive scores here indicate poorer performance. As can be seen, the distribution for the C-N group is skewed toward negative scores – or good performance – whereas the distribution of the S-1 group is slightly skewed toward positive scores – or poorer performance – and has a long tail of poorly performing individuals.

To an extent, a difference between the discriminant score distribution

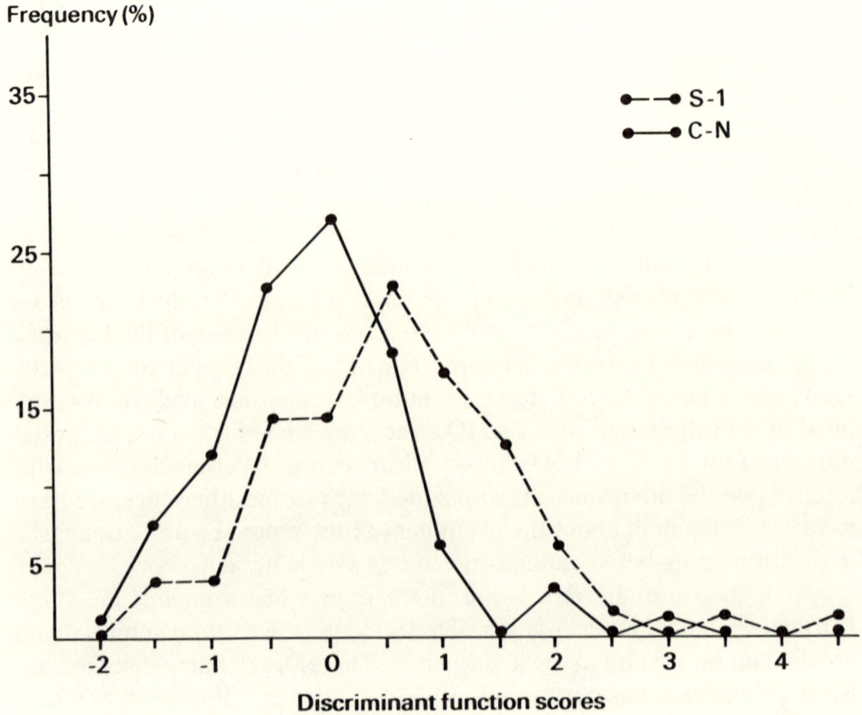

Figure 1.1. Distributions of discriminant function scores for S-1 and C-N. Negative scores indicate good performance; positive scores indicate poor performance.

of the normal comparison group and the group with one schizophrenic parent is to be expected, because the five indexes that entered into the analysis were selected to maximize the differences between these two groups. However, the other two groups (S-2 and C-P) were not involved in the selection of the indexes, and therefore they provide an independent evaluation of the discriminant scores. Table 1.3 shows the means and standard deviations of the discriminant scores for each of the four groups. As can be seen, the S-1 and S-2 groups are very similar, each having positive mean scores indicating relatively poor performance. They also show a considerable amount of variability, as might be predicted in view of the fact that these groups are thought to be genetically heterogeneous for true risk. Interestingly, the C-P group looks like the normal comparison group, with negative mean scores and smaller standard deviations.

If "deviance" on the composite of the five cognitive indexes is defined as scores lying beyond the 95th percentile of the distribution for the C-

Table 1.3. *Discriminant score distributions for five cognitive indexes: Sample A, round 1, all groups*

	S-1 (N = 55)	C-N (N = 92)	C-P (N = 20)	S-2 (N = 12)
Mean	.455	−.275	−.301	.317
SD	1.114	.845	.699	1.108
No. above cutoff point[a]	16	6	1	3
No. below cutoff point	39	87	19	9
% above cutoff point	29	5	5	25

Notes: Complete test data on all cognitive indexes were not available for 26 children whose performances were unscorable on one of the measures. S-1 = group with one schizophrenic parent; C-N = group with normal parents; C-P = group with parents with other psychiatric disorders; S-2 = group with two schizophrenic parents.
[a] The cutoff point was defined as .91.

N group (a discriminant score of .91), 5% of the C-N subjects are arbitrarily classified as deviant. As Table 1.3 indicates, the scores of 5% of the C-P subjects also turn out to lie beyond the cutoff point, but the results for the children of one or two schizophrenic parents are much different: 29% of the S-1 subjects and 25% of the S-2 subjects have discriminant scores that lie beyond the cutoff point. Thus the discriminant function analysis on the set of indexes used here seems to be capable of identifying a subgroup of children who show a deviant composite performance. Substantially more of the children so identified belong to the S-1 and S-2 groups than to either comparison group; this encouraging finding suggests that at least some of the cognitive measures selected for study may be good predictors of later outcome.

Comparison of laboratory data and current clinical status

Although it is premature to try to make statements about the long-term relationship between early impairments in performance on the laboratory measures and the eventual clinical development of the subjects in this study, interim data on the current clinical status of the Sample A subjects can be compared with the discriminant score data on the cognitive indexes. To date, 7 subjects have been hospitalized or treated in an outpatient clinic for serious psychiatric disturbances. Ten others are also in treatment for moderately serious problems. Of these 17, 14 are children of one or two schizophrenic parents. There are another 19 subjects who may be experiencing emotional difficulties, according to our follow-up

Table 1.4. *Comparison of discriminant scores of cognitive measures and current clinical status*

Discriminant score	Clinical status: Deviant	Not deviant	Total	% clinically deviant
All subject groups[a]				
Deviant	7	15	22	32
Not deviant	10	128	138	7
Total	17	143	160	11
S-1 and S-2 (i.e., high risk subjects) only[b]				
Deviant	6	11	17	35
Not deviant	6	35	41	15
Total	12	46	58	21

[a] $\chi^2 = 9.62$ ($p < .01$).
[b] $\chi^2 = 1.99$ ($p < .15$).

contacts with the families, but who have received no treatment thus far. Because the current classification of these 19 subjects is uncertain, they have been removed from the contingency analyses that compare cognitive deviance and early clinical deviance as indexed by hospitalization or treatment for a psychiatric disorder.

In Table 1.4, it can be seen that 11% of the children in all subject groups combined show early clinical deviance. Among the subjects who have deviant scores on the discriminant function analysis of the cognitive data, however, 32% are classified as clinically deviant, whereas only 7% of the subjects with nondeviant discriminant scores show clinical deviance. The contingency relationship between cognitive and clinical deviance is significant at the .01 level.

Table 1.4 also contains a similar analysis of the cognitive and clinical data for the high-risk subjects, that is, S-1 and S-2 alone. Here, although a larger proportion of subjects is classified as clinically deviant – 21% as opposed to 11% for all subject groups combined – the χ^2 value referring to the relationship between the cognitive and clinical data fails to reach a significant level. Nevertheless, there is a trend in the right direction, with 35% of the subjects who have deviant cognitive scores also being clinically deviant. Clinical deviance is found among only 15% of the subjects whose cognitive scores are not deviant. Thus the results of the contingency analyses are at least modestly encouraging.

Comment

Whether the children who showed cognitive deviations on the composite of measures during their first laboratory visit between the ages of 7 and 12 years, and who are now displaying behavioral disturbances in adolescence, are the ones who are going to develop a clear schizophrenic illness remains to be seen with future follow-up. Perhaps there are some false positives to be culled out of the subgroup, and perhaps, if schizophrenia consists of more than one genetic condition, as the high-risk group is followed forward another subgroup with a different pattern of characteristics will emerge. Until the relationship between early patterns of deviance and later clinical patterns is more fully clarified, the development of intervention strategies that would effectively prevent the manifestation of schizophrenia – the long-range goal of this research – will have to wait for information about the specific characteristics and individuals that require intervention.

References

Bender, L., & Freedman, A. M. A study of the first three years in the maturation of schizophrenic children. *Quarterly Journal of Child Behavior*, 1952, *1*, 245–272.

Cornblatt, B. *Evidence of cognitive dysfunctions in children at high-risk for schizophrenia.* Unpublished doctoral dissertation, New School for Social Research, 1978.

Endicott, J., Spitzer, R. L., Fleiss, J. L., & Cohen, J. The Global Assessment Scale: A procedure for measuring overall severity of psychiatric disturbance. *Archives of General Psychiatry*, 1976, *33*, 766–771.

Erlenmeyer-Kimling, L. A prospective study of children at risk for schizophrenia: Methodological considerations and some preliminary findings. In R. Wirt, G. Winokur, & M. Roff (Eds.), *Life history research in psychopathology* (Vol. 4). Minneapolis: University of Minnesota Press, 1975.

Erlenmeyer-Kimling, L. Issues pertaining to prevention and intervention in genetic disorders affecting human behavior. In G. W. Albee & J. M. Joffe (Eds.), *Primary prevention in psychopathology*. Hanover, N.H.: University Press of New England, 1977.

Erlenmeyer-Kimling, L., & Cornblatt, B. Attentional measures in a study of children at high-risk for schizophrenia. In L. Wynne & R. Cromwell (Eds.), *The nature of schizophrenia*. New York: Wiley, 1978.

Fish, B. Biologic antecedents of psychosis in children. In D. X. Freedman (Ed.), *The biology of the major psychoses: A comparative analysis* (Association for Research in Nervous and Mental Disease, Vol. 54). New York: Raven Press, 1975.

Hawks, D. V., & Robinson, K. N. Information processing in schizophrenia: The effect of varying rate of presentation and introducing interference. *British Journal of Social Clinical Psychology*, 1971, *10*, 30.

Heston, L. L. Psychiatric disorders in foster home reared children of schizophrenic mothers. *British Journal of Psychiatry*, 1966, *112*, 819.

Kety, S. S., Rosenthal, D., Wender, P. H., & Schulsinger, F. The types and prevalence of mental illness in the biological and adoptive families of adopted schizophrenics. In D.

Rosenthal & S. S. Kety (Eds.), *The transmission of schizophrenia*. New York: Pergamon Press, 1968.

Koppitz, E. M. *The Bender Gestalt Test for young children*. New York: Grune & Stratton, 1963.

Kornetsky, C., & Mirsky, A. On certain psychopharmacological and physiological differences between schizophrenics and normal persons. *Psychopharmacologia* (Berlin), 1966, *8*, 309–318.

Pearson, J. S., & Kley, I. B. On the application of genetic expectancies as age-specific base rates in the study of human behavior disorders. *Psychological Bulletin*, 1957, *54*, 406–420.

Rosenthal, D., Wender, P. H., Kety, S. S., Schulsinger, F., Welner, J., & Østergaard, L. Schizophrenics' offspring reared in adoptive homes. In D. Rosenthal & S. S. Kety (Eds.), *The transmission of schizophrenia*. Oxford: Pergamon Press, 1968.

Rutschmann, J., Cornblatt, B., & Erlenmeyer-Kimling, L. Sustained attention in children at risk for schizophrenia. *Archives of General Psychiatry*, 1977, *34*, 571–575.

Spitzer, R. L., & Endicott, J. *Schedule for affective disorders and schizophrenia (SADS)* (3rd ed.). Unpublished manuscript, New York State Psychiatric Institute, New York, N.Y., 1978.

Wender, P. H., Rosenthal, D., Kety, S. S., Schulsinger, F., & Welner, J. Cross-fostering: A research strategy for clarifying the role of genetic and experiential factors in the etiology of schizophrenia. *Archives of General Psychiatry*, 1974, *30*, 121–128.

2 Antecedents in first grade of teenage substance use and psychological well-being: a ten-year community-wide prospective study

Sheppard G. Kellam, Marlene B. Simon, and Margaret E. Ensminger

Psychological well-being and use of drugs, alcohol, and cigarettes represent two different kinds of adolescent outcomes, the first internal psychological and the second social behavioral. This chapter is concerned with both their similar and their dissimilar antecedents, and with what these antecedents can tell us about causal mechanisms. This chapter concerns the discovery of theoretically meaningful sets of predictors. It does not include studies of how these predictors actually affect the two outcomes. Studies of mediating paths will be the next stage of our investigations and will be based on the results presented here.

The need for comparison of the antecedents and consequences of dif-

The authors wish to acknowledge the crucial contributions of the Woodlawn community, its families and children, and the board members who over the last 17 years have provided support and guidance for this research and service enterprise. Rose Bates, member of the Community Advisory Committee, has consulted closely with us in the preparation of this chapter. The teachers and principals of the Chicago public schools and the Chicago archdiocesan schools were essential contributors. The school district superintendents, Mr. Byron Minor, Mr. Jack Mitchell, and Dr. Donald Blythe, were extremely helpful. The assistance of Dr. Curtis Melnick, formerly associate superintendent, and Mr. George Flores, also of the Chicago Board of Education, was especially important.

We offer thanks to Jeannette Branch, formerly director of the South Side Youth Program, who has been involved in all aspects of the research and was responsible for the collection of the teacher ratings of social adaptational status when the children were in first grade. We are grateful for the assistance of several present and former colleagues at the Social Psychiatry Study Center – Hendricks Brown, Gary Russell, and Richard Perline – for their work in statistical analytic procedures. Professors George Bohrnstedt, Bruce Dohrenwend, and Barbara Dohrenwend contributed as consultants in measurement and interpretation, although final responsibility is solely the authors'. Joseph Brinley provided important editorial help.

These studies have been supported by the following grants: State of Illinois Department of Mental Health Grant Numbers 17-224 and 17-322; P.H.S. Grant Number MH-15760; a grant from the Maurice Falk Medical Fund; National Institute on Drug Abuse Grant Number DA-00787 (for the follow-up); State of Illinois Department of Mental Health Grant Number DMH 820-02 (for help in analyses of the follow-up data).

ferent psychological and behavioral phenomena has become gradually more apparent. M. L. Kohn (1976), in a recent review of research on social problems, criticizes this research because it has tended to focus on very specific issues. Substance use, juvenile delinquency, psychological disorders, and other outcomes have been studied in isolation from each other. Relatively little work has addressed the question of the similarities or differences in the antecedents and consequences of various social and psychological problems.

This chapter compares the antecedents of two adolescent outcomes, one psychological and one behavioral. We think that understanding the similarities and differences in the antecedents of different outcomes will help identify the processes and conditions important in the development of such outcomes, whether they be biological, social, or psychological.

We are concerned here with the early mental health and family characteristics of a community-wide population of 1966–1967 first graders whom we reassessed in 1975–1976 in a 10-year follow-up. In 1966–1967 we assessed the social adaptational status, psychological well-being, and family characteristics of all the first graders in Woodlawn, a poor, black neighborhood on the South Side of Chicago. In 1975–1976 we located and reassessed the families and the by then teenaged respondents. The reassessments of teenagers included the current mental health status of the population, aspects of family and social involvement, and use of drugs, alcohol, and cigarettes. Both in 1966–1967 (which we shall call Time 1 in this chapter) and in 1975–1976 (Time 2) we also interviewed the mothers or mother surrogates of our population.

The data in this study are prospective, a fact that may help distinguish causes of teenage conditions from effects. The prospective quality also means that the early data are not based on the teenager's own, or anyone else's, memories of the teenager's earlier status, memories that might be inaccurate or prejudiced by his or her current situation.

All the teenagers whom we are studying are of the same age, and all of them spent their first-grade year in the same community. We have discussed the advantages of community studies in Kellam et al. (1975). Age-specific, community-specific studies are necessary complements of broader studies of social and psychological function, such as those on national probability samples. Because community studies focus on defined populations, they may reveal rates of use of certain drugs, for example, that are higher or lower than rates in other communities or in less specific samples. Rutter, Tizard, and Whitmore (1970) also noted the necessity of community studies, saying that one cannot base national-scale planning on nationwide statistics, which do not reflect the differing needs of different areas. Mental health and illness, as well as substance use, have been shown to vary considerably from one community to another, and therefore warrant attention from studies within specific kinds of communities. Indeed, the relationships between social, psychological, and biological variables and later substance use and psychological well-being may vary from one kind of community to another.

The Woodlawn study population, 1966–1967 and 1975–1976

Woodlawn is an urban, poor community on the South Side of Chicago. Between 1955 and 1966, it went from being 40% black to being almost totally black and substantially overcrowded, with lower median income and higher unemployment (de Vise, 1967). It ranked among the four most impoverished Chicago neighborhoods by 1966. However, there was and is heterogeneity within Woodlawn, some sections having higher median income and more home ownership than others.

Our study began with a specific community population and has followed it through time and geographic mobility. Between 1964 and 1969 we made assessments of the mental health of all the first graders in Woodlawn at several points in each school year. Further assessments were made on samples of these children in their third-grade years. We also conducted interviews in the spring of 1965 and the spring of 1967 with the mothers (or mother surrogates) of the children who were in first grade in those 2 years. These assessments were coupled with service and evaluation programs that were partly directed at systematically developing community-wide prevention and early intervention programs (Kellam et al., 1975). In all of these service and research ventures we were supported by a community board composed of leaders from the community's larger citizen organizations. The support and assistance of the board has been essential throughout the course of this work (Kellam & Branch, 1971; Kellam et al., 1972).

For the long-term follow-up study, the target population has been the entire first-grade population of 1966–1967, the 1,241 students who remained in the Woodlawn first-grade classrooms that school year, together with their families. By 1975, when we began our search for families for the follow-up, over two-thirds of this group no longer lived in Woodlawn. In 1975–1976 we located and reinterviewed 939 (75%) of the mothers or mother surrogates of the 1,241 families from the 1966–1967 study. The mothers' refusal rate was 5.9%. An additional 18.5% of the mothers were not reinterviewed because we could not find them, because the families had moved from Chicago, or because their children from the study population were deceased. After the mother was interviewed and had given permission, the teenager was approached. Of the 939 teenaged children of the reinterviewed mothers, 705 (75%) participated in the reassessments, 14.5% refused to participate, and 10.4% could not be found, had moved out of Chicago, or were unavailable because they were in institutions or had run away. The mothers' and teenagers' refusal rates were low by current survey standards and, we think, reflect the efforts of the community board and the fact that services were provided as backup to the research. The study population for this chapter consists of the 705 teenagers whom we reassessed.

To study differences between those reassessed and those not reassessed, we compared three groups from the original population: (1) children who participated in the follow-up as teenagers, all of whose mothers (or mother surrogates) also participated; (2) children who did not participate but whose mothers did; and (3) children who did not participate and whose mothers also did not. We found no differences among the groups in children's or mothers' 1966–1967 psychological well-being, early family income, or welfare status, or in the variety of combinations of adults at home. The third group was somewhat more mobile before and during first grade; the children were more likely to have been in parochial schools in first grade; and the mothers were somewhat younger. It was somewhat harder to trace parochial school students because these schools lacked the centralized, computerized records that the Chicago public school system maintains.

We found significant differences in only 3 of 21 first-grade measures of the children's social adaptation. These 21 measures included IQ and readiness-for-school test scores, along with a set of teacher ratings of each child's functioning as a student. Only maturity as assessed by teachers early in first grade and the grade point averages for both semesters of first grade were different. All three differences were small; moreover, the other 18 measures had no consistent trends that would support any theories about the differences. We conclude that the population of teenagers we assessed did not substantially differ from the groups we did not assess except in early mobility, parochial/public school enrollment, and mother's age. Further information on the follow-up methods is contained in Agrawal et al. (1978).

Collection of data on teenage psychological well-being and substance use

The data on teenage substance use and psychological well-being come from responses to items on two instruments: The "What's Happening" instrument provided data on substance use and the "How I Feel," data on psychological well-being.

The substance-use questions concerned 11 categories, including beer or wine, hard liquor, and cigarettes. The teenagers indicated frequency of their use of these substances (1) during the previous 2 months and (2) during their lifetime. For the substance-use analyses in this report, we use the responses to the latter; analyses based on the "last 2 months" data yield almost identical results.

The "How I Feel" instrument was designed to assess four dimensions of adolescent psychological well-being: (1) psychiatric symptoms, (2) self-esteem, (3) body satisfaction, and (4) self-perception of social adaptation and satisfaction with social adaptation.

In this chapter we will use the measure of psychiatric symptoms as an indicator of psychological well-being. This measure is based on the teenagers' self-ratings on a standardized, multi-item symptom scale. Items for the scale were developed for typical clinical constructs of psychopathology: anxiety, depression, anger/aggression, bizarre/peculiar behavior or feelings, bizarre/paranoid behavior or feelings, obsessions/compulsions, and a global psychopathology construct. This symptom scale was analyzed using Rasch's psychometric model, which is a special case of the more general class of latent trait models (Wright, 1977). The Rasch model provides a method of obtaining scale values for persons and items on an underlying, unidimensional latent trait. In the present application, we were interested in scaling each individual's location on a continuum of psychiatric symptomatology.

In addition to providing interval level measurement of the scale values, the Rasch model also yields statistical tests of fit that allow assessment of how well the items used actually conform to the model. Using these tests of fit, we eliminated 14 items from the original symptom scale; the remaining 35 items fit the model well and yielded Rasch-scaled symptom scores ranging from −4 (least symptomatic) to +4 (most symptomatic).

The adolescents were assessed in groups of usually five to eight. Both questionnaires were administered in one session by black college students in a standardized process that emphasized hearing the concerns of the teenagers, engendering trust, and assuring confidentiality. The assessment questions were presented on slides and on audiotape to rectify reading-ability differences and to standardize the pace in the general administration of the questions (Petersen & Kellam, 1977). During the actual administration of the instruments, the assessors stopped the slides and tape whenever any of the teenagers had questions about either the purpose or the meaning of the items.

We do not know how often teenagers underreport or overreport their substance use, or are less than open about their feelings. Self-report of use of many drugs may be validated by urinalysis within a certain time period after use, and by using urine assay, Robins (1973) found that self-reports of heroin use among Vietnam veterans were reasonably valid. Josephson, Haberman, and Zanes (1971), looking for exaggeration in teenage self-reports of drug use, included a fictitious drug category in a questionnaire; less than 1% of the teenagers reported use of this fictitious drug. In the same study, the authors experimented with three questionnaires that offered differing degrees of anonymity to the respondent: One was completely anonymous, the second had a coded number, and the third had the respondent's name. Increased anonymity did not yield increased self-reports of drug use by teenagers. On the other hand, Horan, Weskott, and Vetovich (1974) found that fewer people reported frequent use of illegal drugs in a face-to-face interview than in a self-administered questionnaire. The incomplete evidence that these studies provide suggests that the privacy at the time of reporting provided by the use of a self-administered questionnaire encourages fuller disclosure. Beyond this, signing one's name does not seem to discourage full reporting.

One can make reasonable inferences concerning the validity of self-reports from the data-gathering situation, from the data itself, from the results of comparable research (Johnston, 1973), and from the results of predictive studies based on the data. We designed our data-gathering sessions to encourage the trust and interest of the respondents in the research and to guarantee confidentiality. In the results we are about to present, the variation of rates of the teenagers' self-reported use of substances – they report high use of some substances and low use of others – suggests that there is no *systematic* overreporting or underreporting. Similar reasoning holds for their reports of symptoms. The predictive studies we report here add weight to the inference that the self-reports are reasonably valid.

Frequencies of teenage substance use

A pattern of substance use that is heavily centered on alcohol, marijuana, and cigarettes is revealed in Table 2.1. In this population males generally reported more use during their lifetimes than females for almost all the substances – an analysis of variance of the five major substance categories shows that males used significantly more beer or wine, hard liquor, and marijuana than did females ($p < .001$). However, both males and females reported frequent use of drugs, alcohol, and cigarettes. A large

Table 2.1. *Lifetime use of drugs, alcohol, and cigarettes reported by teenagers (%)*

Drug categories	Males (N = 345)						Females (N = 360)					
	Never	1–2 times	3–9 times	10–19 times	20–39 times	40+ times	Never	1–2 times	3–9 times	10–19 times	20–39 times	40+ times
Alcohol												
Beer or wine	14.5	20.1	18.9	11.6	11.9	23.0	25.9	24.0	19.2	13.4	6.4	11.1
Hard liquor	53.5	14.0	13.5	5.0	6.4	7.6	61.7	16.8	11.5	4.5	2.0	3.6
Marijuana or hashish	28.6	17.2	10.2	7.6	7.9	28.6	48.6	14.7	12.2	7.8	8.3	11.4
Opiates and other illicit drugs												
LSD or other psychedelics	94.8	2.9	.9	0	.6	.9	95.8	2.2	1.1	.6	0	.3
Uppers, methedrine, or amphetamines	96.8	2.3	.3	0	.6	0	95.3	2.5	.8	0	.8	.6
Downers or barbiturates (unprescribed)	94.8	3.8	.3	.6	.3	.3	93.9	3.3	1.4	0	.6	.8
Tranquilizers (unprescribed)	95.6	3.8	.3	0	.3	0	94.2	3.3	1.4	.6	.3	.3
Cocaine	91.3	6.4	.9	.3	.3	.9	93.6	3.6	.8	1.4	0	.6
Heroin, methadone, opium, or morphine	98.8	.6	0	.3	.3	0	99.2	.3	.3	0	0	.3
Glue, gas, or other inhalants	96.5	2.0	.3	.6	.3	.3	97.8	1.4	0	.3	0	.6
Cough syrup or codeine (unprescribed)	87.8	7.3	2.9	1.2	.3	.6	89.7	5.6	1.4	1.9	.6	.8
	Never	1–2 times	Occasionally	Less than pack/day	Pack/day or more		Never	1–2 times	Occasionally	Less than pack/day	Pack/day or more	
Cigarettes	22.9	21.4	22.6	30.1	2.9		22.9	24.6	26.8	22.3	3.4	

percentage of teenagers reported relatively frequent experience with marijuana and beer or wine (more than one-third of the males and about one-sixth of the females reported use 20 times or more). Hard liquor also was used by a sizable portion of teenagers. Males and females reported smoking cigarettes at about the same frequency. Among the infrequently used drugs, the low rate for heroin stands out; cocaine and unprescribed cough syrup appear to have been more frequent choices than heroin at this age and in this population. These results and others related to the early predictors of substance use may be found in Kellam, Ensminger, and Simon (1980) and in Ensminger, Brown, and Kellam (1981).

First-grade mental health

In the Woodlawn studies we conceptualize mental health in two dimensions: psychological well-being (PWB) and social adaptational status (SAS) (Kellam et al., 1975). In PWB we find the primary components of the traditional psychiatric view of mental health – how the individual feels inside and the status of his or her thought processes. Both are assessed by means of self-reports and/or by psychiatric indicators commonly used by clinicians. In SAS we assess how a significant other – a natural rater – in a particular social field rates the individual's performance on the tasks that the natural rater sets for him or her. Examples of natural raters in social fields are the parent in the child's home, the student's teacher in the classroom, particular other teenagers in the teenager's peer group, and the foreman on the job. On a broader societal level, illicit drug use and delinquency are SAS matters, judged by the courts and the police.

In this project we have defined SAS and PWB as separate concepts and have measured them independently of each other, so that we might study their long-term interrelationships and the outcome of each. In this chapter we report on their long-term relations to both adolescent substance use and psychiatric symptoms.

In 1966–1967 we assessed both the SAS and the PWB of the Woodlawn first graders. Their teachers assessed their SAS in standardized interviews. IQ and readiness-test scores were used as additional measures of SAS, because these tests were tasks the school expected the children to perform. The mothers or mother surrogates, as well as clinicians, reported on their children's PWB.

First-grade SAS

We chose the classroom of the child for the measurement of first-grade SAS, with the teacher as a natural rater, because of the very likely importance of this social field and this natural rater at this point in the life cycle. Our primary instrument, the Teacher's Observation of Classroom Adaptation (TOCA), is comprised of six rating scales to measure SAS: social contact (shyness), authority acceptance (aggressive behavior), maturation, cognitive achievement, concentration, and an overall, global scale of how well the child is performing as a student. Each teacher (all of them were female) rated all of her students in a standardized interview on one 4-point scale for each social task, running from adaptive to severely maladaptive behavior. Teachers made TOCA ratings early in the 1966–1967 school year and at its end. Kellam et al. (1975) contains reliability and validity data regarding these scales.

To construct the TOCA scales, we first requested from the 57 Woodlawn first-grade teachers lists of the ways children demonstrated maladapting to the classroom. From these lists the social tasks expected of first-grade children in this community were inferred. The teachers noted some 450 maladaptive behaviors, which were then grouped independently by two research staff members into five global scales. The following are representative maladaptive items and the five global tasks:

Maladaptive behaviors	*Categories of social tasks*
Is shy; is timid; is alone too much; is friendless; is aloof	Social contact
Fights too much; steals; lies; resists authority; is destructive to others or property; is obstinate; is disobedient; is uncooperative	Authority acceptance
Acts too young physically and/or emotionally; cries too much; has tantrums; sucks thumb; is physically poorly coordinated; urinates in class; seeks too much attention	Maturation
Does not learn as well as he is able; is lazy; does not come prepared for work; underachieves; lacks effort	Cognitive achievement
Fidgets; does not sit still in classroom; is restless; has short attention span	Concentration

In earlier analyses of the TOCA scales, it became clear that those children who were found to be maladapting on one scale were most often rated maladapting on others. In Kellam et al. (1975) we describe the development of a way of typing children according to their pattern of maladapting scales, the various combinations of which we termed social maladaptive modes. In the analyses reported in this chapter a refinement of these typal categories is used, rather than the individual TOCA scales.

We find typal analysis of TOCA often more useful than scale analysis. A child rated adapting on the social contact scale may be rated maladapting on any of the other scales. For example, it would be misleading to contrast all the children not rated shy with those rated shy, because neither the shy children nor the nonshy children form a simple group; some shy ones *and* some nonshy ones are also rated aggressive, some have learning problems, and so on. Typal categories disentangle the shyness and aggressiveness characteristics by placing each child in only one SAS category, the category that reflects the child's *pattern* of maladaptation. As we shall show, the children in the shy category and those in the aggressive category have very different patterns of teenage substance use, and each group has a particular relationship to teenage psychiatric symptoms.

The classification of the first-grade children used here consists of an adapting category and seven social maladaptive patterns or modes. It is based on the presence or absence of shyness – for example, having few friends, sitting alone – and aggressiveness – for example, breaking rules, beating up other children. This distinction was suggested by many investigators in describing children's behavior in the classroom, and our earlier work has shown its usefulness. Shyness and aggressiveness most often occur with learning problems, and this third dimension was therefore taken into account when we defined categories for analysis.

By learning problems we are referring to difficulties with three social tasks assessed by teachers in addition to social contact and authority acceptance: maturation (acting with sufficient independence to accomplish first-grade tasks), cognitive achievement (learning up to ability as the teacher perceives it), and concentration (paying attention for a sufficient span of time to allow for teaching and learning). This concept of learning problems has similarities to M. Kohn and Rosman (1972) and to a learning problems category developed in Lambert's classification of children (Lambert & Nicoll, 1977).

The following categories of first-grade SAS are therefore used in the analyses reported in this chapter:

1. Adapting – rated adapting on all five teacher scales of SAS
2. Learning problems only – rated maladapting on one or more of the learning-problems scales, but not shy or aggressive
3. Mildly shy – rated mildly shy not aggressive, and usually maladapting on learning problems
4. Moderately or severely shy – rated moderately or severely shy but not moderately or severely aggressive, and almost always maladapting on learning problems
5. Mildly aggressive – rated mildly aggressive but not shy, and usually maladapting on learning problems
6. Moderately or severely aggressive – rated moderately or severely ag-

gressive but not moderately or severely shy, and almost always maladapting on learning problems
7. Mildly shy and aggressive – rated mildly shy and mildly aggressive, and usually maladapting on learning problems
8. Moderately or severely shy and aggressive – rated moderately or severely shy and moderately or severely aggressive, and almost always maladapting on learning problems

In addition to these typal categories based on teachers' ratings, we are using two other quasi-SAS measures, the Metropolitan Readiness Test and Kuhlmann-Anderson IQ test. These are considered SAS measures because they represent social tasks presented to the children in the school. The Metropolitan Readiness Test, which measures a child's readiness for school learning (Anastasi, 1968), was administered early in first grade; the Kuhlmann-Anderson IQ test was given toward the middle of first grade by the teachers or staff of the public schools that the first graders attended.

Both tests have been shown to correlate significantly with other SAS measures (Kellam et al., 1975). The readiness-test levels are those defined by the test designers; we have combined the high normal and superior groups in our population for this analysis because of sample sizes. The cutoff points separating the medium-IQ group from the high and low groups are 104 and 92 – plus or minus one-half standard deviation above and below the mean IQ of our population.

First-grade PWB

Two measures of first-grade PWB are used in this chapter. Direct Clinical Observation (DCO), a method of rating first graders on scales of flatness, depression, anxiety, hyperkinesis, and bizarre behavior, and on a global scale, was used early in first grade and at its end by pairs of clinicians who were unaware of the SAS ratings. The second measure is the Mother Symptom Inventory (MSI) completed by the mothers in the home interview in 1966–1967. The MSI is a 38-item inventory adapted from previous investigations of the epidemiology of symptoms among children (Kellam et al., 1975). The mothers were asked to rate their children on each symptom on a 4-point scale from "not at all" to "very much," and the 38 items were grouped in 13 symptom categories. Although unaware of the clinicians' or teachers' ratings, mothers may have been aware of teachers' views of the children's social adaptation.

First-grade SAS and teenage substance use

We used multivariate analyses of variance to study patterns of relationship between the first-grade variables and teenage substance use (Table 2.2)

Table 2.2. *First-grade social adaptational status and lifetime drug use reported at age 16–17: multivariate analyses of variance (main effects)*

	Difference from mean use of drugs in category by males						Difference from mean use of drugs in category by females					
Social adaptational status in first grade (Mean use of drugs in category by sex[a])	*N*	Beer or wine (3.6)	Hard liquor (2.2)	Marijuana (3.3)	Opiates and other illicit drugs (1.4)	Cigarettes (2.7)	*N*	Beer or wine (2.8)	Hard liquor (1.8)	Marijuana (2.4)	Opiates and other illicit drugs (1.4)	Cigarettes (2.6)
Teacher ratings early in first grade												
Adapting	91						151	.4			.1	0
Learning problems only	79						53	−.2			−.1	0
Mildly shy	50						62	−.3			0	−.3
Moderately/severely shy	20						33	−.3			.1	−.1
Mildly aggressive	37						17	−.3			−.2	.5
Moderately/severely aggressive	29						25	.2			.2	.4
Mildly shy and aggressive	20						7	−.2			1.5	.3
Moderately/severely shy and aggressive	11						9	−1.0			−.3	−.7
		ns	ns	ns	ns	ns		*	ns	ns	*	**
	Multivariate significance: ns						Multivariate significance: **					

Teacher ratings at end of first grade												
Adapting	109	−.1	−.2	.2		−.2	167			.1		
Learning problems only	52	−.5	−.3	−.2		−.2	55			−.4		
Mildly shy	36	−.1	0	−.3		−.2	38			.4		
Moderately/severely shy	27	−.9	−.7	−1.4		−.5	22			−.9		
Mildly aggressive	32	.5	.5	.9		.3	32			.2		
Moderately/severely aggressive	44	.4	.7	.6		.2	22			−.1		
Mildly shy and aggressive	16	−.2	−.1	−.3		0	14			.2		
Moderately/severely shy and aggressive	22	.6	.5	.2		.8	11			1.0		
		**	**	***	ns	**		ns	ns		ns	ns
	Multivariate significance: **						Multivariate significance: **					
Metropolitan Readiness Test												
Immature (score: 0–39)	60	−.4	−.1	−.5	.2		51	−.5	−.3	−.4		
Low Normal (40–64)	134	−.3	−.2	0	0		116	−.2	−.1	−.3		
Average (65–79)	74	.2	−.1	.3	−.1		113	.4	.1	.3		
High Normal or Superior (80–100)	34	.9	.7	.8	.3		41	.5	.5	.4		
		**	*	*	*	ns		***	*	*	ns	ns
	Multivariate significance: ***						Multivariate significance: **					
Kuhlmann-Anderson IQ test												
Low (less than 93)	75	−.3					77	−.3				
Medium (93–103)	99	−.1					113	.3				
High (104+)	78	.5					95	.2				
		**	ns	ns	ns	ns		*	ns	ns	ns	ns
	Multivariate significance: **						Multivariate significance: **					

[a] Drug use scores: For all categories except "Cigarettes," 1 = never; 2 = 1 to 2 times; 3 = 3 to 9 times; 4 = 10 to 19 times; 5 = 20 to 39 times; 6 = 40 times or more. "Opiates and other illicit drugs" are all the drugs that are listed under that heading in Table 2.1; a teenager's score on "Opiates and other illicit drugs" is his or her highest score on any drug in that category. For "Cigarettes," 1 = never; 2 = 1 to 2 times; 3 = occasionally; 4 = less than a pack a day; 5 = a pack a day or more.

Significance levels: ns = not significant; * = $p < .05$; ** = $p < .01$; *** = $p = < .001$.

(Bock, 1975). Except for cigarettes, substance use was coded from low usage to high usage on a 1–6-point scale (see the categories of Table 2.1). Use of cigarettes was measured on the 5-point scale shown on Table 2.1. We also present univariate significance levels, along with substance score means wherever the multivariate and univariate significance reaches at least the .05 level (Table 2.2).

Because the teenagers in this population used the drugs that we listed in Table 2.1 in the category "Opiates and other illicit drugs" – psychedelics, uppers, downers, tranquilizers, cocaine, opiates, inhalants, and codeine – far less frequently than any of the other drugs, we have considered them as one drug category, again using the label "Opiates and other illicit drugs." Each teenager's score on this category comes from his or her highest reported rate of use of any of these drugs.

Early first-grade TOCA. Whereas the early first-grade teacher ratings of males show no relation to substance use 10 years later, the ratings of females' SAS do show multivariate significance. In the three substance categories that show univariate significance, the only consistent pattern is that moderately or severely shy and aggressive females used substances less often.

Late first-grade TOCA. The SAS ratings of males at the end of first grade show a clear pattern of relationship. Males rated moderately or severely shy at the end of first grade showed lower substance use 10 years later than their peers in all categories except "Opiates and other illicit drugs." Those rated aggressive, either moderately or mildly, and those rated moderately or severely shy and aggressive always had the three highest mean substance uses for the four substance categories besides "Opiates and others." Parallel results can be obtained by analyzing the proportions of males in TOCA categories who were heavy users and those who had never used substances.

The late first-grade SAS ratings for females, although significantly related to later substance use, do not relate in the same way as the early first-grade ratings. The moderately or severely shy females were using less marijuana at Time 2 than any of the other females, and the moderately or severely shy and aggressive females were the heaviest female marijuana users. Except for marijuana use, no univariate relationship was found between females' SAS at end of first grade and teenage substance use.

The differences between the shy males' and the aggressive males' substance use are clear. Except for the little-used drugs in the "Opiates and others" category, the same pattern exists for all substance categories:

The moderately or severely shy males were at least twice as likely *never* to have used a substance as the moderately or severely aggressive or shy and aggressive males. The moderately or severely aggressive or shy and aggressive males were at least twice as likely as the moderately or severely shy males to report *heavy* use, and were over eight times as likely as the moderately or severely shy males to be heavy users of hard liquor. (By heavy use we mean 20 uses or more.)

First-grade Metropolitan Readiness Test. The more ready children, both male and female, used substances more often 10 years later than the less ready (see Table 2.2).

First-grade IQ. Overall, the males in the high-IQ group used substances most frequently, followed by the middle- and then the low-IQ males (see Table 2.2). This multivariate result had univariate significance for use of beer or wine. The medium- and high-IQ females were heavier substance users than the lower-IQ females; again, beer or wine was most clearly related to IQ.

These results with both IQ and Metropolitan Readiness Test scores are main effects in the multivariate analyses of variance, showing no interaction with teacher ratings of SAS.

First-grade PWB and teenage substance use

We will consider the Direct Clinical Observations (DCO) measure first. Only 12 males and 12 females were rated symptomatic on DCO at the time of first grade. Moreover, most of the symptomatic children were rated only mildly symptomatic, that is, on the second level of a 6-point scale. Of the 24 first-grade children rated symptomatic on the DCO, 2 females and 3 males were heavy users 10 years later of beer and wine, hard liquor, and marijuana, whereas 2 females and 2 males almost completely avoided the use of substances. Given this variability in such small samples, no pattern of substance usage can be established for DCO symptomatic males or females.

When the Mother Symptom Inventory (MSI) was used as a measure of PWB, larger numbers of children were rated symptomatic. In the present analysis a child is considered symptomatic in one of the 13 symptom categories if his or her mother rated her child as "pretty much" or "very much" (i.e., on the third or fourth level of a 4-point scale) on any symptom in that category. There were relatively few associations with substance use 10 years later. For females, 7 significant associations out of 65 opportunities were found; for males, 4 out of 65 were found. The few MSI associations with substance use showed, in every case, symptomatic first-grade children using substances less frequently 10 years later than non-symptomatic first-grade children.

First-grade SAS and teenage psychiatric symptoms

We next examined how the Time 1 SAS measures affected later teenage psychiatric symptoms. The eight TOCA categories and the global teacher ratings are independent variables and the single Rasch score of psychiatric symptoms is the dependent variable in the analyses of variance (see Table 2.3). Adapting children are contrasted in these analyses with each of the seven maladaptive modes and with the mildly and then the moderately or severely maladapting global ratings. The numbers in this table represent standard deviation differences between the various pairs of first-grade contrast groups, adapting being the constant standard against which the other groups are contrasted.

Teacher ratings of SAS early in first grade were not related to females' teenage symptoms, but were related to males' teenage symptoms. By the end of first grade, clear patterns emerged for males: First-grade adapting males were much less symptomatic as teenagers than were males with learning problems only or shy males, most of whom also had learning problems. The first-grade aggressive males showed somewhat higher symptom scores than the adapting children, but the difference appears a bit smaller. The moderately or severely shy and aggressive males (relatively few in number) did not show a difference from adapting males. Males with an end-of-first-grade global teacher rating as mildly, moderately, or severely maladapting were more symptomatic 10 years later than adapting males. Teacher ratings of SAS for females, both early in first grade and at its end, showed no relationship to psychiatric symptoms 10 years later.

Readiness-test scores of males also showed differences in symptom levels 10 years later, with males who were less ready in first grade being more symptomatic as teenagers than the more ready. The readiness-test scores of females showed no relation to their teenage symptom scores.

First-grade IQ scores revealed differences among females 10 years later, with high-IQ females showing lower symptom scores later. Males' IQ scores showed no relation to their symptom scores. These analyses of variance are main effects with very few interactions among the independent variables; the few interactions did not help to clarify the results.

Table 2.3. *Social adaptational status (SAS) in first grade and symptoms 10 years later: analysis of variance (main effects)*

	Females	Males
Teacher ratings of SAS early in first grade		
Eight typal categories	ns	ns
Global teacher rating	ns	**
Adapting (F = 152, M = 94) vs.:		
Mildly maladapting (138, 164)		−.23[a]
Moderately/severely maladapting (71, 86)		−.49
Teacher ratings of SAS at end of first grade		
Eight typal categories	ns	**
Adapting (167, 111) vs.:		
Learning problems only (55, 52)		−.54
Mildly shy (38, 37)		−.59
Mildly aggressive (32, 33)		−.39
Mildly shy and aggressive (14, 16)		−.28
Moderately/severely shy (22, 27)		−.66
Moderately/severely aggressive (22, 46)		−.38
Moderately/severely shy and aggressive (11, 22)		−.04
Global teacher rating	ns	***
Adapting (167, 111) vs.:		
Mildly maladapting (129, 134)		−.45
Moderately/severely maladapting (65, 99)		−.45
Metropolitan Readiness Test in first grade	ns	***
Immature (53, 63) vs.:		
Low average (115, 137)		.48
Average (114, 75)		.71
High normal/superior (41, 34)		.62
Kuhlmann-Anderson IQ test in first grade	***	*ns*
Low (77, 76) vs.:		
Medium (114, 102)	.19	
High (95, 78)	.60	

[a] Standard deviation differences: least squares estimates of the contrast divided by the standard deviation of the dependent variable. Negative values indicate that the base category is less symptomatic than the contrasting category.
Significance levels: ns = not significant; * = $p \leq .05$; ** = $p \leq .01$; *** = $p \leq .001$.

First-grade PWB and teenage psychiatric symptoms

PWB was measured by DCO twice in first grade – early and at the end – and by MSI at the end of first grade. As we described earlier, however, the small number of symptomatic children rated by the clinicians makes interpretation highly speculative. Females who were rated symptomatic

Table 2.4. *First-grade symptom ratings by mothers as antecedents of symptoms in teenage females*

	SD differences in teenage symptoms for symptomatic and nonsymptomatic first-grade females[a]		
13 symptom categories from Mother Symptom Inventory	Symptomatic N	Nonsymptomatic N	Standardized differences
Bizarre behavior	16	345	ns
Sad and worried	37	324	.347
Fears	58	303	ns
Trouble with feelings	67	294	.265
Muscular tension	17	344	.507
Nervous habits	56	305	ns
Sleep problems	26	335	ns
Psychosomatic complaints	34	327	ns
Toilet problems	42	319	ns
Immature behavior	93	268	ns
Speech problems	14	347	.493
Eating problems	113	248	ns
Sex problems	22	339	ns

[a] Standard deviation differences are included for t values significant at $p \leq .05$; positive values indicate that symptomatic first graders have higher symptoms as teenagers.

by their mothers on 4 of the 13 MSI categories – "Sad and worried," "Trouble with feelings," "Muscular tension," and "Speech problems" – had significantly higher symptom ratings as teenagers (see Table 2.4). For males, there were no significant relationships between mothers' ratings of symptoms in first grade and teenage reports of symptoms 10 years later.

Overall, there appears to be some evidence of a relationship between first-grade PWB and teenage symptoms, although it is certainly not very strong. Possibly we can have somewhat more confidence in this result for females than for males. Rutter et al. (1970) report similar results in their long-term follow-up of children's symptoms. It is worth noting that females were more symptomatic on the Rasch scale as teenagers than were males ($p < .02$ by t test).

Aspects of family and teenage substance use and psychiatric symptoms

In this section a set of family characteristics representing central dimensions of family structure and psychological atmosphere are examined in regard to their predictive relationship to teenage psychiatric symptoms and substance use. Analyses were done again by analysis of variance, the numbers on the tables representing standard deviation differences between contrasted groups (see Table 2.5 and its notes).

In this case we classified our independent variables at Time 1 in combination with the same variables at Time 2, in order to determine how change and stability in these family characteristics between the two time periods affected the adolescent's psychiatric symptoms. The family variables in question easily lend themselves to this kind of treatment; the early SAS and PWB variables will also be examined in this way in later reports.

Mother-alone families who remained mother-alone were contrasted with mother-alone families that became mother/second-adult families. Mother/father families that remained mother/father were contrasted with mother/father families that separated and became mother-alone families. Similarly, income above and below the median at Time 1 was categorized along with the same variable above and below the median at Time 2. The mother's expectations at both times about how far her child would go in school and the mother's PWB at both times were classified in similar fashion. Geographic and social mobility was included also. These analyses, then, enable us to see not only how antecedents in these areas operate on psychiatric symptoms and substance measures, but also how chance or stability in a hypothesized good or bad condition in the family affects the teenager's status on these two outcomes.

The results of these analyses suggest that there are no significant differences in psychiatric symptoms or substance use among teenagers from families that were mother-alone households, that were mother/father households, or that changed from one status to the other. Neither change in income nor geographic or social mobility appreciably affected substance use or symptom scores of the teenagers.

The two measures of family psychological atmosphere were related to both adolescent females' symptoms and substance use, however. The mother's self-reports of her PWB related to the teenage female's symptom ratings. Daughters of mothers who reported low PWB at Time 2 had higher symptom ratings than the females whose mothers reported high PWB at both Times 1 and 2 (see Table 2.5).

The mothers' expectations of how far their daughters would go in school related to both the females' substance use and their psychiatric symptoms. Mothers with low expectations at both Times 1 and 2 had daughters who used cigarettes more frequently and reported more symptoms than the daughters of mothers who at Time 2 had high expectations about their daughters' future schooling, regardless of their Time 1 expectations. See Table 2.5 for the results pertaining to symptoms. The results of the mul-

Table 2.5. *Antecedent and concurrent family factors and teenage symptoms: analyses of variance (main effects)*

	Females	Males
Family type		
Ma/Ma vs. MF/MF	ns	ns
(F = 62) (F = 104)		
(M = 77) (M = 77)	ns	ns
MF/MF vs. MF/Ma		
(45)(28)	ns	ns
Ma/Ma vs. Ma/MO		
(44)(53)		
Family income		
Low/low vs. high/high	ns	ns
(105) (119) (108)(98)		
High/high vs. high/low	ns	ns
(52)(35)		
Low/low vs. low/high	ns	ns
(64)(62)		
Change of residence		
Same/worse vs. no move	ns	ns
(99)(93) (68)(69)		
Better vs. no move	ns	ns
(189)(179)		
Mother's (PWB)		
Low/low vs. high/high	.46*	ns
(28)(44) (202)(189)		
Low/low vs. low/high	ns	ns
(91)(67)		
High/high vs. high/low	−.45	ns
(38)(43)		
Mother's expectations about child's education		
Low/low vs. high/high	.42	ns
(128)(141) (84)(51)		
Low/low vs. low/high	.69	ns
(71)(75)		
High/high vs. high/low	ns	ns
(64)(64)		

* Standard deviation differences are included for contrasts where the significant level is at least $p \leq .05$.

Note: Family type is based on the combinations of adults in the household when the children were in first grade and at the time of follow-up when the teenagers were age 16–17. Ma/Ma – Mother alone at both Time 1 and Time 2. Ma/MO – Mother alone at Time 1 and mother plus other adult(s) at Time 2. MF/MF – Mother/father at both Times 1 and 2 with or without other adults. MF/Ma Mother/father with or without others at Time 1 and mother alone at Time 2.

tivariate analysis of variance with substance use as the independent variable are not shown in a table, because there was only one significant relationship with the independent variables.

Discussion

This research strongly suggests that early life conditions of teenagers in the urban, poor neighborhood we studied are important in understanding teenagers' use of substances and their psychological well-being. The sex differences we found suggest that males and females have very different processes of socialization and/or developmental patterns for both substance use and psychiatric symptoms in adolescence. Males not only used more substances but had clearer patterns of antecedents of substance use in the areas of early shyness and early aggressiveness. Males also demonstrated clearer patterns of antecedents of teenage psychiatric symptoms in the area of early school success and failure and in early social involvement (shyness). The patterns of females, in contrast, appear to have weak relations or no relations to these domains of antecedents. Instead, family psychological atmosphere – that is, the mother's expectation for the daughter and the mother's own psychological well-being – appear to be related to the teenage female's use of substances and to her psychiatric symptoms, although causal directions are not altogether clear. These family characteristics, first-grade psychological well-being, and IQ are the antecedents related to adolescent outcomes for females. These antecedents seem more weakly and less clearly related to teenage outcomes than are those for the male teenage outcomes.

Notes to Table 2.5 (*cont.*)

Family income: Low and *high* refer to less or more than the median income at Time 1 and Time 2: $5,000 at Time 1; $7,000 at Time 2.

Change of residence: Better means moved to a better neighborhood by Time 2; *same/worse* means moved within the same, to a similar, or to a worse neighborhood by Time 2; *no move* means no change in residence. Census data were used to determine the status of neighborhoods.

Mother's PWB is measured by her self-reports. The scale runs from "no" to "very frequent" sadness or nervousness. *High* and *low* refer to higher and lower than the median reports by all mothers at both Times 1 and 2 on the combination of two global scales, which indicate how often the mother has days when she is sad or blue and nervous or tense.

Mother's expectations about child's education: High and *low* refer to higher and lower mother's expectations. Lower expectations were "some high school," "finish high school," and "some college"; higher expectations were "finish college" and "beyond college." This breakdown divides the population roughly in half at both Times 1 and 2.

Table 2.6. *Summary of antecedents of teenage drug use and teenage psychiatric symptoms*

	Males		Females	
	Drugs	Symptoms	Drugs	Symptoms
Teachers' ratings of SAS late in first grade				
Learning problems only	—	**↑**	—	—
Shy with learning problems	**↓**	**↑**	↓	—
Aggressive with learning problems	**↑**	↑	—	—
Shy and aggressive with learning problems	**↑**	—	↑	—
First-grade Metropolitan Readiness Test	↑	**↓**	↑	—
First-grade IQ	↑	—	↑	**↓**
First-grade Mother Symptom Inventory	—	—	—	↑
Mother's PWB at Times 1 and 2	—	—	—	**↓**
Mother's expectations of child's education at Times 1 and 2	—	—	↓	**↓**

↑ strong positive relationship; ↑ modest positive relationship — When the level of the factor is high, drug use or symptoms go up too.

↓ strong negative relationship; ↓ modest negative relationship — When the level of the factor is high, drug use or symptoms go down.

When we compare the antecedents of teenage substance use with the antecedents of teenage symptoms we find similarities at the general level, but striking differences at the specific level. First-grade teacher ratings are related to both teenage substance use and psychiatric symptoms for males. However, the patterns differ for the two teenage outcomes. Early shy males used substances less frequently than any other category of males, but they had one of the highest risks of later symptoms. Males with learning problems did not differ from early adapting males with regard to later substance use, but they had a higher risk of later symptoms. On the other hand, males rated aggressive or shy and aggressive in first grade were more likely than any other males to use substances as teenagers, but they had a lower risk of later symptoms than the shy males. Adapting males used a moderate amount of substances, compared to the other males, and had the lowest risk of later symptoms. Table 2.6 summarizes these results.

First-grade IQ- and readiness-test scores are related to both outcomes. Less ready and lower-IQ males and lower-IQ females were likely to use fewer substances later on than their better-performing peers but, in the case of females, were likely to have an increased risk of symptoms. Adolescent males used substances more frequently than females, but teenage females were more symptomatic than teenage males. Females symptomatic in first grade used substances possibly less frequently than other females as teenagers but suffered an increased risk of symptoms.

What these results point toward is that the two outcomes – the psychological and the social behavioral – have antecedents in common areas, and that the specific early characteristics seem to mark children who will take one path or the other as teenagers. It is almost as if these paths are alternatives to each other, and to go one way is not to go the other – and the alternative paths seem set early in life, at least as early as first grade. Those antecedents related to later heavy substance use are often related to better symptom status, and antecedents of low substance use are often antecedents of worse symptom status. Biological (including genetic), psychological, and social structural mechanisms might be, and probably are, all playing roles.

Although predictive studies do not explain how antecedents affect outcomes, they are essential in providing directions for further research. From these studies, we can define several main subsystems that apparently operate from very early in life on later substance use and psychiatric symptoms. First, *social adaptation to school* affects males especially, in particular their psychiatric symptoms as teenagers, with early shyness and aggressiveness influencing later substance use. Second, *early psychological well-being* has a limited effect on later substance use and symptoms. Third, *the family*, in particular its psychological atmosphere, seems important for female substance use and symptoms. We have examined here only a few basic family characteristics; we have yet to explore how family interaction, other aspects of family psychological atmosphere, or other aspects of family structure may influence teenage substance use and psychiatric symptoms.

In beginning to outline how these antecedents may operate on the teenage outcomes in question, several considerations seem important. For many decades it has been a traditional assumption in the social and behavioral sciences that internal developmental patterns are important to adolescent and adult outcomes. Such ideas have historical roots in Western civilization. Maternal deprivation, for example, has been thought to be centrally important to the later psychological development of the child, permanently affecting the child's capacity for later growth and development. In a 1976 monograph, Clarke and Clarke argue that very few studies have differentiated mediation paths between early events and later conditions that are *within the individual* from those that are in the social structure, that is, *outside the individual*. In other words, a child may be raised in difficult conditions and have a poor future mental status either because of the irreversible injury done his or her intellectual and emotional development at the early period or because of the continuing noxious environment.

The social adaptational frame combines both approaches and suggests that internal and external conditions interact with each other to produce outcomes. The child who is raised under poor family conditions early will apparently do badly in his early adaptation to school and in his early psychological well-being. Prior studies on two separate populations of Woodlawn first graders and their families support this inference (see, e.g., Kellam, Ensminger, & Turner, 1977). Subsequently, cognitive skills necessary for success in school may continue to suffer owing to this experience of early failure. Continuing poor external conditions, in the family and possibly in the school, interact with the male child's poor skills and experience of failure to produce poor psychological well-being and poor social adaptation later on.

Paul Weiss (1949) has coined the terms *plastic* and *elastic adaptation*, and these seem useful in this context. By plastic adaptation he means irreversible adaptations of the organism to environmental demand. Elastic adaptation refers to reversible adaptations – those that revert to the original state when the external demand is removed. We have assumed traditionally that an early bad environment produces plastic adaptation in the child. Early maternal deprivation, for example, leads to irreversible or plastic adaptations. This assumption must be reexamined. If environment changes for the better, we may find that the child has more elasticity than we have assumed. Consider, in the family data presented in this chapter, that change in the adult composition of the family after first grade did not significantly influence either teenage substance use or psychiatric symptoms. In first grade such family instability was very important to both SAS and PWB (Kellam et al., 1977).

The mediation of the antecedents reported here on these teenage outcomes could involve either of these two adaptational types, elastic or plastic. If early events and conditions have changed the child in the internal developmental sense, our search for mediation in the psychology of the child will be successful. If these antecedents act on symptoms and substance use by virtue of continuing external conditions, we will find mediation in social structure. Most likely, we must look to both. Where we find mediation will have great importance in understanding the relationships between the child's growth and development and his or her interaction with the social structure in which it occurs.

The generalizability of these relationships to communities other than poor, urban, black communities is not known. It is possible that failure in the first grade for Woodlawn males would have more impact on later psychological well-being and substance use than similar failure in an upper-middle-class, white, Protestant suburb. Without longitudinal studies in other communities, we cannot tell. One may not have as many chances to recoup in an urban, poor neighborhood – in reality and in one's private view of self and society.

References

Agrawal, K. C., Kellam, S. G., Klein, Z. E., & Turner, R. J. The Woodlawn mental health studies: Tracking children and families for long-term follow-up. *American Journal of Public Health*, 1978, *68*, 139–142.

Anastasi, A. *Psychological testing* (3rd ed.). London: Collier-Macmillan, 1968.

Bock, R. D. *Multivariate statistical methods in behavioral research*. New York: McGraw-Hill, 1975.

Brown, C. H., Adams, R. G., & Kellam, S. G. A longitudinal study of teenage motherhood and symptoms of distress: The Woodlawn community epidemiological project. *Research in Community and Mental Health*, 1981, *2*, 183–213.

Clarke, A. M., & Clarke, A. D. B. (Eds.). *Early experience: Myth and evidence*. New York: Free Press, 1976.

de Vise, P. *Chicago's widening color gap* (Report No. 2, Chicago Regional Hospital Study). Chicago: Interuniversity Social Research Committee, 1967.

Ensminger, M. E., Brown, C. H., & Kellam, S. G. Sex differences in antecedents of substance use among adolescents. *Journal of Social Issues*, 1982, *38*(2), 25–42.

Ensminger, M. E., Kellam, S. G., & Rubin, B. R. School and family origins of delinquency: Comparisons by sex. In *Antecedents of Antisocial Behavior*. Hingham, Mass.: Nijhoff, forthcoming.

Fleming, J. P., Kellam, S. G., & Brown, C. H. Early predictors of age at first use of alcohol, marijuana, and cigarettes. *Drug and Alcohol Dependence*, 1982, *9*(4), 285–303.

Horan, J. J., Weskott, T. B., & Vetovich, C. Drug usage: An experimental comparison of three assessment conditions. *Psychological Reports*, 1974, *35*, 211–215.

Johnston, L. *Drugs and American youth*. Ann Arbor, Mich.: Institute for Social Research, 1973.

Josephson, E., Haberman, P., & Zanes, A. *High school drug behavior: A methodological report*. Paper presented at American Association of Public Opinion Research, 1971.

Kellam, S. G., Adams, R. G., Brown, C. H., Ensminger, M. E. The long-term evolution of family structure of teenage and older mothers. *Journal of Marriage and the Family*, August 1982, *44*(3), 539–554.

Kellam, S. G., & Branch, J. D. An approach to community mental health: Analysis of basic problems. *Seminars in Psychiatry*, 1971, *3*, 207–225.

Kellam, S. G., Branch, J. D., Agrawal, K. C., & Ensminger, M. E. *Mental health and going to school: The Woodlawn Program of Assessment, Early Intervention, and Evaluation*. Chicago: University of Chicago Press, 1975.

Kellam, S. G., Branch, J. D., Agrawal, K. C., & Grabill, M. E. Woodlawn mental health center: An evolving strategy for planning in community mental health. In S. E. Golann & C. Eisdorfer (Eds.), *Handbook of Community Mental Health*. New York: Appleton-Century-Crofts, 1972.

Kellam, S. G., Branch, J. D., Brown, C. H., & Russell, G. Why teenagers come for treatment: A ten-year prospective epidemiological study in Woodlawn. *Journal of American Academy of Child Psychiatry*, 1981, *20*, 477–495.

Kellam, S. G., Brown, C. H., Rubin, B. R., & Ensminger, M. E. Paths leading to teenage psychiatric symptoms and substance use: Developmental epidemiological studies in Woodlawn. In Samuel Guze, Felton Earls, & James Barrett (Eds.), *Childhood Psychopathology and Development*, forthcoming.

Kellam, S. G., Ensminger, M. E., & Simon, M. B. Mental health in first grade and teenage drug, alcohol, and cigarette use. *Drug and Alcohol Dependence*, 1980, *5*, 273–304.

Kellam, S. G., Ensminger, M. E., & Turner, R. J. Family structure and the mental health of children: Concurrent and longitudinal community-wide studies. *Archives of General Psychiatry*, 1977, *34*, 1012–1022.

Kellam, S. G., Rubin, B. R., & Stevenson, D. L. *Psychopathology and teacher ratings: Developmental epidemiological studies*. Paper presented at the World Psychiatric Association Symposium, Johns Hopkins University, 1982.

Kohn, M., & Rosman, B. L. A social competence scale and symptom checklist for the preschool child: Factor dimensions, their cross-instrument generality, and longitudinal persistence. *Developmental Psychology*, 1972, *6*, 430–444.

Kohn, M. L. Looking back – A 25-year review and appraisal of social problems research. *Social Problems*, 1976, *24*, 94–112.

Lambert, N., & Nicoll, R. L. Conceptual model for nonintellectual behavior and its relationship to early reading achievement. *Journal of Educational Psychology*, 1977, *69*, 481–490.

Lord, F. M., & Novick, M. R. (with contributions from A. Birbaum). *Statistical Theories of Mental Test Scores*. Reading, Mass.: Addison-Wesley, 1968.

Petersen, A. C., & Kellam, S. G. Measurement of the psychological well-being of adolescents: The psychometric properties and assessment procedures of the *How I Feel*. *Journal of Youth and Adolescence*, 1977, *6*, 229–247.

Robins, L. N. *A follow-up of Vietnam drug users* (Special Action Office Monograph, Series A, No. 1). Washington, D.C.: Special Action Office for Drug Abuse Prevention, April 1973.

Rutter, M. L., Tizard, J., & Whitmore, K. (Eds.). *Education, health and behaviour: Psychological and medical study of childhood development*. New York: Wiley, 1970.

Weiss, P. The biological basis of adaptation. In J. Romano (Ed.), *Adaptation*. Ithaca, N.Y.: Cornell University Press, 1949.

Wright, B. D. Solving measurement problems with the Rasch model. *Journal of Educational Measurement*, 1977, *14*, 97–116.

3 The relative roles of early environment and early behavior as predictors of later child behavior

Thomas S. Langner, Joanne C. Gersten, Thomas A. Wills, and Ora Simcha-Fagan

For predicting a child's behavior 5 years in the future, which is more important, current behavior or the current family and social environment of the child? This chapter examines correlations between early behavior and early environment and attempts to determine the unique contributions of these early influences to later child behavior.

Our question was suggested by data collected in the Family Research Project. The overall purpose of this longitudinal study, now in its 10th year, is to examine influences of the social environment in the etiology of behavioral disorders in children; as in other epidemiological studies, difficulties arise because neither the environmental variables nor the childhood disorders have been well defined. Other purposes of the Family Research Project are to refine definitions of these variables, to improve measurement of the social environment and child behavior, and to develop typologies of children and families based on empirical data.

Previous prediction by environment and by behavior

Prevalence of behavior disorders

Approaches to the epidemiological study of mental disorder have begun with data on prevalence rates. In a random sample drawn from the general

Aside from the authors, present Family Research Project staff members contributed their skills to this paper. Thomas G. Land supervised the statistical analysis; Marjorie J. McMeniman and Daniel Katz performed statistical calculations and helped in editing; computer programming was done by Christopher York.

This investigation is being supported by U.S. Public Health Service Project Grants MH-11545 and MH-18260 of the National Institute of Mental Health Center for Epidemiologic Studies, and by the Center for Studies of Crime and Delinquency grant MH-28182. Previous support was given by the U.S. Department of Health, Education and Welfare, Social and Rehabilitation Service, Cooperative Research and Demonstration Grants Branch grant SRS-CRD-348 (SRS-56006), and the Office of Child Development, grants OCD-CB-348 and OCD-CB-480. The principal investigator is currently supported through Research Scientist Award MH-20868 from the ADAMHA-awarding National Institute of Mental Health, ADAMHA.

child population, one can expect to find about 15% of children with problems severe enough to warrant psychiatric treatment; current estimates range from a median of 10.8% for field studies of teacher-rated maladjustment to a median of 16.0% for field studies of parent-rated maladjustment (see Gould, Wunsch, & Dohrenwend, 1978). These general prevalence rates, of course, include several different types of disorders, such as aggression, antisocial behavior, anxiety, depression, and childhood psychosis. Problems such as aggression and anxiety are much more common among children than is psychosis; for example, Gould et al. (1978) estimated, on the basis of earlier work, that the rate of psychosis in mid-adolescence is about 1 per 1,000.

Identification of children at risk

Methods for identifying groups of children at risk for mental disorder are basic to epidemiological studies. Selection has been approached through several methods: (a) the genetic risk model, focusing on children of schizophrenic parents (see, e.g., DeFries & Plomin, 1978); (b) the use of special characteristics indicative of high risk for psychosis, such as perceptual-motor deviations (see, e.g., Erlenmeyer-Kimling, 1978); (c) the use of selected behaviors that represent potentially continuous domains of psychopathology; and (d) the use of social and family environmental factors that suggest high risk. Because of the small number of psychotic children in the Family Research Project sample, this chapter focuses on the last two methods, those involving continuity and environmental risk.

Continuity model. In a review of treatment studies, Quay and Werry (1972) concluded that when consistency is used as a model for prediction, childhood psychosis and antisocial behavior have significant prognostic power:

> The weight of evidence at the present time is that two kinds of childhood disorders, psychosis and serious antisocial behavior, have gloomy prognoses for adult life. Psychosis in children, whether it begins before puberty or whether it is schizophrenia beginning in adolescence, almost always persists into adulthood. Serious antisocial behavior in childhood is not so uniformly disastrous, but in a large minority of cases it presages life-long problems with the law, inability to earn a living, defective interpersonal relationships, and severe personal distress. [P. 445]

With regard to antisocial behavior, for example, a follow-back study by Robins (1966) found that although only 25% of children referred for antisocial behavior at around age 13 turned out to be antisocial adults, all the adults who were diagnosed as sociopathic personalities had shown antisocial behavior earlier. Gersten et al. (1976) found that among children in the Family Research Project sample, longitudinal analysis over a 5-year period indicated that aggression and conduct disorder continued over time at comparable or increased levels. Similarly, a follow-up of disturbed adolescents into adulthood (Hafner, Quast, & Shay, 1975) indicated that those with conduct disorder, compared with a matched sample with personality disorder, showed lower job stability, more incarcerations, and more divorces.

For behavior problems classified as personality disorder, such as anxiety and withdrawal, findings on continuity have been more complex. Generally, personality problems assessed in early childhood tend to decrease over time (see, e.g., Lefkowitz & Burton, 1978), but children who show more problems at one age level also tend to show more problems at other age levels (Gersten et al., 1976). Long-term studies indicate that personality disorder shows significant continuity only when assessed during early to mid-adolescence (Gersten et al., 1976; Graham & Rutter, 1973). Robins (1966) found continuity for antisocial behavior but not for personality disorder; however, it is probable that, in this study, the differential time of assessment for antisocial and nonantisocial symptoms accounts for their differential predictive power.

Environmental risk. Another approach to prediction involves identification of aspects of the familial or sociocultural environment that indicate risk for psychological disorder. Following is a brief summary of variables that have been found to be associated with psychological impairment; the studies included are primarily cross-sectional rather than longitudinal studies, and hence show concurrent rather than prognostic relationships. Among the familial factors associated with childhood psychopathology are *Parental Coldness and Rejection* (Bowlby & Ainsworth, 1964; Jacob, 1975; McCord, McCord, & Howard, 1961; Snyder, 1977), *Parental Punitiveness* (Baumrind, 1967; Becker et al., 1962; Hetherington, Stouwie, & Ridberg, 1970; Sears, 1961), *Parent Excitability and Inconsistency* (Andry, 1960; Glueck & Glueck, 1950; McCord, McCord, & Zola, 1959), *Parent Psychopathology* (Anderson, 1969; Kellam, Simon, & Ensminger, Chapter 2; Shechtman, 1970; Wolff & Acton, 1968), and *Broken Homes* (Biller, 1970; Douglas, 1964; Glueck & Glueck, 1950; Rutter, 1971). With respect to sociocultural factors, several demographic characteristics, such as age, sex, and socioeconomic status, have been shown to be related to behavior disorders in children, with most studies showing a greater prevalence of disorder among families of minority-group background or low socioeconomic status (King, 1978).

Summary

Prediction is a part of prevention, so it is important to identify aspects of early behavior or early environment that are related to behavior disorders in children. The evidence previously considered indicates that, with regard to early behavior, there is particular prognostic power for antisocial behavior and that, with regard to early environment, a number of variables, both familial and demographic, have predictive power. The purpose of the following sections is to report findings about measurement of behavioral and environmental factors and to determine the relative contribution these make to prediction of behavior disorders on a prospective basis.

Method

The present analysis is based on data from a group of urban families who were the subject of a 10-year longitudinal study initiated in 1967 (Langner, Gersten, & Eisenberg, 1977; Langner et al., 1979). At Time 1 (T1, 1967–1968) 1,034 children aged 6–18 were reported on by their mothers at home during a 2-hour questionnaire interview in a random sample of Manhattan dwelling units.

With the exception of a section on childhood physical illnesses, the behaviors reported on by mothers were all current, within the year preceding the interview. One-quarter of the children were seen by psychiatrists, and the mother's report was rated by at least two psychiatrists on 5-point impairment scales. Five years later (T2) 71%, or 732 mothers, were revisited and again reported on their children's behavior. At this time, a sample of 194 children aged 14 and over were interviewed directly, and record data from schools, police, and family court were obtained. A similar study was done on children in 1,000 welfare families. This second study is described in Eisenberg, Langner, & Gersten (1975) and in Eisenberg et al. (1976).

The stratified clustering plan used for the selection of study children resulted in a sample that was 56% white, 14% black, 29% Spanish-speaking, and 1% from other ethnic backgrounds. The sample was 52% male and 48% female, ranging in age from 6 to 18. Males and females were evenly distributed across the age groups.

Behavior measures

The measures of children's behavior were derived by factor analysis from 222 of the original 654 child behavior items in the questionnaire. A score covering 35 childhood fears and the degree to which these interfered with functioning at home, in school, and with peers was one "item" on the anxiety dimension. The total number of questions used to construct factors was 361. Eighteen relatively independent factors were found. These child behavior factors (presented in decreasing order of reliability) were termed Conflict with Parents, Dependence, Fighting, Regressive Anxiety, Mentation Problems, Competition, Delinquency, Self-Destructive Tendencies, Undemandingness, Conflict with Siblings, Isolation, Repetitive Motor Behavior, Noncompulsivity, Sex Curiosity, Training Difficulties, Weak Group Membership, Delusions-Hallucinations, and Late Development. Reliability ranged from .94 to .69 (Langner et al., 1977). At T2 the factors of Late Development and Training Difficulties were dropped because of the advancing age of the children.

Other items in the T1 questionnaire dealing with the qualities of the parents' marriage and relationship were also subjected to separate factor analyses. Eight parental factors were derived. These were (in decreasing order of reliability) Unhappy Marriage, Unleisurely Parents, Parents' Quarrels, Mother's Physical and Emotional Illness, Isolated Parents, Husband Ill and Withdrawn, Mother's Economic Dissatisfaction, and Traditional Marriage. Reliability ranged from .85 to .66 (Langner et al., 1977). The fourth factor had the greatest predictive power in this factor set.

There were, in addition, five parent–child factors, or ways in which the parents related to the child. They were (in decreasing order of reliability) Mother Traditional-Restrictive, Mother Excitable-Rejecting, Parents Punitive, Mother Supportive-Directing, and Parents Cold. Reliability ranged from .88 to .77 (Langner et al., 1977). The second, third, and fifth factors in this set were most powerfully associated with child behavior.

Family types

Thirteen factor scores representing the family and social environment (8 parental and 5 parent–child factors) were standardized, along with specific demographic variables, and subjected to Hierarchical Cluster Analysis (McKeon, 1967). The profile analysis program determines the cumulative error as each child's family is added to form a group of two families, three families, four families, and so on. By inspection, when the error of classification (error term) makes a large jump, a new group is started. Then the families are reclassified; the sum of each family's squared distances from the average profiles of the subgroups formed serves as a model. The reclassification is necessary, because individuals who were in the center when a group was being formed may have moved to the periphery of the group, or out of it. This technique transforms the factored family and social dimensions into families of various types and yields a set of family patterns that are discrete classifications. The types are named for peaks of .5 standard deviations from the mean or greater, and are not based on judgments or a priori assumptions.

Table 3.1 shows the six T1 family types, including only those families in the follow-up survey at T2, to allow for the construction of regressed change types for the families. The elevations (E) and depressions (D) of the means of the family types are indicated by an E or D, with E indicating more pathology, D indicating less pathology. From the pattern of Es and Ds, the profiles can be visualized. These family types are ordered from left to right according to increasing environmental pathology. The family types are labeled White Affluent Cohesive, White Affluent Discordant, Single Nonbiological Parent and Child, Spanish Low-Status Traditional Cohesive, Spanish Welfare Isolated, and Low Middle Status Ethnic Mix Discordant.

Some demographic characteristics of the family types (in addition to the factor scores) are shown in Table 3.2. Because of its strong contribution to the profiles, ethnic background was included as part of the name of each type. For example, 100% of the White Affluent Cohesive group and 98% of the White Affluent Discordant group were White. These groups were also affluent, as is shown by their average monthly rent at T1 of $140–$145, compared to a range of $57–$68 for the nonaffluent groups. The types were also labeled "cohesive" or "discordant," according to their scores on family relationships (see Table 3.1). In general, as one looks from left to right, or from White Affluent Cohesive to Mixed Ethnic Discordant, the number of children in the family becomes greater, rent decreases, moving to different addresses increases, and the mother's education decreases.

Child types

A typology of children was constructed, using 18 standardized child behavior dimensions. These were clustered in the same manner as the family and social environment. The clusters were formed within four age groups, and then similar clusters were combined across age groups.

The clustering technique groups the factored behavior dimensions into various types. This places each child in a behavior pattern that is discrete, rather than placing him on a single continuum. The child types are named for peaks of .5 to 1 or more standard deviations from the mean. They are not diagnoses, because they are not limited to patients and are not based on clinical judgments; diagnoses are not applicable to the large untreated

Table 3.1. *Parental and parent–child characteristics by family type*

	Family type[a]					
	WAC	WAD	SNB	STC	SW	MED
Parental factor 1: Isolated Parents	D[b].35	—	—	E[b].25	E.42	E.30
Parental factor 2: Unhappy Marriage	D.56	E.25	—	—	E.42	E.75
Parental factor 3: Mother's Physical & Emotional Illness	D.54	—	—	—	E.62	E.47
Parental factor 4: Unleisurely Parents	D.64	D.44	—	E.51	E.78	E.45
Parental factor 5: Mother's Economic Dissatisfaction	D.59	E.26	—	—	E.25	E.56
Parental factor 6: Parents' Quarrels	—	E.92	D.46	D.41	D.67	E.39
Parental factor 7: Husband Ill and Withdrawn	D.32	E.39	—	—	D.26	E.38
Parental factor 8: Traditional Marriage	D.28	D.58	—	E.67	E.56	—
Parent–child factor 1: Parents Cold	D.40	E.64	—	D.31	D.37	E.58
Parent–child factor 2: Mother Traditional-Restrictive	D.79	D.55	—	E.85	E1.14	—
Parent–child factor 3: Parents Punitive	D.26	—	—	—	E.52	E.36
Parent–child factor 4: Mother Supportive-Directing	—	E.35	D.34	—	—	—
Parent–child factor 5: Mother Excitable-Rejecting	D.29	E.75	D.28	D.35	D.27	E.38
Total N = 704[c]	203	112	49	171	36	133

[a] WAC = White Affluent Cohesive; WAD = White Affluent Discordant; SNB = Single Nonbiological Parent and Child; STC = Spanish Low-Status Traditional Cohesive; SW = Spanish Welfare Isolated; MED = Low Middle Status Ethnic Mix Discordant.
[b] D = less of that dimension and E = more of that dimension in *SD* units as compared to the dimension mean of the total sample.
[c] Of the 732 cases in the T2 follow-up, 28 did not fit into any family change type and for this reason were not included in the family typology or in the family change typology.

Table 3.2. *Social-demographic characteristics of family types*

	WAC	WAD	SNB	STC	SW	MED
% white	100	98	53	30	—	19
% black	—	—	6	—	—	68
% Spanish-speaking	—	—	41	70	100	13
% on welfare AFDC	—	—	2	—	100	26
% both natural parents	90	90	4	80	44	45
% always in natural mother's care	100	99	2	96	100	80
% Jewish	49	44	14	—	—	4
% Catholic	25	26	61	91	97	39
% Protestant	16	20	12	6	3	51
% no religion	10	10	12	3	—	6
Mean no. children	2.2	2.3	2.3	3.1	3.8	3.6
Mean monthly rent ($)	145	140	62	57	57	68
Mean no. addresses in New York City	1.8	1.8	2.0	2.4	2.9	2.7
Mean years mother's education	13.9	13.7	9.7	5.7	6.0	9.9

portion of the child population or to the well portion that exhibits personality *types* but not personality disorders. The profile analysis, then, bridges the gap between the quantitative model of dimensions and the class model of diagnoses. Profile types also make possible the acceptance of quantitative procedures by people who give treatment, because the unit of description is a person, not a dimension, and the result is holistic, not fractionated.

The profile types and their T1 frequencies (in the sample of 732 children whose mothers were interviewed at T2) are described briefly here. This information is necessary for understanding of Tables 3.4 and 3.5, which show the six most severely disturbed child types collapsed into two combined groups, C1 and C2. These designations are given at this point, along with the more detailed description of the six types contained in C1 and C2.

Sociable (N = 111 in the T2 sample, 15.2% of T2 sample of 732 cases). These children showed strong Group Membership and little Isolation. They were below average on Mentation Problems (speech, memory, concentration, etc.) and Repetitive Motor Behavior (whirling, head banging, etc.). They showed no elevation in pathology over .25 SD units on any child behavior dimension.

Competitive-Independent (N = 109, 14.9%). In addition to being more Competitive and Independent than the sample average, these children exhibited less Fighting and Isolation and fewer Mentation Problems,

Training Difficulties, Delusions-Hallucinations, and Self-Destructive Tendencies.

Dependent (N = 214, 29.2%). Children in this group were more Dependent than their peers, had less Formal Group Membership, and showed less Conflict with Parents, Conflict with Siblings, Delinquency, Fighting, Competitiveness, Sex Curiosity, and Regressive Anxiety, and fewer Mentation Problems and Self-Destructive Tendencies. The younger children showed more clear-cut dependency.

Moderate Backward Isolate (N = 101, 13.8%). These children showed Later Development, more Isolation, and more Mentation Problems. They also showed some increase in Weak Group Membership, Training Difficulties, Repetitive Motor Behavior, Dependency, and Compulsivity. They were less Competitive than their peers.

Combined groups (C1) (N = 162, 22.1%). This group included the Conflicting Aggressive, Self- and Other Destructive, and Severe Backward Isolate types.

Conflicting Aggressive (N = 100, 13.6%). These children showed more Conflict with Parents and with Siblings, more Fighting, more Delinquency, more Independence, more Anxiety, and less Compulsivity than their peers. The 15- to 18-year-old Conflicting-Aggressives were 1.5 *SD* units higher than average on the Delinquency dimension.

Self- and Other Destructive (N = 23, 3.2%). These children were more than 3 *SD* units over the mean on Self-Destructive Tendencies, and 1 *SD* unit or more higher on Fighting, Conflict with Parents, Delinquency, Regressive Anxiety, and Mentation Problems. They showed more pathology than the average on 14 of the 18 child behavior dimensions.

Severe Backward Isolate (N = 39, 5.3%). These children were 1 or more *SD* units more impaired than their peers on Repetitive Motor Behavior and Isolation, and almost 1 *SD* unit more impaired on Mentation Problems, Late Development, Conflict with Parents, Regressive Anxiety, and Training Difficulties. There is a suggestion of organic damage in this group.

Combined groups (C2) (N = 35, 4.8%). This group, collapsed for presentational purposes, included severely disturbed children. The types in this group were Delinquent Aggressive, Organic, and Delusional.

Delinquent-Aggressive (N = 15, 2.1%). These children had extreme scores (over 1 *SD* unit) on 7 dimensions: Delinquency, Fighting, Delusions-Hallucinations, Mentation Problems, Conflict with Siblings, Conflict with Parents, and Training Difficulties. They also showed somewhat smaller elevations on 8 of the remaining 11 dimensions. Six of these 15 children had been arrested; the group had the highest arrest rate (40%) of any of the child types. The label derives from mother-reported delinquency and from other behavior, rather than from the children's arrest records. This group had the most severe pathology, and it was spread over a wider range of behaviors than in any other type (15 of 18 dimensions).

Organic (N = 8, 1.1%). These children were between 12 and 18 years old and had extreme scores (between 2 and 4 *SD* units) on Mentation Problems, Delusions-Hallucinations, Repetitive Motor Behavior, Isolation, Regressive Anxiety, and Fighting. They had much worse scores than their peers on almost all behaviors, and no scores that clearly showed less than average pathology.

Delusional (N = 12, 1.6%). These children were almost 3 *SD* units above average on the Delusions-Hallucinations dimension and about 1 *SD* unit elevated on Regressive Anxiety. They showed minor elevations on Mentation Problems, Compulsivity, Delinquency, and Isolation. They also showed somewhat less Conflict with Siblings, Late Development, and Dependence.

A description of the clustering of the children from the welfare sample is given in Eisenberg et al. (1976). It is remarkable that in these two follow-up samples of about 700 children each, one representative and the other taken from welfare rolls, the distribution of child types is remarkably similar. When each welfare child is matched to one of the cross-section profile types, the greatest difference is 5%, between the 34% of the welfare and the 29% of the cross-sectional sample classified as Dependent. Only 5% of welfare children could not be matched to cross-section types, because limits were set on the distance their profile might have from the models.

Predictor and criterion variables

The predictors of T2 behavior were based on early behavior or early environment. The former consisted of the T1 child types and seven T1 child behavior dimensions. The environmental predictors were the T1 family types and the Total Stress Score, based on three demographic variables (the number of children in the household, the number of natural parents then living with the child, and the number of addresses at which the child had lived), as well as five parent–child factors, eight parental factors, and four childhood illness scores. (These last scores were a priori scores, and not factors.) Race and social class variables (employed in the family types) were removed from the Total Stress Score to be used as controls, a change that weakened its predictive power but increased its utility.

The criterion variables were T2 outcomes from school and police record data, as well as child behaviors and global measures of impairment based upon the mother's report. The T2 outcomes consisted of (a) police data on whether the individual was ever arrested after T1 and (b) an Adverse Outcome Score ranging from 0 to 4, comprised of the same police data on arrests, school record data on dropping out of school or being held over in school, and the mother's report on expulsion from school. Also from mother's reports, there were seven T2 child behavior dimensions (Mentation Problems, Conflict with Parents, Regressive Anxiety, Delusions-Hallucinations, Fighting, Delinquency, and Isolation). These seven dimensions were moderately or strongly related to impairment ratings. Two global impairment measures were a T2 Total Impairment Rating and the T2 Total Symptom Score. The first measure was based on a simulation of the psychiatric impairment rating using the T1 regression weights assigned to the behavior dimensions, when age and sex were controlled. The T2 Total Symptom Score was the sum of all items considered to be serious symptoms by three of four judges (the project director and the three psychiatrists who rated the children).

Results

Prediction of behavior scores

To test the relative contributions of early behavior and early environment to later behavior, we performed stepwise regression analyses, entering first the T1 stress score and then a behavior score such as the T1 Total Symptom Score, which was composed of the sum of all pathognomonic responses to 654 behavior questions. The scores used were the Total Symptom Score, Mentation, Conflict with Parents, Regressive Anxiety, Fighting, Delusions-Hallucinations, Delinquency, Isolation, and the Total Impairment Rating. The prediction was of various T2 behavior scores.

An example of this procedure is given here, in lieu of a table. The T1 Total Stress Score, entered first, accounted for 4% of the variance in the criterion (Total Symptom Score at T2), whereas the T1 Total Symptom Score, entered second, added 15.2%, bringing the total explained variance up to 19.2%. If the behavior score (or Total Symptom Score) is entered first and the Total Stress Score is entered second, no increment owing to stress is in evidence. Of course, the R^2 or total percentage of variance explained by the stress and behavior measures together remains 19.2%. In all the analysis done on this model, all the increments owing to early behavior were significant, except for Delusions. None of the increments owing to stress was significant (when behavior was entered first) except for Mentation Problems, and that was small in magnitude. In these equations, then, stress (or environment) adds little or nothing over T1 behavior in predicting T2 behavior, whereas behavior dimensions predicting themselves 5 years later add significantly and consistently over the T1 stress contribution.

Although this technique of reversing the order of entry of variables into the regression analysis to test their differential increments in variance is recommended by some and not by other practitioners, the impression that the T1 environmental measures are weaker than the T1 behavior measures in predictive power is problematic because of several methodological issues. Because the behavior dimension showed relatively high internal consistency (by factor analysis), and high stability, as measured by the alpha coefficient, whereas the environmental factors did not exhibit those qualities to such a degree, the results might be attributable to this reliability. Just as problematic is the fact that the measure of behavior is *identical* at T1 and T2, whereas the stress (or environmental) measure at T1 is predicting the T2 behavior dimension in a different domain from itself. It is somewhat unfair to compare the stress measure with the behavior measure, especially in the case where the behavior measure is identical with the 5-year outcome that one is predicting. (See Table 3.5 and discussion.)

Prediction of outcome scores

Table 3.3 shows stepwise prediction by stress and the behavior dimensions to the criterion score of four T2 outcomes in the adverse outcome measure. These outcomes are: arrested, dropped out and held over in school (based on police and school report data that are independent of the questionnaire survey), and expelled from school (based on the mother's report). Here the story is strikingly different. On the left, stress is

Table 3.3. *Stepwise regression analyses: Time 1 (T1) Total Stress Score and T1 Child Behavior Score, predicting Time 2 (T2) Adverse Outcome Score*

Stress entered first	R^2	Behavior entered first	R^2
(1) T1 Stress[a]	3.5	(1) T1 Total Symptom Score	3.4
(2) T1 Total Symptom Score*	4.8	(2) T1 Stress**	4.8
(1) T1 Stress	3.5	(1) T1 Mentation Problems	8.4
(2) T1 Mentation Problems***	9.6	(2) T1 Stress*	9.6
(1) T1 Stress	3.5	(1) T1 Conflict with Parents	0.0
(2) T1 Conflict with Parents	3.7	(2) T1 Stress***	3.7
(1) T1 Stress	3.5	(1) T1 Regressive Anxiety	0.2
(2) T1 Regressive Anxiety***	5.1	(2) T1 Stress***	5.1
(1) T1 Stress	3.5	(1) T1 Fighting	0.2
(2) T1 Fighting	3.5	(2) T1 Stress***	3.5
(1) T1 Stress	3.5	(1) T1 Delusions-Hallucinations	2.0
(2) T1 Delusions-Hallucinations	4.7	(2) T1 Stress***	4.7
(1) T1 Stress	3.5	(1) T1 Delinquency	12.3
(2) T1 Delinquency***	14.0	(2) T1 Stress**	14.0
(1) T1 Stress	3.4	(1) T1 Isolation	0.4
(2) T1 Isolation	3.4	(2) T1 Stress***	3.4
(1) T1 Stress	3.5	(1) T1 Total Impairment Rating	4.9
(2) T1 Total Impairment Rating***	6.0	(2) T1 Stress*	6.0

[a] The T1 Total Stress Score is composed of the following: demographic, parental, parent–child, and child's physical illness score.
* $p = .05$.
** $p = .01$.
*** $p = .001$.

entered first and the behaviors are entered second, and they make significant increments at the .05 level in outcome score variance to 6 out of 9 behavior measures: Total Symptom Score, Mentation, Anxiety, Delusions, Delinquency, and Total Impairment. On the right side, where behaviors are entered first and stress (or environment) is entered second, it makes a significant increment over behavior to T2 outcome variance *in all cases at the .05 level.* Note that when the predictor is in the very same domain as the outcome, for example, mother-reported Delinquency predicting future arrests and school dropouts, and so on, the correlation between T1 Delinquency and the T2 Adverse Outcome Score is necessarily high, and 12.3% of the Adverse Outcome Score is already accounted for by Delinquency. The increment owing to stress, then (1.7%), must necessarily be smaller, because the first-order correlation of Delinquency and outcomes is .35. Anxiety and Isolation, being behavior domains that contrast strongly with Delinquency, allow the environment, or stress score, to make a bigger relative contribution. For example, Anxiety contributes 0.2% to these essentially antisocial outcomes, and when stress is added the R^2 increases to 5.1%. We rarely arrest people for Anxiety; so its contribution to the outcome score based on arrests and school dropouts is almost zero.

The zero-order correlations of the T1 child behaviors, T1 Total Stress Score, and the two criteria (child behaviors at T2 and Adverse Outcome Score at T2) were examined to see if they might explain our results. The correlation or stability of a child behavior at T1 with the same child behavior at T2 is on the average so large (.41) that it eclipses the average correlation of early stress and T2 behavior (.16). However, when T1 child behavior is related to the Adverse Outcome Score as the criterion, the average correlation is .15. T1 stress and Adverse Outcome Score are correlated .19. The predictive power of stress has not changed much (from .16 to .19), but the power of child behavior drops from .41 to .15. This shows that its apparent power was in part an artifact of the self-correlation. (The suggestions raised in the preceding section are supported by this finding.)

The Total Stress Score can therefore contribute much more to the T2 Adverse Outcome Score than it can to T2 behavior scores. One exception is Delinquency, which is correlated .35 with the Adverse Outcome Score. Another exception is Mentation, which has a zero-order correlation of .29 with the T2 outcome score. In all other cases of single domains, such as Conflict with Parents (.00), Anxiety (.06), Fighting (.06), Delusions (.15), and Isolation (.04), the T1 stress score correlation (.19) exceeds the correlation between the T1 behavior score and the T2 outcome score.

Specific behaviors: Mentation Problems and Delinquency

It is of more than passing interest that Mentation Problems predicts moderately well (.29) the school problems in the Adverse Outcome Score. Speech problems, poor memory, and inability to concentrate are symptoms likely to foreshadow school failure. Anxiety, Isolation, and Conflict with Parents are essentially unrelated to the Adverse Outcome Score. Previous analysis has indicated that the more friends a child has, the higher is that child's risk of arrest. In addition, children scoring high on the Self-Destructive factor, which seems to contain the clearly depressive symptoms, had low Delinquency scores and fewer arrests. The isolated, depressed, anxious child is least likely to get arrested and least likely to drop out of school or be held over in grade, or to be expelled. These relationships have not been examined with ethnic and social class groups held constant – a proceeding that may "explain away" the relationship. However, these data are suggestive evidence for the strong influence of peer socialization into the delinquent subculture, as is argued in A. Cohen's *Delinquent Boys* (1955). Is socialized delinquency pathological or is it so widespread in our society that it is statistically normal? We approach statistical normalcy when 20% of white boys and 50% of black boys have been arrested, as in our sample. But that is a relativistic basis for defining psychopathology, and we are supposed to employ absolute standards for judging behavior. Solutions through the usual services seem unlikely, especially when the majority eventually becomes defined as "sick." This is because our services are generally built on a medical model. Perhaps only broad social changes can cope with problems of this magnitude and prevalence.

Four variables make unique contributions to the prediction of mother-reported delinquency: loss of the father, a large number of addresses, having punitive parents, and having cold parents. In our data, social rather than familial factors predominate in predicting delinquency among boys, whereas among girls a series of familial factors tends to dominate (Simcha-Fagan, 1979). However, parental criminal behavior and intrafamilial violence affect boys' delinquency more directly. It is not clear, then, that *only* social changes, and not familial changes, can be effective in preventing delinquency. It is perhaps easier to document the effects of family relationships on children than to document the effects of poverty and prejudice. For that reason, it may appear that the family, rather than society, bears the major responsibility for our epidemic of antisocial behavior. Keniston (1977) has argued very persuasively that the family is not autonomous, and that blaming or educating parents will not solve their children's problems. He emphasizes social class and racial discrimination as the sources of these problems. At this point, we have not been able to demonstrate his contention with our data, except by showing that race has a great deal of residual predictive variance, even when the familial components of being black or Puerto Rican are taken into account (Langner, Gersten, Eisenberg, 1974).

Family and child types as predictors

A second method of comparing environmental and behavioral contributions to prediction of child behavior employs the T1 family typology, representing the environment, and the T1 child typology, representing behavior (see Table 3.4). It is important to know that the family and child

Table 3.4. *Incidence of one or more arrests for T1 family type vs. T1 child type*

Family type[a]	N	% with one or more arrests	Child type[a]	N	% with one or more arrests
White Affluent Cohesive	203	3.0%	Group Affiliative (Sociable)	111	8.1
White Affluent Discordant	112	7.1	Competitive-Independent	109	11.9
Single Nonbiological Parent and Child	49	12.2	Dependent	214	14.5
Spanish Low-Status Traditional Cohesive	171	14.0	Moderate Backward Isolate	101	16.8
Spanish Welfare Isolated	36	19.4	Combined groups		10.5
			Conflicting Aggressive	100	9.0
			Self- and Other Destructive	23	17.4
			Severe Backward Isolate	39	10.3
Low Middle Status Ethnic Mix Discordant	133	30.8	Combined groups		28.6
			Delinquent Aggressive	15	40.0
			Organic	8	25.0
			Delusional	12	16.7
Total	704[b]			732	

[a] Rank ordered by increasing pathology as indicated by means on family dimensions or means on child behavior dimensions.
[b] Of the 732 cases in the T2 follow-up, 28 did not fit into any family change type and for this reason were not included in the new family typology or in the family-change typology.

types are ranked in ascending order of pathology, as measured by the averages of the standard scores used to create the profiles. The White Affluent Cohesives are, for lack of better terms, the best, or healthiest, families, and the Sociable children are the healthiest children. Table 3.4 shows the arrest rates according to family and child types. The best family type has a 3% arrest rate, and the best child type has an 8% arrest rate. Because "healthy" families and children should have low arrest rates, and they do, our attention centers on the difference between their rates. Clearly, healthy families have less than half the arrest rate of the healthy Sociable children; so environment is a better predictor at this end of the scale. The rates of arrest increase generally as one looks down the ranked list of families and children. What of the relative risk from best to worst category? For families, the healthiest type has a 3% arrest rate, as just noted; the worst type (Low Middle Status Discordant) has a rate of 30.8%. This ratio is 10:1, a large relative risk. The relative risk for arrest for the child types ranges from 8% to 28% (a relative risk of 3.5 : 1). Here again, in dealing with outcomes, the environmental measure, the family type, does better at predicting than the behavioral measure.

If we rank the family and child types listed in Table 3.4 from 1 to 6 (from top to bottom) on the basis of their family or individual pathology, we can correlate the rankings with the ranks of their percentage of arrests. If a Spearman rank-order correlation is calculated between family pathology rank and arrest rank, the match is perfect for family types, and the correlation is 1.00. The Spearman rank-order correlation between the child types and percentage of arrests, however, is less, .66.

Table 3.5 shows the percentage of a score of 1 or more, 2 or more, and 3 or more on the adverse outcome measure by family and child types. The rank-order correlation between a score of 1 or more on the adverse outcome measure and the family types is .94; the rank-order correlation between the Adverse Outcome Score and the child type is .69. The relative risk for the family types (4.8, based on 42.9%/8.9%) is also better than the relative risk for the child types (2.6, based on 54.3%/20.7%), a finding that corroborates the strength of the environment.

With respect to a score of 2 or more on the adverse outcome measure, the rank-order correlations are 1.00 for family and .54 for child types. The relative risks are 13 (39%/3%) for family and 4 (40%/10%) for child types. This shows improving power of the family types as a predictor when scores of 2+ on the adverse outcome measure are considered.

When scores of 3+ on the adverse outcome measure are considered, the rank order correlations are .99 for family and .26 for child types. The relative risk for the family type is 44 (based on 22%/0.5%), against the relative risk of 4.6 for the child types (23%/5%). As the number of bad outcomes or malfunctioning areas of the child increases, the family or environmental measure seems to increase in predictive strength, and the child behavior measure seems to remain relatively unchanged in power. The importance of environment for prediction or understanding is amply illustrated by these relative risks.

Effect of family change

Using record data on outcome as a dependent variable, we divided family types into change groups that either were stable over the 5-year period or became better or worse child environments, as measured by regressed change scores (see Table 3.6). The scores of 1 or more on the adverse outcome measure alone are shown. The arrangement of families into affluent families getting better, affluent families getting worse, disadvan-

Table 3.5. *Percentage with one, two, or three or more adverse outcomes at Time 2 by family type and child type* (N = 704)

One or more adverse outcomes				Two or more adverse outcomes				Three or more adverse outcomes			
Family type	%	Child type[a]	%	Family type	%	Child type[a]	%	Family type	%	Child type[a]	%
WAC	9	GA	21	WAC	3	GA	10	WAC	0.5	GA	5
WAD	13	CI	22	WAD	7	CI	8	WAD	2	CI	3
SNB	31	DEP	35	SNB	14	DEP	15	SNB	8	DEP	4
STC	33	MBI	44	STC	16	MBI	18	STC	8	MBI	8
SW	58	C1	26	SW	33	C1	9	SW	19	C1	2
MED	43	C2	54	MED	39	C2	40	MED	22	C2	23

Notes: The adverse outcomes in question are: expelled from school, dropped out of school, held over in school, and arrested. Of the 732 cases in the T2 follow-up, 28 did not fit into any family change type and for this reason were not included in the typology. Rank ordering is by increasing pathology as indicated by means on family dimensions or means on child behavior dimensions.

[a] GA = Group affiliative (Sociable); CI = Competitive-Independent; DEP = Dependent; MBI = Moderate Backward Isolate; C1 is a combined grouping consisting of Conflicting-Aggressive, Self- and Other Destructive, and Severe Backward Isolate types; C2 is a combined grouping consisting of Delinquent-Aggressive, Organic, and Delusional types.

Table 3.6. *Proportion of one or more adverse outcomes (Time 2) by family and change types, grouped to form four ranks comparable to child change types*

Family and change types	Improving or worsening	% with one or more adverse outcomes	Arcsine	Effect size	N	% of total
White Affluent Cohesive	Stable or better	7.4	.55		163	23.2
White Affluent Discordant	Better			.21		
White Affluent Cohesive	Worse	13.8	.76	.75	152	21.6
White Affluent Discordant	Stable or worse					
Single Nonbiological Parent and Child	Better			.53		
Spanish Low-Status Traditional Cohesive	Stable or better			.83		
Spanish Welfare Isolated	Better	36.3	1.29	.62	179	25.4
Low Middle Status Ethnic Mix Discordant	Better			.09		
Single Nonbiological Parent and Child	Stable or worse					
Spanish Low-Status Traditional Cohesive	Worse	40.5	1.38		210	29.8
Spanish Welfare Isolated	Stable or worse					
Low Middle Status Ethnic Mix Discordant	Stable or worse					
Total					704	100.0

taged families getting better, and disadvantaged families getting worse should have produced a fairly smooth progression of increasingly larger percentages of adverse outcomes. This progression does not, in fact, appear.

Almost exclusively white families are seen in the White Affluent Cohesive and White Affluent Discordant groups (see Table 3.6). The adverse outcomes of improving White Affluent families are rarer (7.4%) than those of worsening families of the same general profile (13.8%). The relative risk for worsening families is 2 to 1. Spontaneous improvement in these white families results in a reduction of the rate of poor school outcomes and arrests from approximately 14% to 7%. Gersten et al. (1975) found that improvement by intervention ("nonspontaneous") was of small consequence in recovery, and available to less than half the children at risk in the present sample.

In contrast to the difference between children of improving and worsening White Affluent families, there appears to be little relative difference in rates of one or more adverse outcomes between a group we could call "disadvantaged families improving," who have a poor outcome rate of 36.3%, and "disadvantaged families worsening," with a rate of 40.5%. If our goal is amelioration of the impact of mental disorder and social pathology on human functioning, this result should be extremely depressing. The White Affluent families, with improvement in home atmosphere, marriage, economic status, and other environmental variables, seem to be moderately capable of improving their children's future. Positive changes in poor families, heavily black and Spanish-speaking, on welfare and often without fathers, hardly seem to affect the school and arrest outcome rate of their children. There is little difference between 36% and 40%. The effect size is almost nil (.09).

In Table 3.6 (and Table 3.7) a technique called arcsine transformation is used to measure the size of the effect of the predictor variable, and this effect size can be roughly translated into a statement of power, or correlation (J. Cohen, 1969). An arcsine transformation flattens the distribution and diminishes the problems caused by very long tails. In Table 3.6, there are arcsines for each of the percentages of adverse outcomes (for example, 7.4% = arcsine .55). In assessing the size of the effect, we compared all six possible pairs of percentages. For example, the effect size of the improving or worsening White Affluents (7.4% vs. 13.8%) is obtained by subtracting their arcsines, .55 from .76, yielding an effect size of .21. The effect sizes are given in Table 3.6 and range from .09 to .83; the average is .50. Effect sizes of .20 are equivalent to Pearson correlations of .10, those around .50 are equivalent to Pearson *r*s of .25, and effects around .80 are equivalent to Pearson correlations of .37 to .39. The overall correlation power of the family typology predicting 1+ adverse outcomes is equal to about .25.

Most important in *absolute* terms are the high rates of disadvantaged children (about 40%) compared to White Affluents' children (about 10%) *regardless of change*. The average effect size (J. Cohen, 1969) between change groups, holding family type constant, is .15 (the average of .21 and .09), which is equivalent to a Pearson correlation of less than .10. The average effect size of *T1* environmental types, holding change direction constant, is .68 (.75 and .62), equivalent to a Pearson correlation of approximately .35. For agency outcomes then, change alone is weak; initial family environment (specifically, White Affluent vs. all others) is strong.

Shepherd Kellam (Kellam et al., Chapter 2), following a group of black first graders in Chicago for 10 years, questions whether their early childhood experiences caused irreversible damage, and also whether there is a continuation of a very adverse environment as a constant negative reinforcement, a matter that would make it *appear* that the damage is irreversible. Our present data would not support the idea that early stresses necessarily cause irreversible damage, because children of *improving* White Affluent families showed a somewhat reduced risk on the Adverse Outcome Score (7%). Yet this difference is not large on an absolute basis. It is large only relative to the 14% rate of children from *worsening* white families. In addition, Kellam's idea that negative reinforcement by the broader environment might make it *appear* as if damage is irreversible seems supported by the lack of a large difference between children from improving and those from worsening *disadvantaged* families.

Our final comparison of behavior and environment as predictors is based upon Table 3.7. This table must be contrasted with Table 3.6 if we are to assess the differential contribution to outcome score prediction. Four family types were created, equivalent in number to the child-change types. Again the Adverse Outcome Score was set at 1 or more, because there was a very sharp drop in effect as soon as a score of 2 or more was predicted, and there was no effect whatsoever for a score of 3 or more (a score that involved only 5% of the entire sample).

The largest effect size was .41, based on the difference between the converted percentages of 22.1% of the Stable-Independent and 41.4% of the General Worsening child types. The average effect size, .25, was of course much below this. It is the rough equivalent of a Pearson r of .10. (In Table 3.7 there was no attempt to sort out the effects of change vs. T1 status.) The average effect sizes of family change (Table 3.6) were .50,

Table 3.7. *Proportion of one or more adverse outcomes (T1 → T2) by child behavior change type*

Child behavior change type	% with one or more adverse outcomes	Arcsine	Effect size	*N*	% of total
Stable independent	22.1	.98		226	30.9
			.02		
More aggressive	22.6	1.00	.31	1.46	19.9
			.41		
			.29		
General improvement	36.2	1.29			
			.39	232	31.7
			.10		
General worsening	41.4	1.39		128	17.5
Total				732	100.0
% of total with one or more adverse outcomes	31.0				

Note: The adverse outcomes in question are: expelled from school, dropped out of school, held over in school, and arrested.

equivalent to a Pearson *r* of .25. The contrast of child change (.10) and family change (.25) is considerable, although neither is of great magnitude. The recurrent theme of this chapter is, however, reinforced; knowing the child's environment, or change in environment, can be more of a help in predicting community outcomes than knowing the child's behavior or change in behavior. Note that both environment and behavior are fairly stable over this short span of 5 years, so that change measures do not appear to be as strong as they might in a very rapidly changing society.

How does the family change typology compare in power with the Total Stress Score, which is composed primarily of the same family factors and demographic variables? The Pearson *r* between the T1 Total Stress Score and the T2 Behavior Outcome Score is .19. The family change typology (Table 3.6) is performing at about that level or slightly better ($r = .25$) in predicting the outcome score. This is a built-in check, showing that the family data, whether in the form of a total score or in that of a clustered family typology, has similar predictive power for behavior outcomes based on community records.

The child behavior dimensions, which correlate on the average approximately .15 with the Adverse Outcome Score, are performing at about the same level as the child change typology ($r = .10$). Yet behavior (by dimension or typology) is not as strong as environment when predicting an independent or external behavioral criterion. For adverse outcome prediction, the environmental measures, such as the stress score and the family type, are clearly superior to early behavior measures. For predicting nonindependent dimensions of behavior, however, the T1 behavior is clearly better than the T1 environment, partly because of the artifacts of predictor overlap and consistency of behavior over time.

Summary of findings

1. T1 environmental measures appeared to be weaker than T1 behavior measures in predicting T2 behaviors. This was primarily a function of the fact that the behavior measures were identically measured at both times, and had an average stability coefficient of .41, whereas the environmental (stress) measure was predicting a domain vastly different from itself (T2 behavior).
2. When T1 environmental measures and T1 behavior measures were used to predict T2 adverse outcomes (school and police reports), the environmental (stress) measures were more powerful. The relative strength of the stress measures was enhanced because the behavior measures at T1 and T2 were not identical, nor were they from identical sources (the source at T1 was the mother's report; at T2 it was school and police records).
3. When the T1 family types and T1 child types (created by cluster or profile analysis) were ranked in order of pathology, the family type (environment) was more predictive of later arrest rates than the child type. This was also true of the prediction of adverse outcomes (three school variables plus arrests).
4. Family and child types were divided into those which were stable and those which became better or worse over the 5-year period. The family-change types were moderately related to adverse outcomes ($r \cong .25$). The child change types were minimally related to adverse outcomes ($r \cong .10$).
5. Children from disadvantaged families had a 36%–40% rate of one or more adverse outcomes, whereas children from advantaged (white) families had a rate between 7% and 14%. The effect of change groups, holding family type constant, suggests a correlation of less than .10. The effect of family types, holding change constant, is equivalent to a correlation of .35. Initial environment is stronger; change over 5 years is weaker. Minority children especially do not show any marked improvement in school and police adverse outcome rates even when their families improve.

6. The lack of minority children's improvement with 5-year improvement of the family environment was attributed to negative reinforcement from the extrafamilial environment, and possible effects of the peer group.

Discussion

Knowing about families is crucial for prediction of children's behavior, and perhaps more so when one is considering specific outcomes that our society judges socially undesirable. Records are kept about social disruption, but teachers, parents, the police, and courts are not especially concerned with shy, withdrawn, depressed, or anxious children. Because social control rather than growth of the child seems to be the primary function of all these institutions, our criterion variables from record data tend to be heavily one-sided. This is no doubt a cultural bias, and there may already be some societies that penalize the quiet rather than the disruptive child. (Certainly we have subcultures in which quietness and shyness are risky.) Clinical and social judgment have a way of being fitted to the practical requirements of the society.

If one trusts the mother's reports, because they predict some 5-year outcomes, then we can say that 5-year prediction of asocial behavior (not measured by record data), as well as antisocial, is quite good. The total R^2 for the more asocial kinds of behavior dimensions at T2, when predicted by 32 factors, *including* the same T1 behavior dimensions, is 41.4% for Anxiety, 30.4% for Mentation Problems, and 17.7% for Isolation. At about the same or a slightly higher level of prediction are the more antisocial behaviors: 52.4% for Conflict with Parents, 43% for Fighting, and 34.1% for Delinquency. These proportions of explained variance are high because they have been predicted by both T1 environment *and* T1 behavior. Age and sex have also been included as predictors, and age is highly correlated with antisocial behavior for the age range studied.

If we can account for as much as half of the variance in some aspects of child behavior 5 years later, even by including previous behavior in actuarial fashion, that is probably the maximum we can achieve with our present state of knowledge and crude measurement techniques. Adding predictors from the genetic domain and the physical environment, such as hydrocarbon and carbon monoxide levels; dietary factors, such as protein intake; and pediatric factors, such as birth weight, might improve the prediction somewhat. It should do so, but alas, these variables all overlap social class, ethnic background, and family life-styles and child-rearing practices. The greater the overlap, the less likely it is that a new variable will make a unique contribution or increment. One also pays the price of myriad predictors, because there is a sharp correction downward for the number of predictors used, resulting in the so-called shrunken *R*, which sometimes shrinks out of sight. Understanding the relationships, rather than counting the prevalence of particular disorders or the amount of variance explained, should be our research goal. If parental coldness or punishment results in antisocial behavior across cultures, if maternal excitability rather than loss of parents or other object loss is associated with childhood depression in other societies, if moving around and large families are linked to impaired school functioning worldwide, then specific structural aspects of societies will be linked to specific types of malfunctioning in children. Our measurement techniques may be primitive, but at worst the associations we do find will only have been weakened by our methods. If the associations or predictions are substantial despite this weakening, then we can make a first approach to a science of the social etiology of mental and behavioral disorder.

One source of apparent weakness in the environmental predictors is based on a philosophical concept, namely, that the child's current behavior has incorporated into itself all the influences of the previous and concurrent environmental factors. We start out with children aged 6–18 and look at a 5-year piece of their lives. Yet their environment affected them for between 5 and 17 years *before* we visited them and their families. The previous environment (prior to T1) is hardly measured at all by our study, and emphasis is on the current environment and current behavior, or T1 environment and T2 behavior. At T1, the effects of an average 11 years of previous environmental contact are already found incorporated into the personality and behavior. *These environmental factors continue to operate through the behavior*. They only appear to lose power. Only a few of the predictors, such as early loss of parents, are retrospective. The study that can start at birth and accumulate annual or monthly environmental and behavioral data will have a much better chance of observing the full strength of the environmental stresses in prediction.

Has this been just an academic exercise? Perhaps "The child is father to the man" should be changed to "Show me a child, the child's family, and his or her society, and I will be able to predict about 50% of the child's behavior variation 5 years later. Moreover, if you show me only the child's family and social background, I will often do better at predicting his or her later school and antisocial troubles than I would from seeing only the child's behavior." Of course, both sets of information are needed if we are to do the best possible job of prediction and understanding. The "show me" statement encourages gathering more information on current behavior, family history, and social background, but our findings would eliminate five-sixths of the information often recorded on the grounds that it is irrelevant and makes no unique contribution to prediction or to the etiology of children's disorders, at least in this sample. Of some 70 environmental predictors tested, only 11 made significant unique contributions to many specific behaviors. In rank order of decreasing predictive power these were: being Spanish-speaking, having punitive parents, having cold parents, being black, having an excitable-rejecting mother, having a mother with much physical and emotional illness, being one of a large number of children in the household, coming from a family paying high rent, having a traditional-restrictive mother, having lived at a high number of addresses, and living with a low number of natural parents (see Langner et al., 1977, Table 2-6; Langner et al., 1980).

A large percentage of people who become patients in our society are really environmental, situational, or reactive cases. Their environment should have been changed. This holds for physical as well as emotional problems: Stopping smoking and air pollution is better medicine than a lung operation; exercise and diet are better than a coronary bypass. In the same way, education for marriage and child rearing (along with birth control), adequate jobs, stable communities, elimination of minority status and prejudice, and the reduction of coldness, punitiveness, and liability both in parents and in the larger society are better "medicine" in the long run than the slow repair of psychological damage by individual or group psychotherapy or drugs. The professional, both practitioner and behavioral scientist, should get involved in social change, or at least in the primary prevention of disorder.

References

Anderson, L. M. Personality characteristics of parents of neurotic, aggressive, and normal pre-adolescent boys. *Journal of Consulting and Clinical Psychology*, 1969, *33*, 575–581.

Andry, R. G. *Delinquency and parental pathology*. London: Methuen, 1960.

Baumrind, D. Child care practices anteceding three patterns of pre-school behavior. *Genetic Psychology Monographs*, 1967, *75*, 43–88.

Becker, W. C., Peterson, D. R., Luria, Z., Shoemaker, D. J., & Hellmer, L. A. Relations of factors derived from parent-interview ratings to behavior problems of five-year-olds. *Child Development*, 1962, *33*, 509–535.

Biller, H. B. Father absence and the personality development of the male child. *Developmental Psychology*, 1970, *2*, 181–201.

Bowlby, J., & Ainsworth, M. *Maternal care and mental health*. Geneva: Penguin, 1964.

Cohen, A. K. *Delinquent boys*. Chicago: Free Press, 1955.

Cohen, J. *Statistical power analysis for the behavioral sciences*. New York: Academic Press, 1969.

DeFries, J. C., & Plomin, R. Behavioral genetics. *Annual Review of Psychology*, 1978, *29*, 473–515.

Douglas, J. W. B. *The home and the school.* London: Macgibbon & Kae, 1964.

Eisenberg, J. G., Gersten, J. C., Langner, T. S., McCarthy, E. D., & Simcha-Fagan, O. A behavioral classification of welfare children from survey data. *American Journal of Orthopsychiatry*, 1976, *46*(3), 47–463.

Eisenberg, J. G., Langner, T. S., & Gersten, J. C. Differences in the behavior of welfare and non-welfare children in relation to parental characteristics. *Journal of Community Psychology*, Monograph Supplement, October 1975.

Erlenmeyer-Kimling, L. Genetic approaches to the study of schizophrenia: The genetic evidence as a tool in research. National Foundation, Original Article Series, 1978.

Gersten, J. C., Langner, T. S., Eisenberg, J. G., & Simcha-Fagan, O. Spontaneous recovery and incidence of psychological disorder in urban children. *Psychiatry Digest,* August 1975, pp. 35–43.

Gersten, J. C., Langner, T. S., Eisenberg, J. G., Simcha-Fagan, O., & McCarthy, E. D. Stability and change in types of behavioral disturbance of children and adolescents. *Journal of Abnormal Child Psychology*, 1976, *4*(2), 111–127.

Glueck, S., & Glueck, E. *Unraveling juvenile delinquency*. New York: Commonwealth Fund, 1950.

Gould, M. S., Wunsch, R., & Dohrenwend, B. P. *Formulation of hypotheses about the prevalence of psychiatric disorders in children in the United States*. Unpublished manuscript, 1978. Available from Bruce P. Dohrenwend, Columbia University.

Graham, P., & Rutter, M. Psychiatric disorder in the young adolescent: A follow-up study. *Proceedings of the Royal Society of Medicine*, 1973, *66*, 1226–1229.

Hafner, A. J., Quast, W., & Shay, M. J. The adult adjustment of one thousand psychiatric and pediatric patients: Initial findings from a twenty-five year follow-up. In R. D. Wirt, G. Winokur, & M. Roff (Eds.), *Life history research in psychopathology* (Vol. 4). Minneapolis: University of Minnesota Press, 1975.

Hetherington, E. M., Stouwie, & Ridberg, E. H. *Patterns of family interaction and child rearing attitudes related to three dimensions of juvenile delinquency*. Unpublished manuscript, University of Wisconsin, 1970.

Jacob, T. Family interaction in disturbed and normal families: A methodological and substantive review. *Psychological Bulletin*, 1975, *82*, 33–65.

Keniston, K. *All our children: The American family under pressure*. New York: Harcourt Brace Jovanovich, 1977.

King, L. M. Social and cultural influences on psychopathology. *Annual Review of Psychology*, 1978, *29*, 405–433.

Langner, T. S., Gersten, J. C., & Eisenberg, J. G. Approaches to measurement and definition in the epidemiology of behavior disorders: Ethnic background and child behavior. *International Journal of Health Services* 1974, *4*(3), 483–501.

Langner, T. S., Gersten, J. C., & Eisenberg, J. G. The epidemiology of mental disorder in children: Implications for community psychiatry. In G. Serban (Ed.), *New trends of psychiatry in the community*. Cambridge, Mass.: Ballinger, 1977.

Langner, T. S., Gersten, J. C., Eisenberg, J. G., Greene, E. L., & Herson, J. H. *Children under stress: Family and social factors in the behavior of urban children and adolescents*. New York: Columbia University Press (in press).

Langner, T. S., McCarthy, E. D., Gersten, J. C., Simcha-Fagan, O., & Eisenberg, J. G. Factors in children's behavior and mental health over time: The family research project. In R. G. Simmons (Ed.), *Research in Community and Mental Health – An Annual Compilation of Research*, 1979, Vol. 1, Part II, 127–81. JAI Press, Greenwich, Conn.

Lefkowitz, M. M., & Burton, N. Childhood depression: A critique of the concept. *Psychological Bulletin,* 1978, *85,* 716–726.

McCord, W., McCord, J., & Howard, A. Familial correlates of aggression in nondelinquent male children. *Journal of Abnormal and Social Psychology*, 1961, *62*, 79–93.

McCord, W., McCord, J., & Zola, I. K. *Origins of crime*. New York: Columbia University Press, 1959.

McKeon, J. Hierarchical Cluster Analysis. George Washington University Biometrics Laboratory, Washington, D.C., 1967.

Quay, H. C., & Werry, J. S. (Eds.). *Psychopathological disorders of children*. New York: Wiley, 1972.

Robins, L. N. *Deviant children grown up*. Baltimore: Williams & Wilkins, 1966.

Rutter, M. Parent–child separation: Psychological effects on the children. *Journal of Child Psychology and Psychiatry*, 1971, *12*, 233–260.

Sears, R. R. Relation of early socialization to aggression in middle childhood. *Journal of Abnormal and Social Psychology*, 1961, *63*, 466–492.

Shechtman, A. Psychiatric symptoms observed in normal and disturbed children. *Journal of Clinical Psychology*, 1970, *26*, 38–40.

Simcha-Fagan, O. The prediction of delinquent behavior over time: Sex specific patterns related to official and survey-reported delinquency behavior, in Roberta Simmons (Ed.), *Research in Community and Mental Health* (Vol 1.). Greenwich, Conn.: JAI Press, 1979.

Snyder, J. J. Reinforcement analysis of interaction in problem and nonproblem families. *Journal of Abnormal Psychology*, 1977, *86*, 528–535.

Wolff, S., & Acton, W. P. Characteristics of parents of disturbed children. *British Journal of Psychiatry*, 1968, *114*, 593–601.

Part II

Stressful life events and psychopathology

4 Stress and long-term psychopathology in survivors of the Buffalo Creek disaster

Bonnie L. Green and Goldine C. Gleser

On February 26, 1972, a slag dam constructed by a mining company gave way, unleashing 132 million gallons of churning black slag, debris-filled mud, and water into the Buffalo Creek Valley in West Virginia, carrying away bridges, houses, cars, trailers, and human bodies. Three hours later the last of the water emptied into the Guyandotte River, leaving 125 dead and thousands homeless. Within hours, the local National Guard unit had sealed off the area, and medical units from nearby hospitals had begun to evacuate the badly injured. Volunteer rescue crews were formed and the Red Cross and Salvation Army began bringing in needed supplies. But many weeks went by before the debris could be cleared away and burned, the black muck hauled away from those houses left standing, and some order restored. In the meantime, families stayed with friends or camped in the school gymnasium, and finally were housed in trailers provided by the U.S. government in 13 trailer camps in and near the valley. These were assigned on a first-come–first-served basis, so that friends, neighbors, and kinfolk were split apart. A number of families packed up what few belongings they had left and moved away. The situation was exacerbated by a decision by the state of West Virginia to build a new highway up the middle of the narrow Buffalo Creek Valley. This meant that many who owned their land could not rebuild or move back until a final decision was made regarding where the road would be placed.

The preceding is a brief description of the Buffalo Creek flood disaster of 1972. Several narrative accounts of this disaster exist in book form: Nugent (1973), a journalist, reported on the scene shortly after the flood; Stern (1976), the lawyer handling the lawsuit for the survivors, described the legal aspects; and Erikson (1976), a sociologist, interviewed many of

This project was supported in part by National Institute of Mental Health Grant No. 1 RO1 MH26321. The authors gratefully acknowledge the assistance of Linda Crespo da Silva, Mary Danzeisen, Mary Grace, Mary Kapp, Laurie Levi, and Carolyn Winget at various stages of the study.

the survivors and traced the history of the area, focusing on cultural variables. Several clinical accounts have also been written (Lifton & Olsen, 1976; Newman, 1976; Titchener & Kapp, 1976; Titchener, Kapp, & Winget, 1976).

The clinical accounts, as well as the present research, grew out of a lawsuit filed on behalf of over 600 survivors. The Department of Psychiatry of the University of Cincinnati was hired by the prosecution to complete diagnostic psychiatric interviews on all of the plaintiffs to support a case for "psychic damage." Sixty-five psychiatrists, psychologists, and social workers went to Buffalo Creek twice in the spring of 1974 to interview subjects. Semistructured interview schedules were hastily drawn up in the hope of achieving comparability among the data obtained. In addition, several checklist instruments were included in the packet to be administered whenever possible. The diagnostic reports that resulted from these interviews will henceforth be called the "UC reports." A few months earlier, a neurologist for the defense had interviewed the same subjects and written individual diagnostic reports, which will here be called the "M reports" (from the name of the doctor). All of these data were made available to us subsequent to settlement of the suit in July 1975. We therefore had over 1,200 reports (usually 2 per subject) with which to work.

These materials gave us the opportunity to examine in some detail the effects of a disaster on the lives of a large number of individuals. Although some previous studies have provided in-depth assessments of disaster effects, the current study adds to these by quantifying both psychopathology and various aspects of the stressfulness of the event itself on the individual. The psychopathology is then described statistically and accounted for, using stressfulness together with several other factors. Such a study, it is to be hoped, can add to knowledge about the long-term psychological effects of disasters at an individual as well as a group level. In addition, it suggests a conceptual framework for quantifying certain aspects of disaster in order to examine their separate and combined contribution to later functioning.

The technical aspects of our scaling of psychopathology have been reported in more detail in a previous publication (Gleser, Green, & Winget, 1978). A more thorough report of all aspects of the present study exists in book form (Gleser, Green, & Winget, 1981). This chapter serves as an overview of the project and highlights our major findings.

So far as generalizability was concerned, the current set of data had advantages and disadvantages. The disadvantages were twofold: (1) Data were obtained mainly from those survivors participating in a lawsuit to gain reparation for psychic damage; and (2) the survivors were part of an identifiable subculture (Appalachian). One advantage was that it was a large group spanning the whole range of exposure to the disaster, many of whom might have been unwilling to cooperate with a research project undertaken in another context. A second was that, because we had information on families, we could look at how pathology of one family member affected that of others. Finally, we had two independent assessments of each subject's functioning, as well as the subject's own assessment.

The two independent assessments arose from the two sides of the lawsuit and reflected differences in assumptions about causation of psychopathology. The assumption of the prosecution team (represented by our department) was that these people had functioned adequately, on the average, up until the time of the flood. Following Hocking (1970), Kardiner (1959), Lifton (1967), and Titchener and Kapp (1976), this team saw the traumatic impact of the event as so overwhelming to the majority of victims that even normally adaptive mechanisms were broken down. Psychological impairment then followed, predisposition serving only to determine the amount of stress necessary to trigger a breakdown. The neurologist on the defense team, in contrast, assumed that if psychopathology was present at the time of the interview, it was the result of a lifelong history of psychopathology, unrelated to the flood, because by his definition the flood could produce only a "transient stress reaction."

Description of the sample

Eighty-four couples with children and 32 couples without children in the household were involved in the lawsuit. The latter group included mostly older persons whose children were married or living elsewhere. Sixteen households had only one spouse involved in the suit. Forty-six households were headed by one adult, about three-quarters of these by a divorced or widowed woman.

The age distribution revealed a dearth of people between the ages of 21 and 30. This dearth could be attributed partially to a mass migration in the 1950s and 1960s when the job market became constricted. However, an additional factor was the feeling among many parents that young people were better off getting an education and seeking careers elsewhere than living under constant fear of a mining disaster and the certainty of slow death from black lung disease.

The educational status of the litigants was typical of Appalachians as judged by other reports. The mean education for men was 8.7 years; that for women, 9.5. Approximately 40% of the litigant group had an eighth-grade education or less, and over 60% had not completed high school. Less than 4% of the males and 8% of the females had more than a high school education.

The litigants were *not* typical of the valley inhabitants in racial composition; a somewhat higher proportion were black. Of those people involved in the suit who were aged 16 or older at the time of the flood, about 19% were black, as were 25% of the children, compared to approximately 10% of the total valley inhabitants (Erikson, 1976). This disparity is not difficult to explain. The leading figure in organizing the litigants and hiring the lawyers was a black man who ran the local garage in the heart of the Buffalo Creek area. He was well known throughout the valley, particularly because his son had become a professional football player. Other blacks were undoubtedly encouraged to join by his leadership.

Most of the men worked or had worked in the mines. About a quarter of them had already retired by reason of age or disability and were receiving pensions at the time of the flood. The great majority of the women were housewives, although a number held positions as school teachers or nursing aides or worked in other service-related jobs.

Scaling psychopathology

We decided that the most appropriate measure on which to quantify the interview data was the Psychiatric Evaluation Form (PEF) developed by Spitzer and Endicott (Endicott & Spitzer, 1972; Spitzer et al., 1968). This measure covers 19 dimensions of manifest psychopathology as well as a more global rating of Overall Severity, each scored on a 6-point scale. Though the scales were originally designed to be rated on the basis of a structured interview, the authors had indicated that any additional information available could be used in making the ratings. Three members of the staff trained themselves to use these rating scales, and each scored 20 UC and 20 M reports on the same subjects to determine the feasibility of using this format for unstructured interviews, as well as to estimate scoring reliability.

A generalizability study (Cronbach et al., 1972) was undertaken to obtain estimates of scoring reliability under different rating conditions. For this purpose, variance analyses were performed on ratings of Overall Severity and on three summary clusters. These clusters, based on individual scale intercorrelations from a previous study, were Anxiety, Depression, and Belligerence.

From these analyses we estimated that scoring reliability would range from .60 for Overall Severity to .77 for Belligerence if only one person rated each interview and interviews were randomly assigned to available raters. If two raters were assigned to each interview, there would be an increase in reliability, with estimates ranging from .74 to .86, but this procedure would cost 400 additional scoring hours. We decided, therefore, to use only one rater, randomly assigned, for each interview (Gleser et al., 1978). Minor adjustments in cluster composition were made on the basis of total sample intercorrelations so that the final scales used in the summary clusters were Anxiety (agitation, anxiety, somatic concerns), Depression (suicide, depression, social isolation, daily routine impairment, retardation), and Belligerence (antisocial behavior, belligerence, grandiosity, suspicion-persecution).

After several other possibilities were examined, it was decided to attempt using the PEF for quantifying the children's data as well, even though this instrument had not been previously used with children. Clusters were formed representing the same major dimensions as those from the adult sample, with scales that seemed inappropriate for children dropped.

Interrater reliabilities were analyzed for a sample of 40 reports on 20 cases between the ages of 2 and 15. Average reliability estimates of the M and UC cluster scores ranged from .82 to .88. Because the reliabilities were moderately high and the number of reports large, we decided, as for the adults, to assign one rater randomly per interview. After all of the children's reports had been scored, several more scales were dropped as not useful or not correlating well with other scales in their hypothesized clusters, so that the final composition was Belligerence, from belligerence and antisocial behavior; Anxiety, from somatic concerns and anxiety; and Depression, from social isolation, suicide, depression, and daily routine impairment. In addition, the Overall Severity rating was utilized.

The literature had suggested that we could most appropriately examine the children's data by dividing the sample into age groups for some of the analyses. Therefore, three groups were formed: The youngest group ($N = 51$) was 2 – 7 years old at the time of the flood; the middle group ($N = 74$) was 8 – 11; and the oldest group ($N = 82$) was 12 – 15. In order to make these groupings, we considered school status (preschool, elementary, secondary), developmental status (prelatency, latency, adolescence), and data constraints (so that, for example, 7-year-olds were included in the first group to increase the number of subjects). Because the interviews were obtained 18 months to 2 years after the flood, the age range of the children at the time of the interviews was 4 – 17.

Table 4.1. *Means of standard deviations of Psychiatric Evaluation Form cluster scores for M and UC reports (adults)*

	M reports		UC reports		$r_{\text{M-UC}}$	
	Mean	*SD*	Mean	*SD*	Adults	Children
Overall Severity	3.01	(1.28)	3.85	(.98)	.38	.33
Σ Anxiety	7.56	(2.86)	7.87	(2.68)	.34	.38
Σ Depression-Isolation	8.43	(3.27)	12.03	(3.59)	.28	.34
Σ Hostility-Belligerence	5.93	(2.13)	5.82	(1.85)	.36	.26

A late-adolescent group (16 – 20) was also available ($N = 66$). Because this group was intermediate in age, it was included sometimes with the adults and sometimes with the children in the data analyses. The data from 23 children in the lawsuit were not made use of in any way because they were under the age of 2 at the time of the flood and were not, for the most part, interviewed directly, but evaluated through observation and verbal reports of parents.

Means and standard deviations for the adult cluster scores and Overall Severity for the two reports are shown in Table 4.1. These summary scores for Anxiety, Depression, and Belligerence, along with the scale of Overall Severity, accounted for the major portion of the variance contained in the pathology ratings. The overall levels for the two sets of reports were very similar, with the exception of Depression, where the UC reports were rated considerably higher. Correlations between corresponding cluster scores in the two reports are also shown in Table 4.1. Relationships between the two reports were all highly significant. Thus, in spite of the differences in time (they were done an average of 6 months apart), theoretical orientation, setting (home vs. office), and interviewing styles, these scales seemed to be identifying some valid individual differences in the quality and extent of psychopathology among the litigants.

These results indicated that our ratings of the interview material using the PEF were meaningful and gave us usable and interpretable quantitative information with which to investigate our hypotheses. We therefore combined the ratings from the two reports in order to increase the generalizability of the results.

Two further measurements were available on our sample with which to investigate the validity of our use of the PEF: Symptom Checklists and Clinical Impairment ratings. Symptom Checklists, which had been obtained on 231 adult litigants, were compared to the PEF summary clusters.

Table 4.2. *Correlations of the Psychiatric Evaluation Form (PEF) with Clinical Impairment ratings, by age group*

PEF scales	Age 2–7 (N = 51)	Age 8–11 (N = 74)	Age 12–15 (N = 82)	Adults (N = 380)
Anxiety	.35**	.34**	.26*	.40**
Depression	.27*	.54**	.25*	.43**
Belligerence	−.05	.28*	.18	.14**
Overall Severity	.49**	.65**	.49**	.49**

* $p < .05$.
** $p < .01$.

This instrument was adapted from Parloff, Kelman, and Frank (1954) and has been subsequently revised as the Hopkins Symptom Checklist and the SCL-90. The correlation between Overall Severity for the combined reports and the Symptom Checklist total score was .42 for males and .48 for females. These correlations were comparable to those found in an earlier study (Green et al., 1975), where the PEF scales were rated from the structured interview. Also, despite the high intercorrelations among subscores of the Symptom Checklist, corresponding constructs were generally convergent with both the M and the UC PEF cluster scores. These checklists, filled out by the litigants at the time of the UC interviews, actually correlated higher with the M than with the UC summaries. This may have been because Dr. M. used a symptoms approach in his interviewing; alternatively, the finding may simply reflect the greater unreliability of the UC reports because of the many interviewers involved.

Shortly after the UC interviews were obtained and the reports written, the clinical impairment of the subjects was rated by two psychiatrists (each doing approximately half of the sample). Clinical ratings were based primarily on the diagnosis and the degree-of-impairment statement at the end of the report, and the ratings were utilized by the court to reward settlement money. Not surprisingly, these ratings were more highly related to the UC than to the M reports, particularly on Overall Severity, for which the correlations were .58 and .28, respectively.

The relationships of the combined PEF scores from the M and UC reports with the Clinical Impairment ratings for both children and adults are presented in Table 4.2. As one would expect, the highest correlations are consistently with the more global Overall Severity rating. The Anxiety and Depression scales correlate consistently and significantly with the Clinical Impairment rating, whereas the Belligerence scale shares very little variance with it. Actually, the Belligerence scores are low, in accord with the "disaster syndrome" reported by Titchener and Kapp (1976) in their description of the Buffalo Creek survivors. Anxiety, depression, grief, apathy, and sleep disturbances are reported as the most common symptoms found in this syndrome. It is clear that common criteria were being used by the clinicians and by the raters applying the PEF technique, because relationships emerged from data generated in very different fashions.

It can be seen from Table 4.2 that PEF scores of the children, particularly Overall Severity, converge as well with the Clinical Impairment ratings as do those of the adults. This is true even for the group of children who were only 2 – 7 years of age at the time of the flood. Hence this instrument appears to be a useful one for children as well as for adults, even though fewer scales are relevant and symptoms may take a somewhat different form. Use of this instrument is particularly practical for examining relationships among psychopathology scores within families.

Several behavioral indexes were available from the children's interviews for use in further validity checks and will be briefly summarized. Significant relationships for school-aged children in the two younger groups indicated that a decrease in grades and interest in school was associated with higher levels of psychopathology on the PEF. For the older children, however, the relationships were essentially zero. Relationships of these variables with parental psychopathology suggested that parents' attitudes may have mediated these relationships to some extent, in ways affecting particularly the younger children (e.g., parents may have tended to pick children up from school early when it rained). Secondly, a diagnosis of regressive enuresis was significantly associated with higher Anxiety, Belligerence, and Overall Severity scores for children in the age range 5 – 7 at the time of the flood. It was not so associated for the younger age group, for whom it is probably a more "normal" symptom, and was not diagnosed in the older groups. Finally, diagnosed obesity dating from the flood or a significant weight gain from that point was associated with Depression and Overall Severity for the 8 – 11- and 12 – 15-year-olds. These differential relationships support psychological interpretations of the symptoms from the literature and indicate discriminant validity for our use of the PEF.

Scaling stress

Four scales were formulated for measuring the traumatic impact of the disaster: extent of bereavement in terms of loss of friends, relatives, and family members; the immediate life-threatening impact of the disaster to the individual (S_1); the extent and duration of physical and psychological trauma endured during the 2 weeks following the disaster (S_2); and the extent of displacement from home and community. On this last scale migration to another region was given the highest score (4).

The accuracy of the information coded was dependent upon the recollections of the survivors almost 2 years postflood, and on the completeness of the interview. Additionally, ordering these data into scales required certain assumptions. The Bereavement scale is based on the assumption that extent of bereavement is proportional to the closeness of the relationship. The stressfulness of the flood (S_1) was assumed to be proportional to the extent and duration of the life threat suffered. Stressfulness following the flood (S_2) was assumed to relate to separation, physical hardships, and exposure to death. These assumptions can be validated only as the scales prove useful in predicting long-term pathology. Because the scaling was done on external events that were in some sense measurable, their subjective meaning for the individual was not taken into account, even though it is clear that this is an important factor (cf. Lumsden, 1975). Such differential meaning may be based on past experiences of the individual as well as on broader group differences, such as age, sex, and race.

Estimates of reliability on a sample of 20 cases yielded .77 for Bereavement, .80 for S_1, .82 for S_2, and .91 for Displacement. Perfect agreement was obtained for 70% – 80% of the cases on each of the several scales.

Although we were scaling S_2 with continued death anxiety and the struggle for survival in mind, we thought it likely that some activities could mobilize adaptive coping mechanisms. Therefore, we coded whether or not the individual engaged in such activities as feeding and sheltering others, helping remove debris, and cleaning out his or her own home.

Comparison with other samples

Three samples were available for comparison with the Buffalo Creek litigants in order to give some indication of the extent of psychopathology that was found. The first was with a sample of nonlitigants. An important question to be addressed was whether involvement in the lawsuit caused exaggeration or exacerbation of the litigants' symptoms. Fortunately, we were able to collect Symptom Checklist data on a sample of 40 nonlitigants who lived in the same area and were in the flood. Mean scores for the two groups were very similar and *t* tests revealed no significant differences. This finding provided evidence that presentation of psychopathology was not a conscious effort at impression management for financial gains from the lawsuit. Indeed, Dr. M. was particularly looking for people who might be faking symptoms, but he found only a handful of subjects that he diagnosed as "malingering."

Two samples of psychiatric outpatients were also available for comparison, one from a PEF validation study by the authors of the instrument and one from our own setting. In the first comparison, the averaged M and UC profiles were compared to those of inpatient and outpatient samples rated as part of PEF validation (Endicott & Spitzer, 1972). Though the Buffalo Creek litigants showed somewhat less suicidal ideation and denial of illness, their mean profile otherwise bore a striking resemblance to that of the outpatient sample. The litigants had little, if any, psychotic symptomatology as measured by grandiosity, hallucinations, or denial of illness; neither were they abusing drugs or showing other antisocial behaviors. Their major symptomatology was in the areas of anxiety, agitation, depression, somatic concerns, social isolation, and disturbance of daily routine and leisure-time activities.

The final sample consisted of patients seen in a Cincinnati crisis clinic for brief psychotherapy (Green et al., 1975). These were young, predominantly white females, a third of whom were divorced or separated (crisis often included "loss"). A comparison of scores for this sample with those of the Buffalo Creek litigants showed that Depression and Belligerence scores were slightly lower for the Buffalo Creek sample, whereas Anxiety and Overall Severity ratings were very comparable. Symptom Checklist scores for this group were also available. These scores were in a similar range, except that the clinic patients were somewhat higher on Depression than were the litigants.

These comparisons with samples of psychiatric outpatients make it clear that the Buffalo Creek litigants as a group had symptoms of a proportion to be psychiatrically significant. This finding does not rule out the possibility that their subculture is one that characteristically exhibits many of these same symptoms. However, Erikson (1976) has argued that the people of Buffalo Creek were unlike the old stereotype of the depressed mountaineers in having evolved more self-assurance, orderliness, independence, and dignity. He states, "They had not only worked their way out of the poverty and insecurity that had been the lot of their parents, but they had done so by beginning to erase the emotional and cultural deficits that have so long been the counterpart of want in Appalachia" (p. 132).

Table 4.3. *Correlations of stress scales, helping activities, and demographic variables with Overall Severity*

	Males (N = 131)	Females (N = 163)	Children (N = 273)
Bereavement	.19*	.38**	.19*
S_1	.20*	.25**	.27**
S_2	.18*	.17*	.01
Displacement	.10	.18*	.19*
Helping activities	−.30*	−.11	—
Multiple R	.44	.45	.36
Children in household	.18*	.11	—
Spouse in household	.00	.18*	—
Age	−.11	−.04	.36**
Race	.29**	.21*	.28**
Education	−.24*	−.08	—
Sex	—	—	.15*
Multiple R (including stress)	.57	.47	.54

* $p < .05$.
** $p < .01$.

Prediction of psychopathology

Table 4.3 shows the relationships between, on the one hand, stress, helping activities, and demographic variables and, on the other, Overall Severity on the PEF for males, females, and children.

These correlations indicated that there was, indeed, a positive relationship between extent of victimization as measured by the stress scales and psychopathology up to 2 years after the occurrence of the flood. Both Bereavement and S^1, the initial impact of the flood, were significantly related to Overall Severity for all three groups. These correlations were generally lower for the men than for the women; this was particularly true of Bereavement.

S_2 was significantly but marginally related to Overall Severity for both men and women, whereas Displacement related only for women.

For children, the highest stress correlation was with S_1, the initial flood impact. The relationship with Displacement was primarily attributable to the adolescent group.

For men, the predominant flood-related variable contributing to psychopathology (in a negative direction) was personal helping activity, that is, cleaning out their own houses, removing debris, and feeding or sheltering others.

The combination of these flood-experience variables produced very similar multiple correlations for men and women, although, as mentioned, the multiple for women was determined in larger part by stress, whereas for men helping activities were more important. The multiple for the children was somewhat lower but was also highly significant.

Adding in demographic factors increased the prediction even more for men and children. For the entire sample, white survivors were significantly more disturbed than blacks. Blacks lived in the lower part of the valley and suffered less destruction (and no blacks were lost in the flood); hence their stress scores were lower, a fact that accounts in part for the relationship of race with psychopathology. However, differential stress did not entirely explain the correlation, at least for the men. Partial correlations indicated that differences between black and white men continued to be significant even after equating for stress. For the children as well, race added significantly to the multiple correlation over and above the contribution of stress. This supports Kessler's (1979b) finding that comparable stresses had more impact on whites than on nonwhites and lends credence to his speculation that "if there are any variations in intrapsychic strengths, whites must be disadvantaged relative to nonwhites" (p. 268).

Age was related to psychopathology for the children. Though the cluster scores showed somewhat different trends by age group (i.e., increases occurred at different ages), there were significant differences among the four age groups in all of the cluster scores and on Overall Severity. The latter variable rose fairly steadily from one age group to the next.

Sex was also related to psychopathology in that women had consistently higher scores, with the exception of Belligerence, where this direction was reversed.

Family factors in the form of children in the household for men, and spouse in the household for women, also were related to psychopathology.

Finally, men with more education showed significantly less psychopathology than those with less education.

Adding in the demographic factors substantially increased prediction of Overall Severity for the men and for the children, whereas for the women, the multiple r was almost entirely explained by the stress scales.

The relationship we found between measures of stress and degree of psychopathology of litigant survivors, particularly women, supports Janis's (1971) statement that "the greater the degree of victimization produced by exposure to severe stress, the higher the probability of emotional disturbance afterward" (pp. 24–25). He cites as evidence several studies of victims of bombing in England and Germany.

Also pertinent to the study of the psychological effects of disaster is the research area of stressful life-change events (cf. Dohrenwend & Dohrenwend, 1974b; Raye, 1979). Although recent studies have cast some doubt on the specific etiologic role of such events (Gersten et al., 1977), models for conceptualizing factors affecting the impact of such events have been suggested (cf. Dohrenwend & Dohrenwend, 1974a; Kessler, 1979a), and the area continues to be a fruitful one for exploring the role of stress in the development of psychopathology.

Lumsden's (1975) model of a system under stress includes four stages: impact, appraisal, coping, and outcomes. The impact aspect includes the actual environmental event with its concomitant dimensions. The appraisal phase takes into account the meaning of the event to the individual, mediated by such factors as sex, age, race, and group affiliation. Coping depends upon the preceding stages in the model and includes the individual's attempts to deal with the stressor (behavior, defense mechanisms). Outcomes are either adaptive or maladaptive with regard to the individual's physical and psychological well-being. Lumsden's model is an open system in which, for example, maladaptive responses may become endogenous stressors themselves, starting the process over again, or coping failures may lead to reappraisal, and so on. Though it is clear that all possible variables have not been measured in the present study, the model provides a framework for conceptualizing our findings.

For men, women, and children alike, the original stress of the flood was directly related to eventual outcomes in the psychological realm. For the women, very few subsequent factors were helpful in explaining the long-term picture, with the possible exception of having a spouse in the household. For men and children, mediating factors in the form of demographic variables, particularly education for the men and age for the children, played a role in effecting the eventual psychological outcome. As mentioned, sex was a significant factor for both adults and children. Though higher levels of psychopathology in women have been previously explained as a willingness to report symptoms (cf. Toolan, 1974), recent studies (e.g., Kessler, 1979a) have suggested differential impact of stressors by sex and have related this difference to the use of less effective coping mechanisms by women (Pearlin & Schooler, 1978). For men, the coping activities we were able to measure (personal help) added to the prediction of eventual outcome: Those men who could take some action toward reparation of the damage following the disaster were better off than those who could not. Erikson (1976) points out that the most striking characteristic of the mountaineer is his sense of individualism and independence. He has a "great need to feel self-sufficient and be 'master' in his home" (p. 72). Thus those men who could regain control of their own lives fared better psychologically than those who were left dependent on the government for housing or for permission to go back to their land and rebuild. Furthermore, because of the sharp differentiation of sex roles in Appalachia, most women had little opportunity to experience mastery by such means. In large part, they were sent off with the children to live with relatives or in temporary relief quarters while the men and older boys cleaned up their houses and removed debris, taking some control over the situation.

The role of education in reducing long-term psychopathology, particularly for men, is difficult to unravel from our data. One explanation is that those who had more education understood better the risk that the slag dam entailed and so were better prepared psychologically. This explanation would fit with numerous studies tending to show that, if given accurate warning of impending danger, discomfort, and pain, a normal person is better able to cope with stress and has fewer emotional aftereffects than otherwise (cf. Egbert et al., 1964; Janis, 1958). Another possibility is that the better-educated males had more resources to overcome their loss of self-confidence and mastery (Pearlin & Schooler, 1978). They may have felt less limited occupationally, so that more avenues of escape were open to them, including leaving the valley. They may also have been more likely to have thought through the possibility of a flood and to have made contingency plans or purchased insurance, so that losses were not so devastating. The latter two possibilities in this culture would be determined primarily by the husband and hence not related to the educational level of the wife.

Family relationships

Part of this study focused on the relationships of psychopathology within families. Family members are likely to be more similar than are individuals in general. To explore the extent of this interdependency, we obtained correlations between the psychopathology scores of family members in those families where such data were available. Spouses' corresponding summary scores were significantly related, with the exception of Belligerence and Clinical Impairment (range .16 – .38). Many of the off-diagonal correlations were also significant. Furthermore, the correlations obtained were larger than could be predicted from scores on their common disaster experiences and postflood activities. Apparently interactions between spouses tended to increase or ameliorate psychopathology.

Table 4.4. *Relationships among Overall Severity (OVS) ratings for parents and children by sex and age group*

	Father OVS		Mother OVS	
Age	Male	Female	Male	Female
2–7	−.02	.35	.24	.53*
8–11	.06	.52*	.30*	.36*
12–15	.47*	.11	.27	.36*
16–20	.43*	.09	.28	.39*

* $p < .05$.

A somewhat similar phenomenon was found when children's scores were compared to those of their parents. Although there are several ways to look at relationships between scores of parents and those of children, for purposes of this chapter correlations between Overall Severity in different age groups are presented by sex (see Table 4.4). Several fairly definite patterns emerged. Scores of children of both sexes were more often related to those of their mother. For fathers, girls in the two younger groups showed positive relationships; boys' scores were not related. In the two older groups, the pattern reversed and it was the boys whose scores related significantly to fathers'. Mothers' Overall Severity related to that of both boys and girls of all ages, the relationships with the boys' scores being somewhat lower.

Looking at the same data from another perspective, it can be said that the younger girls' scores related rather strongly to those of parents of both sexes, whereas younger boys' scores related only to those of mothers. In the older groups, there was more evidence of sex typing: The significant correlations for boys were with their fathers and for girls, with their mothers.

It seems, then, that children's reactions to the flood experience were at least partially determined by the extent to which their parents were affected. This conclusion fits in with previous studies about the effects on children of parental response to stress (Carey-Trefzer, 1949; Rakoff et al., 1966).

Kai Erikson and others (Looff, 1971; Weller, 1965) have characterized mountain families as very close in the sense of "interdependent." The individual members do not feel completely whole unless they are "in the fold." On the other hand, these authors note that mountain families are not close in the sense of being really intimate with each other. Our data have shown an interdependence among family members in relation to psychopathology, a finding in line with previous studies (May & Sprague, 1976; Towell, 1977) and one which indicates that intervention in the form of counseling or psychotherapy might best be done within a family context.

Overall, then, we have been able to show that psychopathology present in these disaster victims 18 months to 2 years postflood was predictable from stress suffered at the time of the event; from demographic characteristics, particularly sex, race, and education; from coping behaviors; and from pathology scores of other family members. Although these relationships were modest, taken together they accounted for a substantial portion of the variance in long-term psychopathology. This finding is encouraging, particularly given that the data were not originally collected for research purposes and hence were not as complete and uniform as we would have wished. The positive findings for education and coping activities indicate future possibilities for research and intervention.

This disaster was unusual and needs to be put in perspective (Green, forthcoming). Because it destroyed the landscape and a majority of houses throughout the valley, it could not be easily forgotten. Whereas survivors can often, after a disaster, go back to a community that is untouched, this group had to live with daily reminders of the flood. The new highway being built virtually cut the valley in half and added to the sustained traumatic aspects of the flood, particularly for a culture that has very strong ties to the land (Erikson, 1976). In addition, the disaster relief itself probably had negative effects (Harshbarger, 1973), splitting up families into small trailers in new neighborhoods where noise and delinquency were reported as common problems, and giving no assurances about when the trailers would be taken away. These additional aspects probably contributed to the high chronic levels of psychopathology found in many inhabitants of Buffalo Creek.

Currently, data from a very different type of disaster are becoming available, data with which to compare our findings from the Buffalo Creek flood. A team at the University of Cincinnati Psychiatry Department recently finished a study of survivors of the Beverly Hills Supper Club fire, under the auspices of the Office of Program Evaluation and Research of the Ohio Department of Mental Health and Retardation (Lindy, Grace, & Green, 1981; Titchener et al., 1981). We used the same assessment instruments in order to have some basis for comparison. The PEF interview was given by independent interviewers, and the scales were directly rated. We also used a Symptom Checklist and directly rated extent of stress at the time of and following the fire. Subjects were interviewed 1 year after the fire and followed up 2 years postfire. This disaster took place away from the homes of the survivors, who therefore went back to intact communities. Long-term psychopathology for that group was less than for the survivors at Buffalo Creek, whereas relationships between similar stress measures and psychopathology were quite comparable.

References

Carey-Trefzer, C. The results of a clinical study of war-damaged children who attended the Child Guidance Clinic, The Hospital for Sick Children, Great Ormond Street, London. *Journal of Mental Science*, 1949, *95*, 535–559.

Cronbach, L. J., Gleser, G. C., Nanda, H., & Rajaratnam, N. *The dependability of behavioral measurements: Theory of generalizability for scores and profiles*. New York: Wiley, 1972.

Dohrenwend, B. S., & Dohrenwend, B. P. Overview and prospects for research on stressful life events. In B. S. Dohrenwend & B. P. Dohrenwend (Eds.), *Stressful life events: Their nature and effects*. New York: Wiley, 1974. (a)

Dohrenwend, B. S., & Dohrenwend, B. P. (Eds.). *Stressful life events: Their nature and effects*. New York: Wiley, 1974. (b)

Egbert, L., Battit, G., Welch, C., & Bartlett, M. Reduction of postoperative pain by encouragement and instruction of patients. *New England Journal of Medicine*, 1964, *270*, 825–827.

Endicott, J., & Spitzer, R. L. What! Another rating scale? The Psychiatric Evaluation Form. *Journal of Nervous and Mental Disease*, 1972, *154*, 88–104.

Erikson, K. T. *Everything in its path*. New York: Simon & Schuster, 1976.

Gersten, J. C., Langner, T. S., Eisenberg, J. G., & Simcha-Fagan, O. An evaluation of the etiologic role of stressful life-change events in psychological disorders. *Journal of Health and Social Behavior*, 1977, *18*, 228–244.

Gleser, G. C., Green, B. L., & Winget, C. N. Quantifying interview data on psychic impairment of disaster survivors. *Journal of Nervous and Mental Disease*, 1978, *166*, 209–216.

Gleser, G. C., Green, B. L., & Winget, C. *Prolonged psychosocial effects of disaster: A study of Buffalo Creek*. New York: Academic Press, 1981.

Green, B. L. Assessing levels of psychological impairment following disaster: Consideration of actual and methodological dimensions. *Journal of Nervous and Mental Disease*, forthcoming.

Green, B. L., Gleser, G. C., Stone, W. N., & Seifert, R. F. Relationships among diverse measures of psychotherapy outcome. *Journal of Consulting and Clinical Psychology*, 1975, *43*, 689–699.

Harshbarger, D. *An ecological perspective on disastrous and facilitative disaster intervention*. Paper presented at NIMH Continuing Education Seminar on Emergency Mental Health Services, Washington, D.C., June 1973.

Hocking, F. Extreme environmental stress and its significance for psychopathology. *American Journal of Psychotherapy*, 1970, *24*, 4–26.

Janis, I. L. *Psychological stress: Psychoanalytic and behavioral studies of surgical patients*. New York: Wiley, 1958.

Janis, I. L. *Stress and frustration*. New York: Harcourt Brace Jovanovich, 1971.

Kardiner, A. Traumatic neuroses of war. In S. Arieti (Ed.), *American handbook of psychiatry*. New York: Basic Books, 1959.

Kessler, R. C. A strategy for studying differential vulnerability to the psychological consequences of stress. *Journal of Health and Social Behavior*, 1979, *20*, 100–108. (a)

Kessler, R. C. Stress, social status, and psychological distress. *Journal of Health and Social Behavior*, 1979, *20*, 259–272. (b)

Lifton, R. J. *Death in life: Survivors of Hiroshima*. New York: Random House, 1967.

Lifton, R. J., & Olsen, E. Death imprint in Buffalo Creek. In H. J. Parad, H. L. P. Resnik, & L. G. Parad (Eds.), *Emergency and disaster management*. Bowie, Md.: Charles Press, 1976.

Lindy, J. D., Grace, M. C., & Green, B. L. Survivors: Outreach to a reluctant population. *American Journal of Orthopsychiatry*, 1981, *51*, 468–478.

Looff, D. H. *Appalachia's Children*. Lexington: University of Kentucky Press, 1971.

Lumsden, D. P. Towards a systems model of stress: Feedback from an anthropological study of the impact of Ghana's Volta River Project. In I. G. Sarason & C. D. Spielberger (Eds.), *Stress and anxiety* (Vol. 2). Washington, D.C.: Hemisphere, 1975.

May, J. T., & Sprague, H. A. Chronic stress as a predictor of family health action and health status. In I. G. Sarason & C. D. Spielberger (Eds.), *Stress and anxiety* (Vol. 3). Washington, D.C.: Hemisphere, 1976.

Newman, C. J. Children of disaster: Clinical observations at Buffalo Creek. *American Journal of Psychiatry*, 1976, *133*, 306–312.

Nugent, T. *Death at Buffalo Creek*. New York: Norton, 1973.

Parloff, M. D., Kelman, H., & Frank, J. D. Comfort, effectiveness and self-awareness as criteria of improvement in psychotherapy. *American Journal of Psychiatry*, 1954, *111*, 343–352.

Pearlin, L. I., & Schooler, C. The structure of coping. *Journal of Health and Social Behavior*, 1978, *19*, 2–21.

Rakoff, V., Sigal, J. J., & Epstein N. B. Children and families of concentration camp survivors. *Canada's Mental Health*, 1966, *14*, 14–16.

Raye, R. H. Life change events and mental illness: An overview. *Journal of Human Stress*, 1979, *5*, 2–10.

Spitzer, R. L., Endicott, J., Mesnikoff, A. M., & Cohen, M. S. *The Psychiatric Evaluation Form*. New York: Biometrics Research, 1968.

Stern, G. M. *The Buffalo Creek disaster*. New York: Random House, 1976.

Titchener, J. L., & Kapp, F. T. Family and character change at Buffalo Creek. *American Journal of Psychiatry*, 1976, *133*, 295–299.

Titchener, J. L., Kapp, F. T., & Winget, C. The Buffalo Creek syndrome: Symptoms and character change after a major disaster. In H. J. Parad, H. L. P. Resnik, & L. G. Parad (Eds.), *Emergency and disaster management*. Bowie, Md.: Charles Press, 1976.

Titchener, J. L., Lindy, J. D., Green, B. L., Grace, M. C., & Lindy, J. G. *Disaster in the crucial year after: The Beverly Hills Fire, Final Report*. Unpublished manuscript, University of Cincinnati, Department of Psychiatry, December 1981.

Toolan, J. M. Depression and suicide. In G. Caplan (Ed.), *American handbook of psychiatry* (Vol. 2, 2nd ed.). New York: Basic Books, 1974.

Towell, R. F. Anxiety state-trait levels between parents and children in a family practice unit. In C. D. Spielberger & I. G. Sarason (Eds.), *Stress and anxiety* (Vol. 4). Washington, D.C.: Hemisphere, 1977.

Weller, J. E. *Yesterday's people: Life in contemporary Appalachia*. Lexington: University of Kentucky Press, 1965.

5 Remote and recent life events and psychopathology

Bruce P. Dohrenwend and John M. de Figueiredo

Three bodies of literature suggest that stressful life events may be an important impetus to psychopathology in adults from the general population. The first consists of studies of extreme situations such as natural disasters and, especially, exposure to combat during wartime (see B. P. Dohrenwend & Dohrenwend, 1969; Hocking, 1970; Kinston & Rosser, 1974). The second focuses on the impact of recent exposure to accumulations of more ordinary stressful life events, such as birth of a first child, being laid off a job, divorce, physical illness or injury, and death of a loved one (see B. S. Dohrenwend & Dohrenwend, 1974; Gunderson & Rahe, 1974). The third involves research on the impact of more remote events during childhood, events such as separation from parents owing to their deaths or to other causes (see Chen & Cobb, 1960; Granville-Grossman, 1968; Gregory, 1958; Heinicke, 1973).

Although all three bodies of literature are suggestive, no one of them provides a clear demonstration that environmentally induced stress is an important factor in the etiology of any of the major types of severe psychopathology in adults from the general population. Thus, for example, although research on extreme situations has shown conclusively that under some conditions, environmentally induced stress can produce a wide range and variety of psychopathology in previously normal adults (see B. P. Dohrenwend & Dohrenwend, 1969, 1977), the situations involved have few obvious counterparts in civilian populations in times of peace. With regard to the impact of more usual stressful events, neither

This research was supported in part by Research Grant MH 10328 and by Research Scientist Award KO5-MH 14663 from the National Institute of Mental Health, U.S. Public Health Service. It was also supported by the Foundations' Fund for Research in Psychiatry. We are grateful to Carmi Schooler for pointing out the relevance of Inbar's *The Vulnerable Age Phenomenon* for our findings. We would also like to thank Diana Cook for her valuable help with the difficult job of constructing the indicators of events involving loss and family structure during childhood.

the literature on exposure to such events in childhood nor studies of recent experience with them as adults shows consistently strong relationships with psychopathology. Some of the investigations report inconsistent findings (see Granville-Grossman, 1968), much of the evidence is correlational and frequently retrospective (see B. P. Dohrenwend & Dohrenwend, 1977; Heinecke, 1973), and, especially where research focuses on combinations of recent life events, there are serious problems of measurement that lead, in some studies, to a confounding of the measure of life events with the measure of psychopathology (see Brown, 1974; B. P. Dohrenwend, 1974).

Clearly, then, each set of studies has weaknesses as well as strengths with regard to investigation of the role of socioenvironmentally induced stress in psychopathology. It seems reasonable, therefore, to think that research strategies combining elements of more than one of these sets would be more productive than those focusing on any of them alone. That the former strategies do not tend to be implemented has more to do with tradition and practicality than with logic.

We have set forth elsewhere our thoughts about the important counterparts of extreme situations that are sometimes formed by combinations of more usual life events in general populations (see B. S. Dohrenwend & Dohrenwend, 1978). Briefly, we have hypothesized that a pathogenic triad of conditions approximating some of those that obtain in extreme situations is formed when the following types of events are experienced in close proximity to one another: serious physical illness or injury that exhausts the individual physically; fateful loss events, such as death of a loved one, whose occurrence is outside the individual's control; and other events that disrupt the individual's usual sources of social support–for example, a move from a rural to an urban area or from one country to another, a divorce, a change in jobs.

In the present chapter, we focus more on the role of remote events than we and most researchers interested in investigating stressful life events have done in the past. More specifically, our concern is with certain major "landmark" events, especially events involving losses before age 19, experienced by members of a small probability sample of adult residents of New York City. Our aim is to examine the possible role of such remote events in relation to these subjects' adaptations to the life events they experienced in the 12 months prior to the interviews we conducted with them.

In this analysis, we have been particularly influenced by the results of several studies in which the investigators have distinguished between earlier and later loss of parents during childhood in relation to various types of adult pschopathology. Their findings suggest that inconsistent results from other studies may be due in part to failure to make this distinction, because it is loss of one or both parents before the child has reached age 11, rather than later in childhood, that appears to be important (see Gregory, 1958). Five of the investigations reporting the impact of early loss focused on psychiatric patients rather than on psychopathology in the general population (Barry, 1949; Birtchnell, 1972; Greer, Gunn, & Koller, 1966; Norton, 1952; Oltman, McGarry, & Friedman, 1952). Two more, however, were based on samples from the general population; both of these reported data on the relation between earlier, by contrast with later, loss of one or both parents during childhood and adult psychopathology (Brown, Harris, & Copeland, 1977; Langner & Michael, 1963).

Langner and Michael's (1963) study was based on data from a sample consisting of about 1,600 adults from a predominantly white, non-Puerto Rican section of Manhattan in New York City. These investigators found that in the sample as a whole, individuals whose homes were broken by death or other causes before they were 7 years old were more likely than the average to be rated as having impairing psychiatric symptoms (pp. 166–167). The relationship was strongest for those lowest in socioeconomic status, where death of the mother before age 7 appeared to play a particularly important role (pp. 162, 169). By contrast, respondents from homes broken while they were age 7–16 did not differ in psychiatric impairment from respondents whose homes remained unbroken during their childhoods (p. 167).

More recently, Brown et al. (1977) compared depression in a random sample of 458 women living in a section of London with depression in a sample of 114 psychiatric patients, also women. They found that loss of the mother by death or other causes before age 11 was the only type of loss or separation from parents during childhood that was related to depression in adulthood in *both* the general population sample and the psychiatric patients.

Method of procedure

Most of the data to be reported from our own research come from two structured interviews averaging about an hour and a half each and conducted about a week apart with each person in a sample of 166 New York City adults, age 21–64.

The sample of respondents

The purpose of these interviews was primarily methodological. Our goal was to develop measures of remote and recent stressful life events and of various types of psychiatric symptomatology. We were concerned that our measures be applicable, reliable, and valid for comparing contrasting sex, class, and ethnic groups in epidemiological studies of environmental stress and psychopathology in general populations. We could not afford a large sample for these purposes. We did, however, need to be able to stratify the sample we obtained on the basis of known demographic characteristics, so that, for example, we could oversample blacks and Puerto Ricans from higher social classes in order to unconfound ethnic and class background. To secure the necessary information about demographic characteristics without going to the great expense of conducting preliminary interviews in a very large number of households, we decided to draw our sample from subjects for whom the necessary information had already been provided in a study conducted 4 years earlier.

This sampling procedure resulted in certain consequences that should be considered in relation to the present results. Our 166 subjects are not representative of adults in New York City. Rather, they represent a part of a group who lived there 4 years earlier and still could be located within the city. I say "a part" because our nonresponse rate was higher than we expected. We obtained initial interviews with only 60 percent of the 331 subjects who fell into our stratified sample and were locatable, and we lost another 33 of these who refused our follow-up interview 1 week after the initial interview. Thus our 166 subjects tend to be unusually stable residentially and to overrepresent the public-spirited majority.

"Demoralization" and the measurement of maladaptive outcome

The symptom items in our interview were selected from various of our previous studies (e.g., B. P. Dohrenwend & Crandell, 1970; B. P. Dohrenwend et al., 1978) and from relevant literature. These symptoms were grouped by a consensus of two out of three psychiatrists in our research unit into clinically meaningful potential scales.

In the process of examining the characteristics of these scales, 25 of them in all, we located a subset of 8 scales that tended to be correlated with each other almost as highly as their reliabilities would permit. These scales were:

Poor self-esteem
Helpless-hopeless
Dread
Anxiety
Sadness
Confused thinking
Psychophysiological symptoms
Perceived physical health

Taken together, they appear to describe something very similar to what Jerome Frank (1973) means by demoralization. Moreover, a series of additional analyses reported elsewhere (B. P. Dohrenwend, Shrout, Egri, & Mendelsohn, 1980) suggests that the label not only fits in terms of content but is useful in explaining why the commonly used psychiatric screening instruments (e.g., Langner, 1962; Macmillan, 1957) that provided most of the items in several of the 8 scales relate as they do to outside variables such as social class, physical illness, going to college, being a suburban housewife, and experiencing combat during wartime (B. P. Dohrenwend et al., 1980).

Frank (1973) suggests that "a person becomes demoralized when he finds that he cannot meet the demands placed on him by the environment, and cannot extricate himself from his predicament" (p. 316). Among the sources of the predicament, Frank mentions environmental stresses, giving the examples of wartime experiences (p. 316); constitutional defects (p. 316); learned incapacity (p. 317); existential despair (p. 317); all physical illnesses, especially chronic physical illnesses (pp. 46–47); and "crippling [psychiatric] symptoms" (p. 315). We have formed a composite scale of demoralization by treating each of our eight subscales as a separate component and standardizing the scoring of each subscale to control for differences in number of items. The resulting composite scale of demoralization has a range of scores of 0–32 with a mean of 7.60 and a standard deviation of 4.73 in our sample. Its internal consistency reliability is .91, and it provides us with our main measure of adaptation in the present investigation.

Recent life events

Near the end of the interviews, each respondent was asked, "What was the last major event that, for better or worse, changed or interrupted your usual activities?" This question was followed by probes concerning the participants in the event and its date. After these questions, respondents were told, "Now I'll ask you about a number of other experiences that people have. Some of these things happen to most people at one time or another, while some of these things happen to only a few people." At this point respondents were presented with 10 lists describing 102 events in various areas of activity, such as school, work, and family, and asked for each list, "During the last 12 months, did any of these things happen to you, or to a member of your family or to another person who is important to you?"

In addition, magnitude scores were obtained for each of the 102 events from a small parallel sample of judges consisting of 92 New York City residents (B. S. Dohrenwend et al., 1978). Moreover, four additional judges from our research staff classified each event to determine whether, objectively, it was likely to represent gain or loss or was ambiguous in this regard, and whether it was likely or not to be fateful and hence independent of both the subject's physical health and his or her psychiatric condition (B. S. Dohrenwend et al., 1978).

Remote life events

One of the reasons that we and others have focused on recent life events rather than remote life events is a practical one having to do with problems of recall. The longer the period over which events are to be recalled, the greater is the loss of accuracy owing to faulty recall (see, e.g., Ulenhuth et al., 1977). Nevertheless, there are certain landmark events that are unlikely to be forgotten by anyone – for example, deaths of parents or other major separations from parents while growing up. In the present interview, therefore, we made provision for eliciting such landmark events over the entire life course of each individual. Those that we report here have to do with separations from parents because of death or other reasons before the respondent was 19 years old.

We report on two main indexes. The first focuses on deaths of parents and contains the following categories:

No parent died during the respondent's childhood, that is, up until the respondent was about age 18.
At least one parent died while the respondent was between the ages of 11 and 19, but none before the respondent reached age 11.
At least one parent died before the respondent was age 11.

We chose the age-11 cutoff to distinguish earlier from later bereavement during childhood because findings from other studies, mentioned earlier, suggested that it might be important to do so. Our small sample size does not permit much finer distinctions.

Our second index focuses on separations resulting from causes other than deaths of parents (or, in one or two instances, stepparents). Here again, the small sample size limited us in the number of distinctions that could reasonably be made, and our index is as follows:

There were no separations for causes other than death from any parent before the respondent was 19.
There were separations for causes other than death from one or more parents or parent surrogates lasting less than a year.
There were separations from one or more parents or parent surrogates lasting more than a year.

To provide a context for interpreting these two indexes, we also constructed an index of family structure during the respondent's childhood containing the following classifications:

> The respondent was raised by both natural parents for most of the time before he or she reached age 19.
> The respondent was raised by two or more adults, one or both of whom were not natural parents, for most of the time before he or she reached age 19.
> The respondent was raised by a single female or, in a small minority of cases, a single male for most of the time before he or she reached age 19.

In this index, we gave special weight to whether one or more than one parent or parent surrogate was involved in rearing the respondent. Our reason is that Kellam, Ensminger, and Turner (1977) found that presence of a second adult was associated with almost as good adaptation of black school children in the first grade as the presence of both parents, whereas the presence of a mother alone was associated with poor outcome. The subjects in the present research are, of course, adults rather than first graders, and only a minority of these adults are black. Nevertheless, the distinction seems interesting, and our small sample size again limits the number of variations in family type that we can usefully examine.

Distribution of remote losses

In our society, the majority of children under 18 live with their natural parents, according to figures from the Population Reference Bureau quoted in the *New York Times* in the late 1970s (Nordheimer, 1977). A surprisingly large proportion of children, fully a third, do not. For example, 16% live with their mothers alone and 1% with their fathers alone. An additional 13% live with two parents, one of whom is not the child's natural parent. The remaining 3% live with other custodians. These figures are consistent with information reported by our respondents, a third of whom were not raised by both their natural parents for half or more of the time before they were about 18 years old. Against this background, the rather startling amount of childhood loss involving parental figures in our sample may not seem so unusual.

Our measure of maladaptive outcome is a score on the scale of demoralization that is 1 standard deviation or more above the mean for the sample, excluding Puerto Ricans, who are scored separately according to the mean of their own group. Our reason for scoring Puerto Ricans separately is that, as we have found in previous research, there is a subcultural difference in their mode of expressing distress that must be allowed for on measures of this kind. We estimate that respondents in our general population sample who score at or above these cutting points are showing a level of demoralization that would be characteristic of a mixed sample of psychiatric inpatients and outpatients from the same demographic groups (B. P. Dohrenwend et al., 1980).

Results

Relation of remote events to maladaptive outcome

Let us consider first the relation of the remote events and circumstances to maladaptive outcome. On this matter, our first two findings are negative. Type of family structure during childhood appears to have little relation to whether or not our respondents were highly demoralized when we interviewed them as adults. If anything, the group raised by a single parent, the group we thought most likely to be demoralized, included the lowest proportion of the highly demoralized.

Nor does separation for causes other than deaths of parents during childhood appear to be related to adult demoralization in our sample. We considered in detail the reasons for separation. Although the numbers are small, none seems associated with demoralization. Thus, for example, not one of the five respondents who had a parent in a mental hospital or nursing home for a mental or emotional problem was highly demoralized, nor were any of the four respondents whose parents or parent surrogates were in jail at some time during the respondents' childhoods.

At this point in the analysis, we wondered whether we had an unusually hardy group of survivors in New York City as a result of our sampling procedures, or, alternatively, whether maladaptive behavior among persons who had experienced such losses during childhood was expressed in other ways. The latter conclusion, is not, however, suggested by our analysis of other measures, such as drinking problems and antisocial history.

Against this background of negative results, it is almost startling to see in Table 5.1 that there may be a relationship between demoralization and bereavement during childhood. There is a tendency – and this conclusion is consistent with Brown et al.'s (1977) findings on depression and with Langner and Michael's (1963) findings on psychiatric impairment – for the proportion of demoralized adults to be highest among respondents who experienced the death of one or both parents before age 11. In our data, however, in contrast to these earlier results, this outcome is as likely

Table 5.1. *Demoralization in a sample of New York City adults according to their childhood experiences with deaths of parents*

	Earlier bereavement: One or both natural parents died before respondent reached age 11	Later bereavement: One or both parents died during respondent's childhood but neither before respondent was 11	Both natural parents alive during respondent's childhood
% highly demoralized	25.0	0	12.6
N	28	19	119

Note: $\chi^2 = 6.31$; 2 *df*; $p < .05$.

for deaths of fathers as for deaths of mothers, even for our female respondents.

Note also in Table 5.1 that the most striking contrast with the early bereaved group is provided by the respondents who experienced the death of a parent when they were age 11 or at a later time during their childhood. Not one of this group turned out to be demoralized at the time we interviewed them as adults. Is it possible that the later experience with bereavement has somehow inoculated these individuals against the demoralizing effects of contemporary loss, whereas bereavement earlier in life has the effect of increasing vulnerability to contemporary loss (see Bornstein et al., 1973)? Or is it just that the two groups, those suffering earlier bereavement and those suffering later bereavement during childhood, are different on other background variables associated with demoralization?

As Table 5.2 shows, the two groups are remarkably similar on the main background variables that we have found to be related to scores on the demoralization scale: sex, marital status, ethnic background, and educational level. They may differ somewhat in age, but there is no relation between age and demoralization in our sample.

Relation of remote loss to adaptation to recent loss

Let us return to our questions about the vulnerability or the resistance to recent loss that may result from early or late childhood bereavement.

Table 5.3 shows that demoralized subjects, regardless of early bereavement, have had recent experiences with more loss events and losses of greater magnitude than nondemoralized subjects. The latter difference is

Table 5.2. *Selective demographic characteristics of respondents who experienced earlier and later childhood bereavement*

	Bereavement during childhood	
Demographic characteristics	Early (N = 28)	Late (N = 19)
% under 40	50.0	31.6
% female	67.9	63.2
% married	67.9	73.7
Ethnicity (%)		
Puerto Rican	35.7	36.8
Black	32.1	31.6
Other	32.1	31.6
Education (%)		
Less than high school graduation	60.7	52.6
High school graduation	21.4	31.6
College graduation	17.9	15.8

statistically significant at the .05 level. Moreover, the sharpest contrast is with fateful loss events that are unlikely to be confounded with the respondent's psychiatric condition. Clearly, recent loss events play a part in demoralization. Does early bereavement during childhood make individuals more vulnerable to such losses?

If early death of one or both parents increases vulnerability to later loss events, we would expect demoralized subjects who experienced early bereavement to have fewer recent loss events than demoralized subjects who did not lose one or both parents during childhood. As Table 5.3 shows, there is indeed a tendency for the recent loss events faced by those who experienced early bereavement to be smaller in magnitude (an average of 525.4) than the recent losses of those who had not experienced early bereavement (an average of 768.8). Although this difference is not statistically significant with the small numbers involved, note the pattern of differences between the demoralized who experienced early death of one or both parents and the demoralized whose parents remained alive during their childhood. More of the latter group were exposed to losses, and their average number of losses was greater. Moreover, they were far more likely to have experienced physical illness or injury. Because those who suffered the early death of one or both parents apparently became demoralized after smaller losses in adult life, these results are consistent

Table 5.3. *Recent stressful loss events of demoralized and nondemoralized respondents according to their experience with bereavement during childhood*

	Demoralized respondents			Nondemoralized respondents			
Recent loss events	One or both parents died before respondent reached age 11 (N = 7)	Both parents alive during respondents' childhood (up to about age 18) (N = 15)	Total demoralized (N = 22)	One or both parents died before respondent reached age 11 (N = 21)	One or both parents died during respondent's childhood but not before respondent was 11 (N = 18)	Both parents alive during respondent's childhood (up to about age 18) (N = 104)	Total nondemoralized (N = 143)
% experiencing one or more recent losses	71.4	86.7	81.8	52.4	61.1	69.2	65.7
Mean number of losses	1.57	2.13	1.96	1.33	1.28	1.56	1.50
% experiencing one or more recent loss events							
Physical iliness or injury	0	40.0	27.3	14.3	22.2	17.3	17.5
Fateful events other than physical illness or injury	71.4	66.7	68.2	38.1	44.4	54.8	51.0
Other loss events	28.6	33.3	31.8	33.3	22.2	32.7	31.5
Mean magnitude scores for loss events in which respondent was the central figure	525.4	768.8	690.6	422.6	433.3	426.7	426.9

Notes: Data on life events were missing for one respondent, who is omitted from this table. It should also be recalled that none of the subjects who experienced childhood loss of one or both parents after age 10 was demoralized: Hence the apparently missing column under the heading "Demoralized respondents."

with a hypothesis of greater vulnerability associated with the early death of one or both parents.

What about the group of respondents who experienced later bereavement during childhood? It will be recalled that none of these respondents scored high on our measure of demoralization at the time of interview. This finding prompted us to raise the question whether their childhood experience with bereavement, coming as it did after age 10, when they may have been less vulnerable to severe damage than earlier in childhood, somehow inoculated them against the effects of loss later in life. If so, we would expect these respondents to withstand exposure to an unusually great amount of recent loss without becoming demoralized.

As Table 5.3 shows, however, those respondents who experienced later bereavement during childhood appear to have been exposed to fewer recent loss events than demoralized respondents who experienced no bereavement during childhood, and fewer also than demoralized subjects who may have been vulnerable as a result of having suffered early bereavement. In fact, so far as the magnitude of the recent loss events to which they have been exposed is concerned, those experiencing later bereavement during childhood do not differ from nondemoralized subjects in general. There is thus no evidence in the results we have presented that bereavement between the ages of 11 and 18 inoculates against the demoralizing effects of contemporary loss events later in life.

Discussion

Several limitations need to be emphasized with regard to these results. Two of them stem from the small size and special character of our sample of subjects. First, the small sample has left us with very small numbers in some of our most important cells, for example, the demoralized respondents who suffered early bereavement. This difficulty has led us to argue on the basis of meaningful trends and tendencies in some of the comparisons, rather than on the basis of the results of tests of statistical significance. Second, given the fact that the sample overrepresents residentially stable and public-spirited citizens, it is quite possible that a substantial percentage of persons showing different types of maladaptive responses to remote and recent loss events are being missed. For example, very few subjects in our sample score high on our measures of antisocial history, drinking problems, or drug abuse – any or all of which are maladaptive responses that should be considered in investigating relations between remote losses and adaptation to contemporary stressful life events. Moreover, there are stressful events during childhood other than those involving separation from parents, for example, separation from siblings and the child's own experiences with physical illness and injury. In addition, there is need for attention to a whole period of development between childhood and the time we interviewed our subjects, the majority of whom (61%) were between the ages of 40 and 65.

Meanwhile, though preliminary to more complete coverage of early losses and replication with larger samples, our results seem sufficiently compelling even now to warrant some further speculations about their possible theoretical and practical implications. The reason is that our finding about the role of early bereavement does not stand alone. It is consistent with the results of Brown et al.'s (1977) research on depression and Langner and Michael's (1963) studies of psychiatric impairment in general populations, and with the findings of Barry (1949), Birtchnell (1972), Brown et al. (1977), Greer et al. (1966), Norton (1952), and Oltman et al. (1952) on psychiatric patients.

In brief summary of the results so far, our data suggest that early bereavement during childhood increases vulnerability to contemporary loss events in adulthood. By contrast, there is no evidence that later bereavement during childhood either increases such vulnerability or inoculates against the effects of contemporary events involving loss. What might be the sources of this early damage, and why should it occur before age 11?

In the view of Brown et al. (1977), the major way in which such early loss increases vulnerability is by impairing self-esteem at a critical period of development. Though it seems reasonable that the impact should be greater earlier than later in childhood, there is no readily apparent reason why the period should extend beyond the preschool years or stop at around age 10. Although our samples are small, our data suggest that bereavement between ages 6 and 10 is at least as likely as bereavement during the still earlier period to leave the subject vulnerable to demoralization in the face of loss events in later life. Presumably, most of the other studies just cited also found the period 6–10 important, or they would have used an earlier cutoff.

It may be more than an intriguing coincidence, therefore, that Inbar (1976, p. 1) describes this particular period, age 6–11, as a vulnerable age of transition with regard to school achievement measured by number of grades completed. He points out that this is the beginning of the child's formal education. His argument is that a child may be affected more negatively during this period than either younger children or older children by changes that interfere with schooling. Loss of the help of one or both parents and, in some cases, change in schools as a consequence of the breakup of the home would be such disruptive experiences.

In our sample, at least, deaths that occurred while the respondent was age 0–5 were slightly more likely to be deaths of mothers (11 out of 20 cases). By contrast, deaths that occurred while the respondent was age 6–11 were most likely to be deaths of fathers (9 out of 12 cases). We would expect that the financial loss and logistics of remarriage would be more likely to lead to disruption of schooling in the case of deaths of fathers. Although he is not specific about the age of his subjects at the time of loss, Schooler (1972) provides some possibly relevant data on the character of the vulnerability that may be induced by the death of the father. He found in a large sample of employed U.S. males that loss of the father by death during the subject's childhood tended to be accompanied by less ideational flexibility and more attitudinal rigidity when the child became an adult. It seems possible that these characteristics are related to the nature of the vulnerability to stress that arises under the impact of such disruption and loss during the early school years.

If substantiated by further research, this explanation in terms of a vulnerable period during the early school years could have important implications for efforts at primary prevention. It suggests both a locale, the elementary school, and the classes within it, the first five grades, for intervention. Such intervention could be aimed at providing social support to help modify the immediate impact of bereavement; a more ambitious aim would be to try to prevent any decline in the child's abilities and attitudes of mastery. The net result would be a kind of social-psychological inoculation against some of the pathogenic effects of contemporary loss events in later life.

Assuming it to be more apparently obvious, we have said less about the nature of the impact of parental death on children up through age 5, the preschool years. This may well be the type of loss that was related to psychiatric impairment in adulthood in the study by Langner and Michael (1963), though these investigators did not restrict the cause of the loss to death. Similarly Brown et al.'s (1977) results point to the importance of loss of the mother as a factor in adult depression, though the period they considered extended to age 11 and, like Langner and Michael, they included losses by causes other than death. It is impossible to tell from the way the results in these studies are reported just how important in the aggregated findings was loss of the mother by death before the child reached age 6. Our guess would be that it was very important.

Overall, our results perhaps explain why some researchers, including Brown et al. (1977), have found loss of the mother before age 11 to be important, whereas others have found loss of the father to be important as well (e.g., Birtchnell, 1972). Specifically, our findings point to loss of the mother before age 6 and/or loss of the father between ages 6 and 10 as significant. To test the matter further, we investigated the proportion of losses of either of these two types in our 7 demoralized subjects who lost one or both parents prior to age 11 and in the 21 respondents who suffered early childhood bereavement but were not demoralized when we interviewed them as adults. The results are striking. Fully 86% of the former showed one or the other of these two types of early loss, by contrast with only 38% of the latter. Although the numbers are small, the difference is large and is statistically significant at the .05 level.

We would like to close by venturing our tentative conclusion. Where maladaptive responses by adults to contemporary stressful events involving loss take the form of marked subjective distress, there are at least two sets of childhood deprivations that may be involved as predisposing factors. One is loss of the mother by death during the preschool years; the other is loss of the father by death during the first 5 years of formal schooling. In the first, loss of maternal love and nurturance during childhood induces the vulnerability to later loss. In the second, disruption of the early process of formal education is the culprit. It is quite possible that each in a different way renders an individual's self-esteem unusually vulnerable to losses later in life.

References

Barry, H., Jr. Significance of material bereavement before age of eight in psychiatric patients. *Archives of Neurological Psychiatry*, 1949, *62*, 630–637.

Birtchnell, J. Early parent death and psychiatric diagnosis. *Social Psychiatry*, 1972, *7*, 202–210.

Bornstein, P. E., Clayton, P. J., Halikas, J. A., Maurice, W. L., & Robins, E. The depression of widowhood after thirteen months. *British Journal of Psychiatry*, 1973, *122*, 561–566.

Brown, G. W. Meaning, measurement, and stress of life events. In B. P. Dohrenwend & B. S. Dohrenwend (Eds.), *Stressful life events: Their nature and effects*. New York: Wiley, 1974.

Brown, G. W., Harris, T., & Copeland, J. R. Depression and loss. *British Journal of Psychiatry*, 1977, *130*, 1–18.

Chen, E., & Cobb, S. Family structure in relation to health and disease. *Journal of Chronic Disease*, 1960, *12*, 544–567.

Dohrenwend, B. P. Problems in defining and sampling the relevant population of stressful life events. In B. P. Dohrenwend & B. S. Dohrenwend (Eds.), *Stressful life events: Their nature and effects*. New York: Wiley, 1974.

Dohrenwend, B. P., & Crandell, D. L. Psychiatric symptoms in community, clinic, and mental hospital groups. *American Journal of Psychiatry*, 1970, *126*(11), 1611–1621.

Dohrenwend, B. P., & Dohrenwend, B. S. *Social status and psychological disorder*. New York: Wiley, 1969.

Dohrenwend, B. P., & Dohrenwend, B. S. The conceptualization and measurement of stressful life events: An overview of the issues. In J. S. Strauss, H. M. Babigian, & M. Roff (Eds.), *Origins and course of psychopathology*. New York: Plenum, 1977.

Dohrenwend, B. P., Shrout, P. E., Egri, G., & Mendelsohn, F. S. Nonspecific psychological distress and other dimensions of psychopathology: Measures for use in the general population. *Archives of General Psychiatry*, 1980, *37*, 1229–1236.

Dohrenwend, B. P., Yager, T. J., Egri, G., & Mendelsohn, F. S. The psychiatric status schedule (PSS) as a measure of dimensions of psychopathology in the general population. *Archives of General Psychiatry*, 1978, *35*, 731–735.

Dohrenwend, B. S., & Dohrenwend, B. P. (Eds.). *Stressful life events: Their nature and effects*. New York: Wiley, 1974.

Dohrenwend, B. S., & Dohrenwend, B. P. Some issues in research on stressful life events. *Journal of Nervous and Mental Disease*, 1978, *166*, 7–15.

Dohrenwend, B. S., Krasnoff, L., Askenasy, A. R., & Dohrenwend, B. P. Exemplification of a method for scaling life events: The PERI life events scale. *Journal of Health and Social Behavior*, 1978, *19*, 205–229.

Frank, J. D. *Persuasion and healing*. Baltimore: Johns Hopkins University Press, 1973.

Granville-Grossman, K. L. The early environment in affective disorder. *British Journal of Psychiatry*, 1968, Special Publication No. 2, 65–79.

Greer, S., Gunn, J. C., & Koller, K. M. Aetiological factors in attempted suicide. *British Medical Journal*, 1966, *2*, 1352–1355.

Gregory, I. Studies of parental deprivation in psychiatric patients. *American Journal of Psychiatry*, 1958, *115*, 432–442.

Gunderson, E. K. E., & Rahe, R. H. *Life stress and illness*. Springfield, Ill.: Thomas, 1974.

Heinicke, C. M. Parental deprivation in early childhood. In J. P. Scott & E. C. Senay (Eds.), *Separation and depression*. Washington, D.C. American Association for the Advancement of Science, Publication No. 94, 1973.

Hocking, F. Extreme environmental stress and its significance for psychopathology. *American Journal of Psychotherapy*, 1970, *24*, 4–26.

Inbar, M. *The vulnerable age phenomenon*. New York: Russell Sage Foundation, 1976.

Kellam, S. G., Ensminger, M. E., & Turner, R. J. Family structure and the mental health of children. *Archives of General Psychiatry*, 1977, *34*, 1012–1022.

Kinston, W., & Rosser, R. Disaster: Effects on mental and physical state. *Journal of Psychosomatic Research*, 1974, *18*, 437–456.

Langner, T. S. A twenty-two item screening score of psychiatric symptoms indicating impairment. *Journal of Health and Human Behavior*, 1962, *3*, 269–276.

Langner, T. S., & Michael, S. T. *Life stress and mental health* (Vol. 2). London: Free Press of Glencoe, 1963.

Macmillan, A. M. The health opinion survey: Technique for estimating prevalence of psychoneurotic and related types of disorder in communities. *Psychological Reports*, 1957, *3*, 325–329.

Nordheimer, J. The family in transition. *New York Times*, Nov. 27, 1977, p. 1.

Norton, A. Incidence of neurosis related to maternal age and birth order. *British Journal of Social Medicine*, 1952, *6*, 253–258.

Oltman, J. E., McGarry, J. J., & Friedman, S. Parental deprivation and the broken home in Dementia Praecox and other mental disorders. *American Journal of Psychiatry*, 1952, *108*, 658–694.

Schooler, C. Childhood family structure and adult characteristics. *Sociometry*, 1972, *2*, 255–269.

Ulenhuth, E. H., Balter, M. D., Lipman, R. S., & Haberman, S. J. Remembering life events. In J. S. Strauss, H. M. Babigian, & M. Roff (Eds.), *The origins and course of psychopathology*. New York: Plenum, 1977.

Part III

Measurement and data analysis in psychopathology

6 Definition and assessment of childhood depressions

Maria Kovacs

Introduction

Two clinical observations first aroused my curiosity about juvenile depressions. Several years ago, I interviewed a large number of hospitalized suicidal adults for a research project. It seemed to me that, of the patients who reported preadolescent depressive episodes, a notable number were suffering from a schizoaffective disorder at the time of the interview. Thus I began to wonder whether juvenile depressive episodes are predictive of subsequent affective or schizophrenic disorders. I made a later observation during my involvement in a treatment outcome study with adult outpatients that utilized cognitive therapy as one intervention for depression. One of the goals of cognitive therapy was to "uncover" and to modify the assumptions and attitudes that are relevant to, and presumably underlie and support, the patient's dysfunctional depressive cognitive set (Beck, 1967/1972; Beck & Rush, 1978; Kovacs & Beck, 1978, 1979). It appeared that many patients reported having learned their depression-relevant cognitive schemata during their childhood and preadolescent years. I therefore became curious to learn whether such schemata could be discerned in youngsters in general, and in depressed children in particular.

My interest was further heightened by a pilot study of depression in school-aged children (Albert & Beck, 1975), which revealed that the youngsters had high rates of symptomatology as assessed by an adult self-

Preparation of this chapter was supported by NIMH Grant MH 30925-01. The pilot study was partially supported by NIMH Grant MH 19989-05.

Appreciation is due to Aaron T. Beck, M.D., for his encouragement and support in the early phases of this project; to Nila G. Betof, M.A., Jeffrey E. Celebre, M.A., Paul A. Mansheim, M.D., Leonora K. Petty, M.D., and Jan T. Raynak, M.D., who helped to conduct the pilot study; and to Robert A. Steer, Ph.D., for statistical advice.

Data from the Canadian study were made available through the courtesy of Lenora F. Butler, Ph.D., and Solveiga Miezitis, Ph.D., of the Ontario Institute for Studies in Education, Toronto, Canada, to whom I am much indebted.

rated depression inventory. I wondered whether the results would be similar if a children's inventory was administered.

As these recollections indicate, much of my initial curiosity about juvenile depression concerned its possible relationship to the adult disorder. When I actually began to study depression in preadolescents and adolescents, I did not anticipate that my eventual work would have to revolve around issues of instrumentation and clinical definition, and that it would become focused on the nosology of childhood depressive disorders.

In this chapter, I review some of the problems in the longitudinal study of depression among *school-aged* children, describe the results of a pilot investigation, and consider the pilot project's future directions.

Problems in the longitudinal study of childhood depressions

The existence of childhood depressive disorders is somewhat controversial. Their study is made difficult by the absence of agreed-on, reliable, and valid diagnostic criteria, the lack of assessment tools, and sparse information on what settings are most likely to provide appropriate subjects.

Does childhood depression exist?

"Depressive" affective and behavioral displays are by no means rare in juvenile populations (Lessing & Zagorin, 1971; Rutter & Graham, 1968). However, recent reviews (Conners, 1976; Gittelman-Klein, 1977; Kovacs & Beck, 1977) have noted questions about whether such displays represent a nosologic entity, namely, a distinct aggregate of psychopathological signs and symptoms with a characteristic course, duration, and treatment responsitivity.

Skepticism about the existence of childhood depression as a diagnostic entity could reflect (a) an accurate assessment of the state of affairs (that is, there may be an absence of the disorder in children owing to some biological – for example, endocrine – factors); (b) a theoretical orientation that colors the clinician's observation (for example, according to traditional psychoanalytic principles, children's immature personality structure and superego weakness preclude the development of adultlike depressive states; see Rie, 1966, for an overview); (c) an observational or expectational set derived from models of adult depressive disorders (for instance, one argument against the existence of juvenile depressive episodes is that children who apparently manifest the syndrome are generally responsive to environmental interventions, that is, can be cheered up with little difficulty; thus this argument presupposes that the frequently observed intractability of adult depressions also has to be a sine qua non of childhood depressive episodes); (d) a developmental perspective which posits that the observed symptoms represent adaptive psychobiological affective reactions (Sandler & Joffe, 1965); and finally (3) an antilabeling bias, as can be seen in some workers' readiness to view all except the most deviant or disabling clinical pictures in juveniles as "adjustment reactions."

In the final analysis, however, the validity of childhood depression as a diagnostic entity can be proven or disproven only through controlled and systematic nosological study of carefully selected and well-described samples.

Diagnostic criteria for childhood depressions

Proponents of the existence of childhood depressions have yet to arrive at agreed-on definitions or diagnostic criteria. According to recent reviews (Conners, 1976; Kovacs & Beck, 1977), there is a lack of consensus not only on the range and type of signs and symptoms that characterize depressed youngsters, but also on whether childhood depression is "overt" and readily observable or presents itself in a "masked" form.

In the relevant literature, the terms *overt* and *clinically depressed* refer to symptom pictures that are similar to the clinical presentations seen in depressed adults. Correspondingly, this alleged childhood disorder is described as encompassing symptoms such as dysphoria or similar mood disturbance, poor self-esteem or self-deprecation, social withdrawal, reduced initiative, anhedonia, sleep disturbances, morbid or suicidal thoughts, and impaired ability to do schoolwork (for reviews see Conners, 1976; Kovacs & Beck, 1977). Some researchers have proposed operational definitions derived from adult diagnostic criteria (e.g., Ling, Oftedal, & Weinberg, 1970; Weinberg et al., 1973). Others have described diagnostic subtypes based on the children's clinical pictures and their differential treatment responsivity. Clinical subtyping is exemplified by Frommer's (1968) categories of enuretic and/or encopretic depression, depressive phobic anxiety states, and uncomplicated depression, and by McConville, Boag, and Purohit's (1973) categories of affectual depression, negative self-esteem depression, and guilt depression.

In contrast to this viewpoint, the masked-depression advocates contend that the familiar manifestations of the adult depressions are rarely observable in youngsters. Instead, the disorder's expression is allegedly concealed by behaviors that are more developmentally appropriate, including acting out, disobedience, temper tantrums, fire setting, or somatic complaints. The underlying depressive elements can be ascertained through careful interviewing and through analysis of the child's dreams, daydreams, and drawings (for a review, see Kovacs & Beck, 1977).

As Kovacs and Beck (1977) noted, however, there is an overlap in the clinical descriptions of overtly depressed children and of those who are said to suffer from masked depression. For example, whereas some workers consider temper tantrums as a masking symptom, others define tantrums as overt manifestations of childhood depression. Moreover, some behaviors that presumably mask childhood depression can be viewed more parsimoniously as presenting complaints or as associated rather than core features of the syndrome.

Thus, although the available clinical descriptions provide a useful starting point for an empirical study of childhood depressive disorders, the fact remains that the proposed characterizations or criteria do not have sufficient reliability or validity data in their support (Werry, 1976).

Table 6.1 illustrates the need for reliable description. As can be seen, the percentage of children reported to be clinically "depressed" ranges from 0 to 61 across the different studies. The variability of these rates may be due to the nonequivalence of the samples on parameters such as age and psychiatric status. In part, however, the figures in Table 6.1 seem to fluctuate as a function of how the clinical data were obtained, how stringently the syndrome was defined, and how the symptoms were rated. For instance, in order to designate a child as "depressed," Gittleman-Klein and Klein (1973) and Kovacs et al. (1977), who reported two of the lowest percentages of depressed youngsters in their study samples, required not only that certain symptoms be present but that these symptoms be of a predefined degree of severity.

Table 6.2 groups some of the salient symptoms that have been said to characterize childhood depression and illustrates both the overlap and the diversity of the various clinical descriptions. According to Weinberg et al. (1973), for instance, overtly depressed children manifest the group of symptoms on the topmost part of Table 6.2. Connell (1972), Frommer (1968), and others have offered both the bottom left and the topmost group of symptoms as characteristics of childhood depression. All three groups of symptoms listed in Table 6.2 constitute salient aspects of the clinical picture of masked depression (e.g., Cytryn & McKnew, 1974; Glaser, 1968). The variability of the data illustrated in Tables 6.1 and 6.2 underscores the need for reliable consensual diagnostic criteria for childhood depressive disorders and also argues for uniformity in assessment methods.

Table 6.1. *The prevalence of depressive syndromes in children*

Study	Subjects	Type of assessment	Diagnostic criteria	% rated as "depressed"
Frommer, Mendelson, & Klein, 1972	210 psychiatric OP[a] (age: < 5)	Interview and case notes	Not stated	58
Gittelman-Klein & Klein, 1973	34 school phobic OP (age: 6–14)	Interview	Observable depression (modified Inpatient Multidimensional Psychiatric Scale Items)	35
Kovacs, Betof, Celebre, Mansheim, Petty, & Raynak, 1977	39 psychiatric IP[b] and 20 normals (age: 8–13)	Structured interview	Symptom cluster	14 0
Ling, Oftedal, & Weinberg, 1970	25 neurology headache OP (age: 4–16)	Retrospective case history analysis	Operational 4 of 10 symptoms	40
Pearce, 1977	547 psychiatric IP/OP? (age: 1–17)	Not stated	Not stated	23
Petti, 1978	73 psychiatric IP (age: 6–12)	Semistructured interview plus referral documents	Weinberg et al. (1973) criteria	61
			Bellevue Index (quantified Weinberg et al., 1973, criteria)	59
Weinberg, Rutman, Sullivan, Penick, & Deitz, 1973; Brumback, Dietz-Schmidt, & Weinberg, 1977	72 education diagnostic center OP (age: 6–12)	Interview	Operational; 4 of 10 symptoms	58

[a] OP = outpatients.
[b] IP = inpatients.

Table 6.2. *Selected childhood "depressive" symptoms*

	Dysphoria/mood change Withdrawal Diminished socialization Negative self-concept Self-deprecation Vegetative disturbances Somatic complaints	
Plus ↙		↖ Plus ↘
Irritability Negative thought content/fantasy Suicidal behaviors Anergia Enuresis/encopresis Changed school performance	——— Plus ———→	Antisocial behaviors Temper tantrums Running away Phobias Hyperactivity Truancy Anxiety

The follow-up interval

As a natural sequela to the diagnostic confusion and the lack of uniform clinical assessment procedures, there are few reliable data on the short- or long-term vicissitudes of the signs, symptoms, and behavioral manifestations of juvenile depression or on the course of the syndrome itself. Long-term follow-up is important not only in life history research in psychopathology, but also as one means of validating nosological categories (Feighner et al. 1972). In turn, a longitudinal nosological study must have guidelines defining what constitutes a reasonable follow-up interval.

Because the available literature on childhood depression provides little information on the duration of these disorders or on the time interval within which symptomatic youngsters may be at high risk for relapse or for recurrence of an episode, a researcher may wish to turn for help to the literature on adults.

However, the information on the course of adult depressive disorders is sufficient to discourage a fledgling researcher. First, the data indicate that, within the adult life span, there is no particular age range at which individuals are most at risk for depression (Secunda et al., 1973). Thus, if the depressive disorders of childhood represent chronologically earlier manifestations of the adult illness, their longitudinal study is likely to be a very long-term enterprise with relatively low immediate yield.

Second, although there are data to suggest that individuals with unipolar depressive illness have their first episodes at younger ages than those whose first depression is part of a bipolar affective disorder, in both cases decades or more can pass before another depressive episode occurs (Perris, 1966). However, the symptom-free intervals between depressive episodes tend to become shorter with increasing age. If we extrapolate backward from these data, we may thus hypothesize that depressed youngsters will have very long symptom-free periods; consequently, a 5–15-year follow-up could yield misleading information on the eventual psychiatric course of these juvenile disorders. This situation may be contrasted with longitudinal research on schizophrenia, for instance, wherein a 15-year follow-up of either high-risk or clearly symptomatic youngsters is likely to yield valid data on the course of the disorder over time.

Research strategies for the study of childhood depressions

As this brief overview indicates, it is imperative that empirical investigations of childhood depressions encompass explicit and replicable clinical or psychometric assessment, reliable description of the children's symptom picture, and systematic selection criteria.

There are numerous research strategies that may be useful for the definition of childhood depressions (see the Recommendations of the Subcommittee on Assessment, in Schulterbrandt & Raskin, 1977). The specific paradigm would necessarily have to accommodate the interest of the investigator, be it clinical description, treatment response, or hypothesis testing. For example, one approach could be the reliable and systematic description of behavioral alterations that characterize recently bereaved school-aged children. Based on the assumption that mourning is a naturally occurring "nonpathological" variant of depressive disorders, youngsters whose behavior and symptom pictures clearly *deviate* from the sample norm may exemplify one form of clinical depression. On the other hand, an investigator may decide that certain symptoms are cardinal components of a depressive syndrome; the full range of symptomatology of children who manifest the target symptoms could then be carefully described.

Investigation of whether the diagnosis of depression can be validated by biological markers is yet another strategy. For instance, there have already been attempts to assess EEG sleep patterns (Coble et al., 1977) and cortisol secretion levels (Joaquim Puig-Antich, personal communication, 1977) in ostensibly depressed children. The work of Weinberg et al. (1973) and Ling et al. (1970) illustrates case selection in accordance with operationally defined and modified adult diagnostic criteria. This is an especially pragmatic strategy for the assessment of treatment interventions that have demonstrated efficacies for adult depressive disorders. Although the selection of depressed children through operationally defined criteria has been lauded (Werry, 1976), it is important to note that, at present, such criteria constitute *working definitions*. Empirical data are yet to be gathered to support their diagnostic validity.

A descriptive, nosologically oriented research project on childhood depressions

My actual entry into childhood-depression research was piecemeal and unsystematic. As I have already noted, I was interested in several issues: (a) the relationship between childhood depression and the adult disorder, (b) the cognitive characteristics of depressed children, and (c) the actual prevalence of depression among juveniles.

What was puzzling, however, was that authoritative texts and publications on the affective disorders conveyed the impression that depressive illness was primarily an "adult" condition (e.g., Beck, 1967/1972; Grinker et al., 1961; Mendels, 1975; Secunda et al., 1973). Even family studies of depressives rarely, if ever, seemed to pay attention to affective disorders in relatives prior to the age of 16 years (see e.g., Perris, 1966). Though the childhood psychopathology literature was far more informative, it did not provide explicit, reliable, and valid criteria for childhood depressions, nor did it suggest a pragmatic way of assessing or screening youngsters. In addition, the literature did convey the impression that clinically significant depressive disorders are by no means prevalent in school-aged populations.

Consequently, I thought that it would be useful to have a quick assessment device that would facilitate the screening of large samples in order to locate index cases for further study. Because self-rated symptom inventories are easily administered and economical, the Albert and Beck (1975) project gave me the idea of altering an existing adult depression inventory for children. I also decided to validate this planned instrument against clinical ratings of depression.

When I approached several clinicians from the Philadelphia Child Guidance Center in order to initiate a validation study, it became evident that our uses of the term *childhood depression* were not in concert. Basing our decisions on the literature, we arrived at a tentative working definition of what signs, symptoms, and behaviors should be assessed and what a global clinical rating of "depression" should signify. The next hurdle to overcome was the variability of interviewing styles and theoretical stances – matters that influenced what data were obtained in the interview with the child and how the information was weighted.

In a short time, it became overwhelmingly clear that the development of assessment technology and of a systematic nomenclature of childhood depressions had to take priority over more theoretically oriented research paradigms. My interest thus became focused on the definition and the diagnoses of juvenile depressions. I eventually decided to pursue two strategies that have been recommended for the validation of a diagnostic entity, namely, reliable clinical description and follow-up (Feighner et al., 1972). Because my long-term goal is to gather data on the "natural" course of childhood depressions, the research focus is on common trends rather than on individual differences.

Problems of instrumentation

Because no clinical rating scales were available 5 years ago for the assessment of childhood depression, as I have already noted, the development of a systematic interview became one of the initial project goals. At the start, our rating form included those symptoms or behaviors that were most often cited in the literature as characteristic of childhood depression. However, numerous discussions and the results of pilot testing eventually yielded a far more comprehensive schedule than we first anticipated: the Interview Schedule for Children (ISC). The ISC itself has undergone several major revisions. The data to be presented are from our first pilot investigation of childhood depression using the ISC-Form A.

The ISC-Form A was designed to be administered by a clinician in a face-to-face interview with the child. The schedule encompassed 37 symptoms and symptom clusters, including (a) manifestations of overt as well as masked childhood depression, (b) aspects of a mental status examination, and (c) behavioral observations. Some of the observational items were adapted from the ECDEU assessment battery (Guy, 1976).

The interview schedule defined the symptoms and behaviors that were to be assessed. In order to standardize the procedure of obtaining the relevant information from the child, the schedule also encompassed a set of pertinent questions that were to be asked for each item (symptom). On each page of the ISC-Form A, each symptom definition, with its corresponding inquiries, was followed by a severity rating scale so that the interviewer could immediately enter his or her rating.

Most symptoms or behaviors were rated on a scale from "0 – not at all'' to "8 – severe.'' The scale points were explicitly defined in terms of symptom frequency and severity, with a special emphasis on whether the symptom was associated with functional impairment. A number of items, such as "hallucinations,'' were rated on a 0–2-point scale wherein 0 = not at all, 1 = probable, and 2 = definite. The completed interview schedule consequently yielded a set of symptom ratings, not a differential diagnosis.

The self-rated questionnaire for children that I was first interested in validating was designated as the Children's Depression Inventory (CDI). The initial version of the CDI was a semantic modification of the 21-item Beck Depression Inventory for adults (Beck, 1967/1972; Beck & Beamesderfer, 1974). On the basis of pilot testing with children between the ages of 8 and 14 years, several content areas that appeared to be of little relevance to this age group were eliminated. Additional testing led to further refinement of the items, including alterations in content and vocabulary, and to attempts to standardize the qualitative or quantitative dimension underlying the item choices. Several items were adapted from a questionnaire by Albert and Beck (1975) and were added to the inventory. Eventually, the CDI underwent three major and several minor revisions as a result of large-scale testings of schoolchildren and the findings of the pilot study, to be discussed next.

The data to be presented are from an *early* version of the 27-item CDI. The items were designed to reflect overt childhood depressive symptoms, such as sadness, low self-esteem, decreased interest, difficulty in schoolwork, suicidal ideation, and irritability. Four possible responses were presented with each item, such that choice of the response scored 0 represented absence of the symptom and choice of the response scored 3 signified a severe symptom. For example, on "sadness,'' the item choice that was keyed 0 read "I do not feel sad,'' whereas the statement "I am so very sad that I can't stand it'' was the item choice that was keyed 3.

Selected data from the pilot study

Our pilot study eventually had multiple aims, namely, determination of (a) whether the ISC-Form A was a viable and reliable means of symptom rating, (b) whether the symptoms encompassed in the ISC-Form A would cluster together to form a "depressive syndrome,'' and (c) whether the self-rated depression inventory score correlated with the clinicians' overall ratings of the severity of the child's depression.

The subjects were 39 children in the Philadelphia Child Guidance Clinic's inpatient or day care units. Most of the children had been referred to the clinic because of acting out or unmanageable behavior. Because our initial aims necessitated a correlational study, we needed youngsters with a diversity of clinical pictures. Thus our subjects were consecutive admissions who had to meet only the criteria of being between 8 and 13 years of age and not mentally retarded.

We also interviewed 20 "normal" children in order to gather data on the applicability of our instruments to nonclinical populations. These youngsters were obtained from families of neighbors of the interviewing clinicians and staff of the guidance center. For the nonclinical group, we controlled only for age range, absence of mental retardation, and no history of psychiatric treatment. Thus it is important to emphasize that the nonclinical children constituted *not* a control group but an unmatched comparison group.

Each child was individually interviewed by one of the project clinicians, using the ISC. The interrater reliability of the instrument was determined by having a second clinician observe some of the interviews and independently rate the ISC items.

The CDI was administered to the child in a separate session, independently of the clinical interview. The child was given a copy of the CDI, and a research assistant read each item aloud as the child read along and circled his or her answers.

The characteristics of the samples, the reliability of the symptom ratings, and the major findings have been described in detail elsewhere (Kovacs et al., 1977).

Table 6.3 presents selected data from this pilot study. Unless otherwise noted, the numerical column entries reflect the percentage of children who received ISC-Form A ratings from 5 (moderate symptom) to 8 (severe symptom). For the items listed on Table 6.3, interrater reliability coefficients ranged from .55 to .98 on a sample of $N = 39$.

The two topmost items in the table should be noted first. The phrase *Global depression* refers to a depressive *syndrome* that was defined in the ISC-Form A as encompassing the familiar manifestations of overt (or adultlike) depression. On the basis of this operational definition, 14% of the clinic children manifested "moderate" to "severe" depression. However, the clinicians were also provided with the opportunity to enter a separate 0–8-point global depression rating based on "clinical hunch." When the definition of the syndrome to be rated was this lax, the percentage of clinically depressed children jumped to 55. The discrepancy between the operationally defined global depression and the undefined depression-by-hunch figures provides a nice illustration of the extent to which prevalence rates may vary as a function of syndrome definition. It

Table 6.3. *Prevalence of moderate to severe symptoms by clinical interview rating*

ISC-Form A item	Clinical sample (N = 37)	Nonclinical sample (N = 20)
Global depression (operationally defined)	14%	0%
Global depression (''clinical hunch'')	55%	6%
Depressed mood	11%	0%
Depressed thinking	6%	0%
Social withdrawal/diminished motivation	11%	0%
Depressed demeanor	11%	0%
Psychomotor retardation	6%	0%
Decreased sleep/appetite	14%	0%
Current suicidal behavior	6[a]	0[a]
Suicide ideation – current or past	49[a]	45[a]
Suicide attempts – current or past	8[a]	0[a]
''Phobic'' school avoidance	8%	5%
Fighting/temper outbursts	54%	5%
Truancy	14%	5%
Antisocial behavior	28%	6%

Note: The entries are selected items and represent only a fraction of all the symptoms assessed in the ISC-Form A.
[a] Rated as present on a present–absent scale.

also illustrates the need for specification of the behaviors that are to be assessed.

An additional interesting aspect of the data in Table 6.3 is the variable symptom distributions in the clinical sample. For instance, whereas 54% of the group had had marked fighting and temper outbursts, only 6% evidenced moderate to severe pessimism, hopelessness, and low self-esteem (depressed thinking). Although all the symptoms in Table 6.3 have been said to characterize childhood depression, their variable distributions suggest that they might not constitute one syndrome.

To determine the dimensions underlying the ISC-Form A and to assess whether the alleged depressive symptoms fall into a cluster, we subjected the data to a principal component analysis using varimax rotation. Cattell's (1966) scree test was used to determine the number of components to be retained for rotation. Table 6.4 depicts the five derived components that account for 60.4% of the total variance. In interpreting the components, only item loadings ≥.45 were considered salient. For purposes of this presentation, the table lists only those symptoms that loaded on *one* component. As the entries indicate, the first component reflects overt

Table 6.4. *ISC-Form A symptom clusters*

I	II	III	IV	V
Psychomotor retardation	Hyperactivity	Global depression ("hunch")	Hallucinations	Suspiciousness
Constricted affect	Anger/hostility	Fighting/temper outbursts	Delusional thinking	Current suicidal behavior
Depressed demeanor	Pressure of speech	Antisocial behavior	Suicide attempts – past or present	
Global depression (operationally defined)	Euphoria/elation	Depressed thinking	Suicide ideation – past or present	
Underproductive speech	"Silly" affect	Nervous mannerisms		
Depressed mood		Truancy		
Social withdrawal/ diminished motivation				
Anxious demeanor				

Note: The entries represent only those ISC items that had loadings of $\geq .45$ on *one* component.

depressive symptomatology. Items with the heaviest loadings were those assessing nonverbal, behavioral manifestations of depression.

Suicidal behaviors, pessimism/hopelessness, and low self-esteem (depressed thinking) did not cluster with the other "depressive" symptoms. It is also notable that acting-out or behavior problems are on a separate dimension, although the masked depression position would have led us to expect some or all of them on the "depressive" component. The items on Component II show an uncanny resemblance to the adult clinical picture of hypomanic or manic states. The data in Table 6.4, however, must be interpreted in view of the fact that a principal components solution forces orthogonality between the resultant factors. Thus we cannot know the actual degree of relationship *between* the components.

The results of this pilot study suggested that our descriptive approach toward the eventual definition of childhood depressive disorders was worth pursuing. The ISC-Form A interrater reliability figures implied that the face-to-face interview with the child can be standardized and that it can provide viable data. A "postmortem" on ISC items with less than desirable interrater agreement revealed that one source of difficulty was lack of specificity, or overinclusiveness, of some items, flaws that have been remedied by subsequent ISC revisions. Results of the principal components analysis were encouraging and pointed to one way of discovering meaningful order underlying the clinical data.

Results from the self-rated CDI were similarly promising. First, CDI total scores correlated at $r = .55$ ($p < .001$, $N = 54$) with clinicians' global depression ratings. In spite of the newness of the scales involved, this coefficient is in the range that has been reported for established clinical and self-rating depression scales for adults (Becker, 1974).

As an alternative way to assess the relationship between self-rated depressive symptoms and clinicians' ratings of the severity of depression, the ISC-Form A global depression ratings were used to group the children into three classes: no or minimal depression, mild depression, and moderate to severe depression. The mean CDI scores of the children in the three depression categories were in the expected direction; namely, with increments in the clinically rated severity of depression, there was a progressively higher mean CDI score.

Table 6.5 presents the distribution of item choices 2 and 3, that is, moderate to severe (or clinically significant) symptoms, for selected CDI items. The data are from the pilot study subjects and from a group of fifth- and sixth-grade schoolchildren in Toronto, Canada, who were tested in their schools as part of a large-scale project conducted by the Ontario Institute for Studies in Education.

Table 6.5. *Prevalence of moderate to severe "depressive" symptoms according to children's self-ratings (in %)*

CDI item	Canadian school sample (N = 127)	U.S. nonclinical sample (N = 20)	U.S. clinical sample (N = 39)
Sadness	5	<1	13
Pessimism	5	5	13
Sense of failure	20	0	26
Anhedonia	6	0	13
Self-dislike	6	0	8
Self-devaluation	8	0	11
Self-blame	20	5	37
Suicidal ideation	5	0	11
Withdrawal	9	0	16
Negative body image	14	10	21
Insomnia	24	25	29
Anorexia	20	10	18
Fatigue	12	0	18
Somatic complaints	13	0	26
Loneliness	10	0	24
Decreased marks	8	0	29
Schoolwork difficulty	14	15	27

Note: The entries represent selected CDI items.

The data from Tables 6.3 and 6.5 indicate that self-ratings of comparable "symptoms" or behaviors tend to yield a slightly higher prevalence figure than interviewer ratings. For example, on the ISC-Form A interview, 11% of the clinical sample showed moderate to severe social withdrawal. However, 16% of these children rated *themselves* as being considerably socially withdrawn. Such discrepancies are probably due to the greater stringency of clinical ratings.

The data in Table 6.5 also illustrate that isolated "depressive" symptoms are quite frequent among the nonclinical groups of children. For example, anorexia was relatively prevalent in both *non*clinical samples, and this rate was similar to the figures reported by Brumback, Dietz-Schmidt, and Weinberg (1977) for clinical populations. Comparable portions of the U.S. clinical sample and the Canadian nonclinical group of children reported a marked sense of failure. The prevalence of self-reported insomnia was also similar across the three samples. In general, however, the nonclinical groups seemed somewhat less likely than the clinical children to endorse items that reflect significant symptoms: From 5% to 24% of the Canadian children and from 0% to 25% of the U.S.

nonclinical sample reported troublesome symptoms; the clinical children's endorsements ranged from 8% to 37%.

These self-report data have a number of implications. First, the variability of answers across CDI items argues against a response set. Second, the rather high endorsement rates on some item choices suggest that isolated "symptoms" must not be equated with a clinical syndrome or a psychiatric illness. For example, some endorsements may mirror the presence of transient medical illness. On the other hand, the choice of responses may also represent developmentally appropriate concerns or phenomena. A more definitive statement of the meaning of the self-rated "symptoms" must await replication with much larger clinical and nonclinical samples. Although the CDI data must be viewed with caution, the findings do suggest that nonretarded children between the ages of 8 and 13 years are able to complete self-rated inventories and can discriminate between item choices and variable item content.

Future directions

The difficulties that were encountered in implementing our pilot study and in constructing the ISC-Form A underscore the need for systematic and reliable symptom description in child psychopathology. In fact, the actual day-to-day pragmatic issues that arose have led to an increased specificity of research goals and to a more systematic and complex design.

The findings that have been summarized in this chapter have proven useful in refining the clinical interview schedule. Discussions of items that did not yield sufficiently high interrater agreements have led to revisions that encompass (a) the separation of clinically obvious components of an item and their independent ratings, (b) the elimination of nonprofitable or ambiguous inquiry questions, and (c) the addition of inquiry questions that allow the interviewer to ascertain that interviewer and child are talking about the same thing. Further pilot testing resulted in an extensively revised and more comprehensive schedule, the ISC-Form C. At the present time, administration of the ISC-Form C has been extended to a separate interview with the parent *about* the child. As already noted, the CDI has also been revised. On the basis of available data, the items have been completely rewritten and their formats have been altered. This form is currently being validated.

Ultimately, questions about the existence of a distinct juvenile depressive syndrome and its parameters can be answered only through systematic and reliable large-scale data gathering. The question whether this putative syndrome has the characteristics of a psychiatric *disorder* can be addressed through follow-up and through family studies. Thus, my work has evolved into a nosological study that includes the extensive clinical evaluation and follow-up of children recruited from both psychiatric and medical settings. Demographic, developmental, and life-events data are also being gathered. The parents of the youngsters are independently assessed, and familial psychiatric histories are being obtained. The children and their parent(s) are reevaluated several times a year subsequent to the research intake interview.

In summary, however, I would like to mention my discomfort with several aspects of the childhood depression literature and with work currently in progress, my own included. First, I am struck by the relative absence of a reliable system of inquiry that seems specifically tailored to the problems of the juvenile years. Second, I remain puzzled by the extent to which the field is permeated by theoretical approaches, problem-solving strategies, and research paradigms (including those employed in my nosological work) that are "borrowed" from the study of adult psychiatric and psychological disorders. As of yet, it is hard to know whether these features of our research reflect an impoverishment in our thinking and clinical strategies, an inevitable tendency of adult problem-solvers to ask and to solve questions in cognitively and experientially familiar terms, or the best possible approach to an interesting and puzzling clinical issue.

References

Albert, N., & Beck, A. T. Incidence of depression in early adolescence: A preliminary study. *Journal of Youth and Adolescence*, 1975, *4*(4), 301–307.

Beck, A. T. *Depression: Clinical, experimental, and theoretical aspects*. New York: Hoeber, 1967. (Republished as *Depression: Causes and treatment*. Philadelphia: University of Pennsylvania Press, 1972.)

Beck, A. T., & Beamesderfer, A. Assessment of depression: The depression inventory. In P. Pichot (Ed.), *Psychological measurements in psychopharmacology: Modern problems in pharmacopsychiatry* (Vol. 7). Basel: Karger, 1974.

Beck, A. T., & Rush, A. J. Cognitive approaches to depression and suicide. In G. Serban (Ed.), *Cognitive defects in the development of mental illness*. New York: Brunner/Mazel, 1978.

Becker, J. *Depression: Theory and research*. Washington, D.C.: Winston & Sons, 1974.

Brumback, R. A., Dietz-Schmidt, S. G., & Weinberg, W. A. Depression in children referred to an educational diagnostic center: Diagnosis and treatment and analysis of criteria and literature review. *Diseases of the Nervous System*, 1977, *38*, 529–535.

Cattell, R. B. The scree test for number of factors. *Multivariate Behavioral Research*, 1966, *1*, 247–276.

Coble, P., Kupfer, D., Petti, T., Conners, C. K., Kane, J., & Jameson, P. The EEG sleep of hospitalized boys with depressive symptomatology. *Proceedings of the Association of the Psychophysiological Study of Sleep*, Houston, Tex., 1977.

Connell, H. M. Depression in childhood. *Child Psychiatry and Human Development*, 1972, *4*, 71–85.

Conners, C. K. Classification and treatment of childhood depression and depressive equivalents. In D. M. Gallant & G. M. Simpson (Eds.), *Depression: Behavioral, biochemical, diagnostic and treatment concepts*. New York: Spectrum, 1976.

Cytryn, L., & McKnew, D. H. Factors influencing the changing clinical expression of the depressive process in children. *American Journal of Psychiatry*, 1974, *131*, 879–881.

Feighner, J. P., Robins, E., Guze, S. B., Woodruff, R. A., Winokur, G., & Munoz, R. Diagnostic criteria for use in psychiatric research. *Archives of General Psychiatry*, 1972, *26*, 57–63.

Frommer, E. A. Depressive illness in childhood. *British Journal of Psychiatry*, 1968, Special Publication No. 2, 117–123.

Frommer, E. A., Mendelson, W. B., & Reid, M. A. Differential diagnosis of psychiatric disturbance in pre-school children. *British Journal of Psychiatry*, 1972, *121*, 71–74.

Gittleman-Klein, R. Definitional and methodological issues concerning depressive illness in children. In J. Schulterbrandt & A. Raskin (Eds.), *Depression in childhood: Diagnosis, treatment, and conceptual models*. New York: Raven Press, 1977.

Gittleman-Klein, R., & Klein, D. F. School phobia: Diagnostic considerations in the light of imipramine effects. *Journal of Nervous and Mental Disease*, 1973, *156*, 199–215.

Glaser, K. Masked depression in children and adolescents. *Annual Progress in Child Psychiatry and Child Development*, 1968, *1*, 345–355.

Grinker, R. R., Miller, J. B., Sabshin, M., Nunn, R. & Nunnally, J. C. *The phenomena of depressions*. New York: Hoeber, 1961.

Guy, W. *ECDEU assessment manual for psychopharmacology* (Rev. ed.; DHEW Pub. No. [ADM] 76-338). Washington, D.C.: U.S. Government Printing Office, 1976.

Kovacs, M., & Beck, A. T. An empirical-clinical approach toward a definition of childhood depression. In J. Schulterbrandt & A. Raskin (Eds.), *Depression in childhood: Diagnosis, treatment, and conceptual models*. New York: Raven Press, 1977.

Kovacs, M., & Beck, A. T. Maladaptive cognitive structures in depression. *American Journal of Psychiatry*, 1978, *135*, 525–533.

Kovacs, M., & Beck, A. T. Cognitive-affective processes in depression. In C. E. Izard (Ed.), *Emotions in personality and psychopathology*. New York: Plenum, 1979.

Kovacs, M., Betof, N. G., Celebre, J. E., Mansheim, P. A., Petty, L. K., & Raynak, J. J. *Childhood depression: Myth or clinical syndrome?* Unpublished manuscript, University of Pennsylvania, 1977. (Available from M. Kovacs, Western Psychiatric Institute and Clinic, 3811 O'Hara Street, Pittsburgh, Pa. 15261.)

Lessing, E. E., & Zagorin, S. W. Dimensions of psychopathology in middle childhood as evaluated by three symptom checklists. *Educational and Psychological Measurement*, 1971, *31*, 175–198.

Ling, W., Oftedal, G., & Weinberg, W. Depressive illness in childhood presenting as severe headache. *American Journal of Diseases in Children*, 1970, *120*, 122–124.

McConville, B. J., Boag, L. C., & Purohit, A. P. Three types of childhood depression. *Canadian Psychiatric Association Journal*, 1973, *18*, 133–138.

Mendels, J. (Ed.). *The psychobiology of depression*. New York: Spectrum, 1975.

Pearce, J. Depressive disorder in childhood. *Journal of Child Psychology and Psychiatry*, 1977, *18*, 79–82.

Perris, C. A study of bipolar (manic-depressive) and unipolar recurrent depressive psychoses: 11. Childhood environment and precipitating factors. *ACTA Psychiatrica Scandinavia Supplementum*, 1966, *42*, 45–57.

Petti, T. A. Depression in hospitalized child psychiatry patients. *Journal of the American Academy of Child Psychiatry*, 1978, *17*, 49–59.

Rie, H. E. Depression in childhood: A survey of some pertinent contributions. *Journal of the Academy of Child Psychiatry*, 1966, *5*, 653–685.

Rutter, M., & Graham, P. The reliability and validity of the psychiatric assessment of the child: I. Interview with the child. *British Journal of Psychiatry*, 1968, *114*, 563–579.
Sandler, J., & Joffe, W. G. Notes on childhood depression. *International Journal of Psychoanalysis*, 1965, *46*, 88–96.
Schulterbrandt, J. G., & Raskin, A. (Eds.). *Depression in childhood: Diagnosis, treatment and conceptual models*. New York: Raven Press, 1977.
Secunda, S. K., Katz, M. M., Friedman, R. J., & Schuyler, D. *The depressive disorders* (DHEW Publication No. [HSM] 73-9157). Washington, D.C.: U.S. Government Printing Office, 1973.
Weinberg, W. A., Rutman, J., Sullivan, L., Penick, E. C., & Deitz, S. G. Depression in children referred to an educational diagnostic center: Diagnosis and treatment. *Journal of Pediatrics*, 1973, *83*, 1065–1072.
Werry, J. S. (Commentary). In D. M. Gallant & G. M. Simpson (Eds.), *Depression: Behavioral, biochemical, diagnostic, and treatment concepts*. New York: Spectrum, 1976.

7 Childhood and young adult predictors of schizophrenic outcome

Raymond A. Knight and James D. Roff

Although a number of studies examining the issue of prognosis in schizophrenia have been undertaken, most of these have simply correlated a set of variables assessed at some early time in the course of the disorder with some subsequent outcome criterion. Any prospective differentiation within the samples studied has been most often limited to the dichotomization of particular dimensions (e.g., Garmezy, 1970). The potentially fruitful follow-up of empirically derived preschizophrenic or early schizophrenic types has been neglected. Moreover, as Vaillant (1978) has astutely pointed out, many prognostic studies have taken a narrow unidirectional approach to analyzing data – either prospective differentiation, to be correlated with a subsequent outcome criterion, or outcome differentiation, to be used to assess the predictive validity of earlier symptoms. Finally, the outcome criteria employed in many of these studies have often been vague or disorderly (Stephens, 1978), have been narrowly defined and often unidimensional (Strauss & Carpenter, 1978), and have typically been assessed at only a single follow-up time. In this chapter we will present the major results of a child guidance study of preschizophrenics in which, unlike many earlier researchers, we adopted a multivariate, bidirectional, multidimensional, multitemporal strategy.

Our project involves a combination of a follow-back study from young adulthood to child guidance records and a follow-up study from young to middle adulthood. The major question addressed in this chapter is whether clear paths to adult schizophrenia can be discerned in the histories of preschizophrenics and early schizophrenics. To investigate this possibility we have applied a number of multivariate techniques to a relatively small sample. Our strategy, though solving some of the dilemmas of previous research, immediately fuels the fires of debate about the appropri-

The authors wish to thank Eleanor Wertheim, Joffree Barrnett, and Denny Marvinney, who helped rate and analyze the childhood and adult data, and John Moss, who helped analyze the data.

ateness of such statistics for small samples. We will argue from our data that, as long as we keep clearly in mind both the tentative nature of the results of such analyses and the need for replication and cross-validation, such techniques can serve, even in small samples, as tools for unraveling the complex nexus of symptoms and behaviors in schizophrenia. Important interactions may go completely undetected without them.

Some portions of these data have been presented in previous publications on the project (Knight et al., 1979; J. D. Roff & Knight, 1978; J. D. Roff, Knight, & Wertheim, 1976a, 1976b). Because the new data that we will present here build upon previous analyses, we will briefly summarize some of the essentials of these previously reported results.

Method

Subjects

Our sample included 45 males who had their initial psychotic break in the service in the 1940s and early 1950s and were diagnosed as schizophrenic. All had previously been seen as outpatients in child guidance clinics in Minnesota, Wisconsin, Illinois, or New York, and had been part of a follow-up study of a large number of child guidance cases into the military service (M. Roff, 1970). Because of the childhood outpatient treatment contact of these cases they are appropriately called "disturbed preschizophrenics."

We collected information on this sample from three independent record sources – child guidance records (average age = 10.9), service records (average age = 21.7), and Veterans Claim files (average age = 43.7). Thus our information spanned more than 30 years, some of it predating the first psychiatric hospitalization.

In choosing this sample we used a hospital diagnosis of schizophrenia with full awareness of the overinclusive nature of this procedure. It should be mentioned, however, that both authors independently agreed that all included cases had been psychotic. Thus, though some of these cases might have been excluded had more stringent criteria been applied, they all clearly fit into the broad *Diagnostic and Statistical Manual*-II definition for schizophrenia. Some cases initially diagnosed as schizoid personality, but subsequently rediagnosed as schizophrenic by the VA, were included as part of this sample.

It is important to specify clearly the sampling limitations of this project, because they restrict the generalizability of our findings and indicate the need for cross-sample replication by other investigators. The most obvious limitation is that all subjects had childhood treatment contact prior to their service hospitalization. Therefore the generalization of these findings to schizophrenics who have not had early clinic contact must remain tenuous. Moreover, compared to previous child clinic studies (Ricks & Berry, 1970; Robins, 1966), our sample contained relatively fewer juvenile court referrals and more school referrals. This sample also excluded those rejected for military service for psychiatric reasons. Actually, acceptance for military service served as a rough screening, in that those hospitalized during adolescence or with grossly psychotic clinical status were rejected at induction. Thus early onset cases, who would possibly become the most deteriorated cases (Astrup & Noreik, 1966), were excluded. Subjects whose initial onset occurred after discharge from the service (late-onset, better-prognosis cases) were also not represented. Finally, the sample was all male.

Because we were interested in within-sample comparisons, however, it is important to note that all subjects were similar with respect to child clinic contact, military service hospitalization, and diagnosis as schizophrenic.

Procedure

Symptoms were abstracted and scales rated independently from the childhood, young adult, and middle adult sources by research assistants. For each of the adult file sets separately, the two authors independently made global clinical judgments on 5-point scales of the severity of thought disorder and of affective deficit, and rated outcome clinical status on a 7-point scale. Adequate reliability was obtained for the symptom extraction and scale ratings by the assistants and for the global clinical judgments. All reliability data and details about the scales, ratings, and clinical judgments have been previously presented (cf. J. D. Roff et al., 1976a, 1976b, for the childhood data, and Knight et al., 1979, for the adult data). A summary list of the major scales, ratings, and judgments made at each stage is included in Table 7.1.

Using the independent clinical judgments, especially outcome clinical status, and remaining blind to both the young adult and the childhood data, the two clinicians established a consensus summary outcome rating for each case on a 6-point scale. The development of this scale has been described elsewhere (J. D. Roff et al., 1976b). Outcome 1 reflected recovered patients who had clearly been psychotic, but who at outcome were considered not schizophrenic. Outcome 2 indicated doubtful cases of process schizophrenia with predominantly neurotic or characterological

Table 7.1. *Variables assessed at each stage*

Childhood	Young adult	Middle adult
I. Revised symptom scales	I. Social competence	I. Social competence
Schizoid	Discipline problems scale	Employment history
Acting out	Service performance scale	Marital status
Neurotic	Social adjustment scale	II. Thought
Aggressive	Prehospital time in service	Conceptual disorganization[b]
Neurological	II. Thought	Paranoia[b]
II. Rating Scales	Conceptual disorganization[b]	Disorientation[b]
School conduct	Paranoia[b]	New Haven Schizophrenia Index[c]
Home conduct	Disorientation[b]	Thought disorder symptom scale
Peer adjustment	New Haven Schizophrenia Index[c]	Thought disorder clinical judgment
Internalizing-externalizing orientation[a]	Thought disorder symptom scale	III. Affectivity
Relation to clinic	Thought disorder clinical judgment	Affectivity scale
Relation to therapist	III. Affectivity	Affectivity clinical judgment
III. Additional variables	Affectivity scale	IV. Outcome
Age at initial clinic contact	Affectivity clinical judgment	Chronicity
IQ		Consensus outcome
Teacher comment that child disturbed		

[a] Achenbach, 1966.
[b] Hautaluoma, 1971.
[c] Astrachan, Harrow, Alder, Brauer, Schwartz, Schwartz, & Tucker, 1972.

deficits. Outcome 3 included paranoid cases with hostile affect or emotionally unstable character structure. Outcome 4 contained schizoid cases with minimal thought disorder, but with predominantly flat affect. Outcomes 5 and 6 were judged to be definite process schizophrenics, the former in partial remission or improved for lengthy periods, the latter deteriorated or unimproved.

This system closely parallels those used by other investigators (e.g., Astrup & Noreik, 1966). Concurrent validation for these outcome ratings was provided by highly significant correlations in the appropriate directions with other outcome indexes (length of hospitalization, level of VA compensation, unemployment, and marital status).

Results

Childhood

The childhood data were analyzed independently from the adult information. We grouped a subset of the symptoms into five rational scales. To maximize the homogeneity of these scales, we calculated symptom–scale point biserials and retained only those symptoms that correlated significantly with the total scale score. The five revised scales are listed in Table 7.1. The symptoms comprising each of these scales can be found in J. D. Roff et al. (1976b). These five symptom scales were combined with the 10 additional variables cited in Table 7.1, factor analyzed, and rotated to varimax. Four significant factors emerged: unsocialized aggressiveness, low IQ–poor school achievement, neuroticism, and schizoid syndrome. A partial replication on 36 cases rejected for military service for psychiatric reasons with a diagnosis of schizophrenia, but with no follow-up information, produced a similar factor structure for the first four factors extracted (congruency coefficients = .94, .95, .87, .98). The four dimensions are also similar to those reported by others with large samples not restricted to preschizophrenics (Achenbach, 1966; Lorr & Jenkins, 1953). Two of these factors, low IQ and schizoid syndrome, predicted poorer consensus outcome, $ru_{(43)}$[1] = .32 and .36, $p < .03$, respectively. Unsocialized aggression correlated with more positive outcome, $r = -.33$, $p < .03$, whereas the neurotic factor did not correlate with consensus outcome, $r = .04$.

To establish types or clusters, factor scores for the 45 subjects were generated for these four factors, and a Mahalanobis distance measure (D^2)[2] was computed between each subject and every other subject across the four factor scores. The resulting D^2 matrix, which consists basically of the distance of every subject from every other subject, was factor analyzed. The five factors produced by this analysis represent types or clusters of subjects, and assignment to a particular type is determined by relative factor loading size. Tryon and Bailey (1970) have presented the rationale for and a detailed description of this methodological approach.

After type assignment to one of the five types, a mean profile of factor *T* scores was calculated for each type. These profiles are presented in Figure 7.1. Each type can be named by its major profile elevation: Type 1 is Low IQ; Type 2 is Unsocialized Aggression; Type 3 is Schizoid; Type 4 is Neurotic/Low IQ; and Type 5 is Neurotic. The point biserials between type assignment and consensus outcome were $r = .03$, $-.27$ ($p < .10$), .42 ($p < .01$), .29 ($p < .05$), and $-.64$ ($p < .01$), respectively, for the five types. Type 1, Low IQ, was not related to outcome. Type 2, Unsocialized Aggression, and Type 5, Neurotic, were related to good outcome. Type 3, Schizoid, and Type 4, Neurotic with Low IQ, were related to poorer outcome.

Adulthood

In analyzing the adult data, we have focused on two of the fundamental symptom complexes of schizophrenia, thought disorder and the affective deficit, and on social competence measures. Table 7.1 presents a list of some of the measures we have used. We have already briefly described the global clinical judgments. The affectivity and thought disorder scales were formed from factor analyses (at young and middle adulthood) of the symptoms most frequently checked by the research assistants. The affectivity scale included apathy, poor peer relations, seclusion or withdrawal, and flat affect. The thought scale included hallucinations, delusions, bizarre or psychotic thinking, and confusion. The details of the thought and affectivity scale construction, of the social competence measures, and of the other thought disorder scales have been presented in Knight et al. (1979).

In a previous paper (Knight et al., 1979)[3] we examined the concurrent validity of the thought, affect, and social competence measures at both young and middle adulthood. In general, measures of disordered thought showed high interrater reliability and good convergent and discriminant validity both at initial hospitalization and at outcome. Measures of affectivity were somewhat less reliable at onset; and though equal to thought disorder measures in concurrent validity at onset, they evidenced poor discriminant validity at outcome. Measures of social competence did not show even convergent validity.

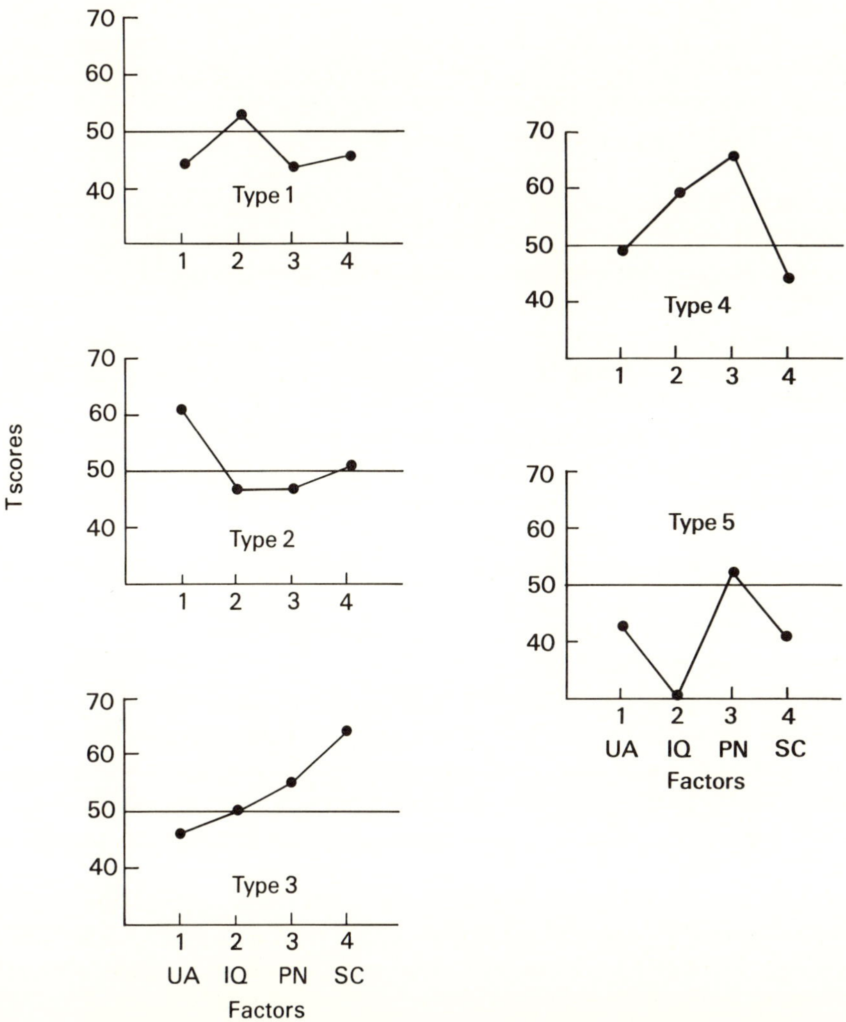

Figure 7.1. Mean factor scores for four factors for the childhood types (UA = unsocialized aggressiveness; IQ = low IQ–poor school achievement; PN = neurotic; SC = schizoid).

A completely different picture emerged, however, when we looked at the predictive validity of these domains from initial hospitalization to middle adulthood (cf. Knight et al., 1979). Of all the thought disorder measures, only the clinical judgment predicted chronicity and consensus outcome. Only the clinical judgment and conceptual disorganization evidenced any stability over time (i.e., correlated with themselves at outcome). Although possessing somewhat inferior concurrent credentials, both affectivity measures, on the other hand, predicted chronicity and consensus outcome ($p < .01$), and both had impressive temporal stability ($p < .001$). Strikingly, the affectivity scale predicted five of the six outcome thought measures better than the same thought measures predicted themselves. Social adjustment and job performance in the service also predicted chronicity and consensus outcome, and were related to outcome affectivity but not to outcome thought disorder measures.

To elucidate the longitudinal relation between thought disorder and affectivity and to examine the possibility of a causal connection between the two, we calculated cross-lagged panel analyses for both the scales and the clinical judgments. This technique is a special case of the multitrait–multimethod matrix, developed by Campbell (1963) to assess longitudinal trait relations. It requires that two traits (here affectivity [A] and thought disorder [T]) be measured at Times 1 and 2 (the methods). The two constructs and two times generate four variables (A_1, A_2, T_1, and T_2), and the four variables generate six correlations. The method compares the cross-lagged correlations, which are expressed as a cross-lagged differential ($r_{A_1T_1} - r_{A_2T_1}$). According to Campbell, if A caused T, then the cross-lagged differential should be positive, and if T caused A, the differential should be negative.

Figure 7.2 presents the cross-lagged panel correlations for the thought and affectivity scales and clinical judgments. In both sets of measures the assumption of synchronicity of measurement (Kenny, 1975) was clearly met. Kenny's second cross-lagged assumption, that of stationarity, was met only for the judgments. The synchronous correlations for both variable sets increased, and for the scales this increase was significant, $z(45) = 2.78$, $p < .01$ (Peters & Van Voorhis, 1940). Thus the possibility that cross-lagged differentials might be produced by a spurious third variable cannot be completely discounted. Both cross-lagged differentials were in the same positive direction, $r_{A_1T_2} > r_{A_2T_1}$. For the scales this differential was highly significant, $z(45) = 3.29$, $p < .001$, and for the judgments it approached significance, $z(45) = 1.52$, $p < .15$. Because cross-lagged panel analysis has low power and most often requires large samples ($N > 300$) to get significance (Kenny, 1975), these results are somewhat impressive. The measure that had less bias (the scales) showed the greater cross-lagged differential. Because the clinicians were making global assessments, their concurrent ratings of thought and affect might have been somewhat confounded. This possible bias might account for the lack of a significant cross-lagged differential in their judgments. Nevertheless, the direction of the cross-lagged differentials was consistent across both measures, suggesting the causal primacy of an affective deficit. Although

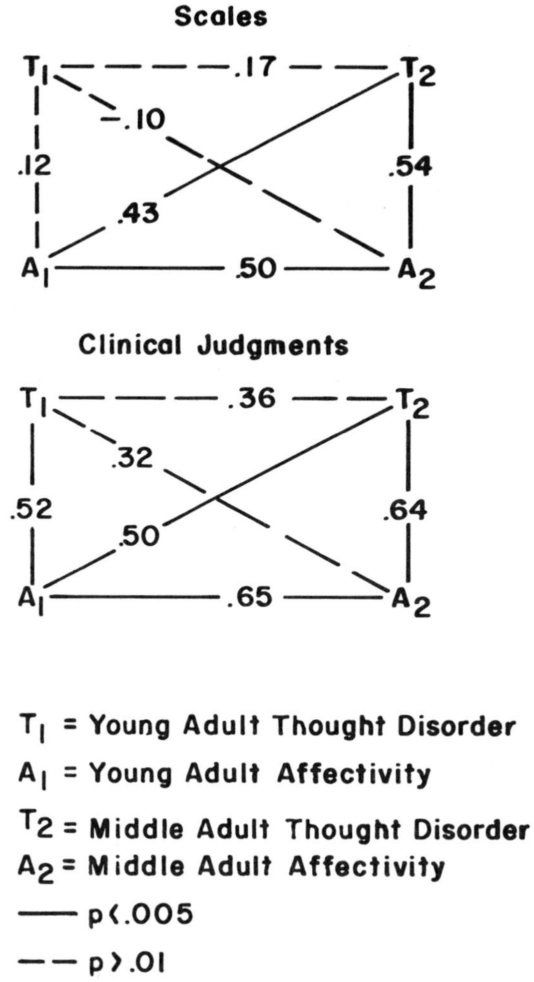

Figure 7.2. Cross-lagged panel correlations for the scales and clinical judgments of young adult and middle adult thought disorder and affectivity.

the possibility that these differentials were produced by a spurious third variable cannot be ruled out, these data clearly indicate the secondary role that thought disorder played.

Childhood through adulthood

The results of the cross-lagged panel analysis of the adult data, just mentioned, when combined with the inherent unidirectionality imposed by the temporal progression, provided a solid base for the generation of a path analysis model that included both the childhood and the adult variables. *Path analysis* refers to a family of statistical methods for interpreting the linear relationships among a set of variables. These methods allow one to assess the strength of causal links, when the direction of these links has been set a priori (cf. Kim & Kohout, 1975; Spaeth, 1975). We applied the simplest of the path models, based on multiple regression, to the three life stages of our sample and assumed the causal primacy of affectivity in the two adult stages. Thus the direction of causation was assumed to go from childhood factors through young adult symptoms to middle adult symptoms to outcome, and in adulthood from affect deficit to thought disorder. In this form, path analysis is essentially a sequence of standardized partial regression analyses, presented graphically to simplify the interpretation of complex hypothesized causal relations.

Two separate path analyses were computed – one including the thought and affect clinical judgments in the adult stages and a second including thought and affect scales. Because we will be comparing the results of these two analyses it is important to specify at the outset the particular focus of each measurement type. In making the judgments, the clinicians assessed the more modal or characteristic aspects of a person's affective response and rated the severity and persistence of disordered thought. The scales, on the other hand, simply reflected the presence or absence of individual affective and thought symptoms or behaviors. We will concentrate on these essential measurement differences in describing the patterns that emerged in each path analysis.

Figures 7.3 and 7.4 present the traditional pictorial presentation of the judgment and scale path analyses, respectively. These diagrams depict the linear additive relationships among the variables in the model (Spaeth, 1975). In both analyses we have included as exogenous variables (the initial predictors, not determined by the operation of the model) the three childhood factors that significantly correlated with the consensus outcome. The young and middle adult variables and consensus outcome were included as endogenous variables; that is, they were assumed to be determined by variables within the model as well as by a residual variable (E), which represents the effects of all variables outside the model, $\sqrt{(1 - R^2)}$. The arrows connecting two variables indicate the direction of the a priori hypothesized causal relations between variables. The size of the standardized partial beta coefficients (*b*) reflects the causal importance of these hypothesized relations. In the figures, according to convention, all significant regression coefficients (solid lines) and all regression coefficients greater than .15 in a significant multiple regression analysis (broken lines) are represented.[4]

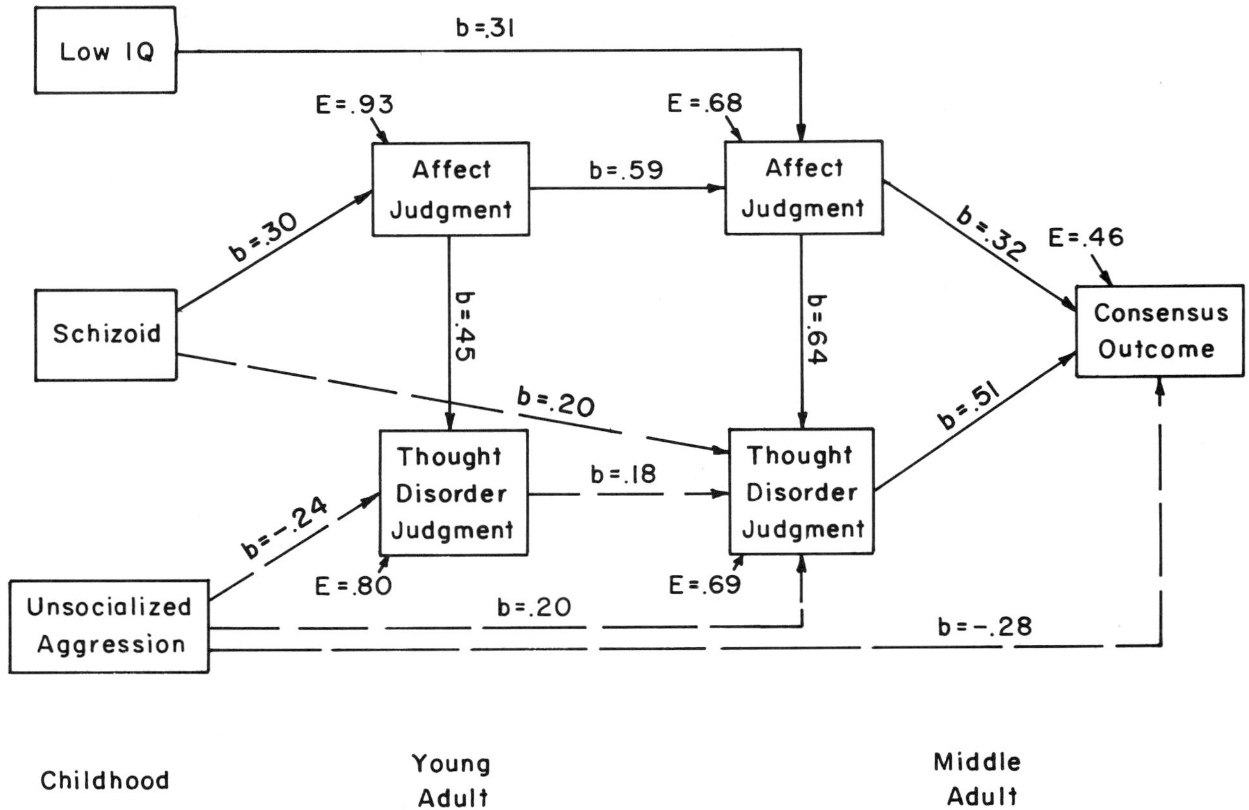

Figure 7.3. Path analysis diagram of the childhood factors, adult affect deficit and thought disorder clinical judgments, and consensus outcome.

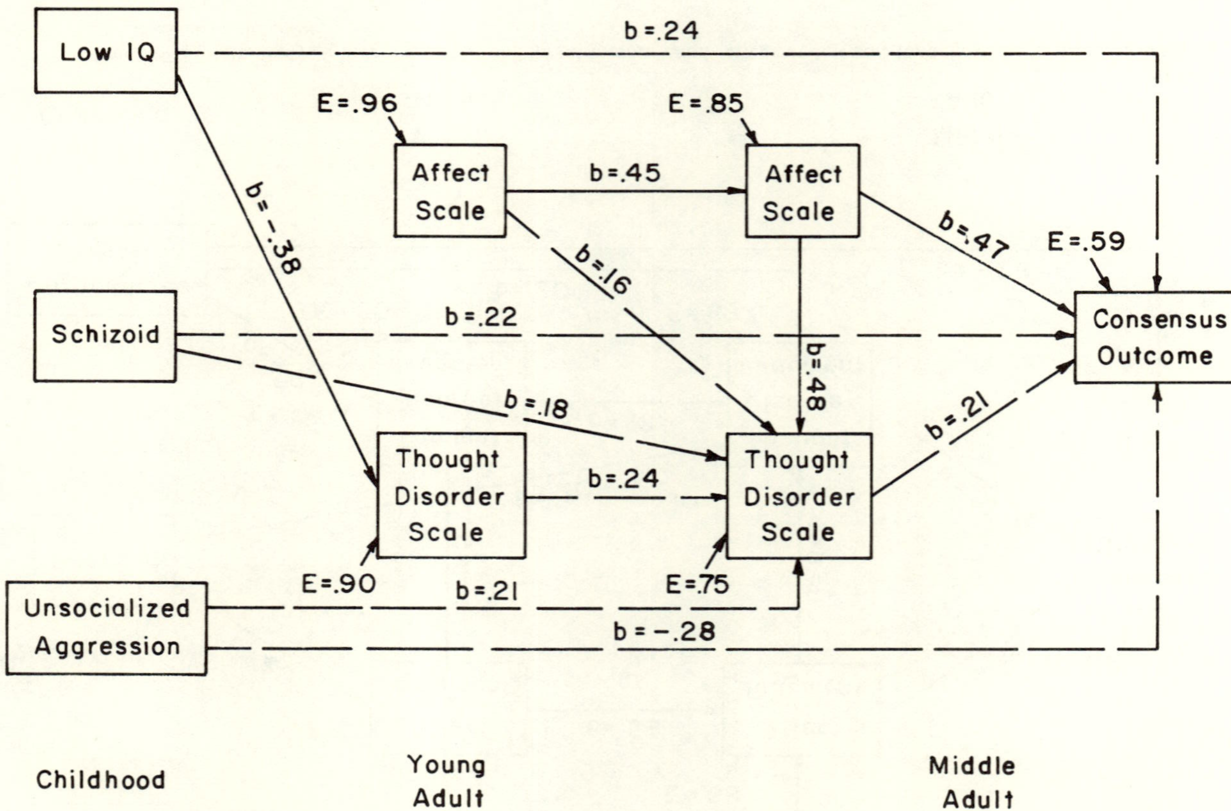

Figure 7.4. Path analysis diagram of the childhood factors, adult affectivity and thought disorder scales, and consensus outcome.

Table 7.2. *General decomposition of the childhood factors and the affectivity and thought clinical judgments*

		Causal effects		
Variables[a]	Total effect (r)	Direct (b)	Indirect	Noncausal effects
IQ,A_1	.05	.05	—	—
IQ,T_1	−.10	−.12	.02	.00
IQ,A_2	.34	.31	.03	.00
IQ,T_2	.12	−.08	.20	.00
IQ,O	.32	.13	.19	.00
SC,A_1	.30	.30	—	—
SC,T_1	.25	.11	.14	.00
SC,A_2	.22	.04	.18	.00
SC,T_2	.37	.20	.15	.02
SC,O	.36	.12	.24	.00
UA,A_1	−.20	−.20	—	—
UA,T_1	−.33	−.24	−.09	.00
UA,A_2	−.26	−.14	−.12	.00
UA,T_2	−.02	.20	−.22	.00
UA,O	−.33	−.28	−.05	.00
A_1,T_1	.52	.45	—	.07
A_1,A_2	.65	.59	—	.06
A_1,T_2	.50	−.02	.46	.06
A_1,O	.52	.03	.35	.14
T_1,T_2	.36	.18	—	.18
T_1,O	.28	−.13	.09	.32
A_2,T_2	.64	.64	—	.00
A_2,O	.77	.32	.33	.12
T_2,O	.75	.51	—	.24

[a] IQ = Low IQ–poor school achievement; SC = Schizoid syndrome; UA = Unsocialized aggression; A_1 = Young adult affectivity judgment; A_2 = Middle adult affectivity judgment; T_1 = Young adult thought disorder judgment; T_2 = Middle adult thought disorder judgment; O = Consensus outcome.

The regression equations underlying the path model permit the total effect (r) of one variable on another to be partitioned into direct, indirect, and noncausal (spurious) effects (Kim & Kohout, 1975). This decomposition of effects for the clinical judgments and scales analyses is presented in Tables 7.2 and 7.3, respectively. Direct effects (b or beta) specify the proportion of the standard deviation of a criterion variable that is ac-

Table 7.3. *General decomposition of the childhood factors and the affectivity and thought scales*

		Causal effects		
Variables[a]	Total effect (*r*)	Direct (*b*)	Indirect	Noncausal effects
IQ,A_1	.10	.10	—	—
IQ,T_1	−.36	−.38	.02	.00
IQ,A_2	.15	.10	.05	.00
IQ,T_2	.03	.03	.00	.00
IQ,O	.32	.24	.08	.00
SC,A_1	.19	.19	—	—
SC,T_1	−.12	−.15	.03	.00
SC,A_2	.21	.12	.09	.00
SC,T_2	.28	.18	.04	.06
SC,O	.36	.22	.14	.00
UA,A_1	−.17	−.17	—	—
UA,T_1	−.06	−.02	−.03	−.01
UA,A_2	−.16	−.08	−.08	.00
UA,T_2	.09	.21	−.12	.00
UA,O	−.33	−.28	−.05	.00
A_1,T_1	.12	.19	−.07[b]	.00
A_1,A_2	.50	.45	—	.05
A_1,T_2	.43	.16	.26	.01
A_1,O	.39	−.05	.30	.14
T_1,T_2	.17	.24	−.07[b]	.00
T_1,O	−.13	−.01	.05	−.17
A_2,T_2	.54	.48	—	.06
A_2,O	.69	.47	.10	.12
T_2,O	.48	.21	—	.27

[a] IQ = Low IQ–poor school achievement; SC = Schizoid syndrome; UA = Unsocialized aggression; A_1 = Young adult affectivity scale; A_2 = Middle adult affectivity scale; T_1 = Young adult thought disorder scale; T_2 = Middle adult thought disorder scale; O = Consensus outcome.

[b] Indirect suppressor variable effect.

counted for by the predictor variable when all other hypothesized causal variables are partialed out. Indirect effects are obtained by calculating the sum of the products of all coefficients in every indirect path (i.e., through an intervening variable or variables) between the predictor and criterion variables. Spurious or noncausal effects equal the differences between the total effect and the sum of the direct and indirect effects (cf. Kim & Kohout, 1975).

The path analysis of the clinical judgments (Figure 7.3 and Table 7.2) taken by itself seems relatively straightforward. The childhood low IQ factor bypassed the young adult measures and was significantly related to a withdrawn, flatter, or more inappropriate modal affective adaptation at middle adulthood, $b_{IQ,A_2} = .31$, $p < .05$. As can be seen in the decomposition table (Table 7.2), most of the relation of low IQ to poorer outcome, .19 of .32, was mediated indirectly.

The schizoid childhood factor was related directly, $b_{SC,A_1} = .30$, $p < .05$, to more severe young adult affect deficit and indirectly, .18, to more severe middle adult affect deficit. Interestingly, the schizoid factor was more related to the severity of middle adult thought disorder than to the severity of young adult thought disorder, and the greater portion of this relation to middle adult thought disorder was direct, $b_{SC,T_2} = .20$ (of total .37).

Of the three childhood factors the unsocialized aggression factor had the most complex relation to the adult clinical judgments. The complexity of these relations is most clearly presented in the decomposition table (Table 7.2). Unsocialized aggression correlated significantly with young adult thought disorder, $r_{UA,T_1} = -.33$, $p < .05$, and most of this relation was direct, $b_{UA,T_1} = -.24$. More childhood aggression was related to less severe thought disorder in young adulthood. Childhood aggression did not, however, correlate with middle adult thought disorder. Oppositely signed direct, $b_{UA,T_2} = .20$, and indirect, $-.22$, effects combined to cancel each other. Although no causal lines between childhood aggression and adult affectivity appear in the path diagram, the decomposition table reveals that the combined direct, $b_{UA,A_2} = -.14$, and indirect (through young adult affectivity), $-.12$, effects resulted in a trend, $r_{UA,A_2} = -.26$, $p < .10$, which suggests that lower childhood aggression was related to greater middle adult withdrawal and flat or inappropriate affect.

It is important to point out the most salient result for unsocialized aggression. Despite the complex trends described, the largest proportion (85%) of childhood aggression's correlation with a better consensus outcome was *not* mediated by the severity of adult affect and thought deficits, $b_{UA,O} = -.28$, $p = .06$.

The relations among the clinical judgments of affectivity and thought deficits in the young and middle adult stages essentially confirmed the previously reported cross-lagged panel analysis of the clinical judgments.

The severity of the young adult affectivity deficit was stable through middle adulthood and predicted both thought disorder and consensus outcome. Most of its variance was causal, but much of its effect was mediated indirectly through the middle adult affectivity deficit. The young adult thought disorder clinical judgment showed relatively weak stability, $b_{T_1,T_2} = .18$, and did not predict consensus outcome. When significant thought disorder correlations did emerge (e.g., $r_{T_1,T_2} = .36$, $p < .05$), a larger portion of each of these relations was shown to be spurious (e.g., for this correlation, the noncausal effect = .18).

In general, except for two differences that will be discussed shortly, the overall pattern (i.e., the directions of the total correlations in the decomposition tables) of the path analysis of the scales (see Table 7.3) was congruent with the pattern of the path analysis of the clinical judgments. The major overall difference between these two analyses was that the relations were consistently weaker for the scales than for the clinical judgments.[5] That the scales mediated less well than the judgments between childhood symptoms and outcome is indicated in the considerable direct effects, bypassing the symptoms, of the low IQ and schizoid factors on consensus outcome in the path analysis of the scales, $b_{IQ,O} = .24$ and $b_{SC,O} = .22$, respectively (see Figure 7.4). In the clinical judgments the greater portion of causal variance between childhood and outcome for these two childhood factors was indirect, .19 and .24, respectively, for low IQ and the schizoid syndrome, and thus was mediated through the affect and thought judgments.

Only two results in the path analysis of the scales deviated in nontrivial ways from this general trend of pattern consistency with the judgments, but at a lower level.[6] The first involved the relation of low IQ to the young adult thought disorder scale. As is evident in Figure 7.4, low IQ significantly predicted the presence of fewer thought disorder symptoms in young adulthood, $b_{IQ,T_1} = -.38$, $p < .02$. This finding was consistent in direction with the same relation in the judgments, $b_{IQ,T_1} = -.12$, but was stronger rather than weaker. The second deviation is evident only in the decomposition tables. The schizoid factor was related to more severe young adult thought disorder (clinical judgment), $r_{SC,T_1} = .25$, $p < .10$, but to fewer thought disorder symptoms (scales), $r_{SC,T_1} = -.12$. If one disregards the latter correlation as nonsignificant, one could consider this result as also covered by the general summary, but the difference between these correlations (.37) is large.

Thus a close scrutiny of these two path analyses revealed more consistency than inconsistency, and indicated that the greatest discrepancy was in the strengths of the relations rather than the pattern of these relations. These overall consistencies across the two analyses can be summarized in the following general trends:

1. Lower childhood intelligence was related to fewer young adult thought disorder symptoms and to a more withdrawn, more flat or inappropriate middle adult affective adjustment.
2. The childhood schizoid syndrome consistently correlated with greater affective deficit in young and middle adulthood, and was more related to middle than to young adult thought disorder.
3. Childhood aggression tended to predict less severe young adult thought disorder and less severe affect deficit in middle adulthood.
4. Young adult affectivity was stable through middle adulthood and predicted both thought disorder and consensus outcome. Most of its variance was causal, and much of its effect was mediated indirectly through middle adult affectivity.
5. Young adult thought disorder was not stable and did not predict consensus outcome. Much of its variance was spurious.

A perusal of both path diagrams reveals a number of instances in which the childhood factors bypassed the young adult symptoms and predicted middle adult symptoms (e.g., in the clinical judgments, low IQ bypassed young adult affect to predict middle adult affect). A closer examination of the correlations in the decomposition tables indicates that of the 12 relevant comparisons between young and middle adulthood, the childhood factors predicted middle adult measures better in 5 instances, whereas they predicted young adult measures better in 3 instances. Because a finding that temporally distal measures were better predicted than proximal measures is contrary to the general trend in developmental research (e.g., Olweus, 1979), we examined the relation of distal to proximal prediction more directly with multiple correlation. The combined childhood factors (all variables stepped in together) predicted middle adult consensus outcome, $R(3, 41) = .58$, $p < .001$, better than either the combined young adult scales, $R(2, 40) = .42$, $p < .025$, or the combined young adult judgments, $R(2, 35) = .52$, $p < .005$, predicted outcome. For predicting specific symptoms, the combined childhood data by themselves were able to predict significantly the middle adult affective judgment, $R(3, 40) = .48$, $p < .025$, but this combination could predict none of the four young adult measures significantly. The trend in these analyses is the superior prediction of more distal measures.

The path analyses indicated that the childhood low IQ factor score had predictive validity in this sample. Yet the Low IQ Type that we described earlier (also cf. J. D. Roff et al., 1976b) was not related to outcome. There was also evidence from the path analyses that low IQ and low aggressiveness combined to contribute to a more schizoid, lower socially competent middle adult outcome. The combined predictive ability of low

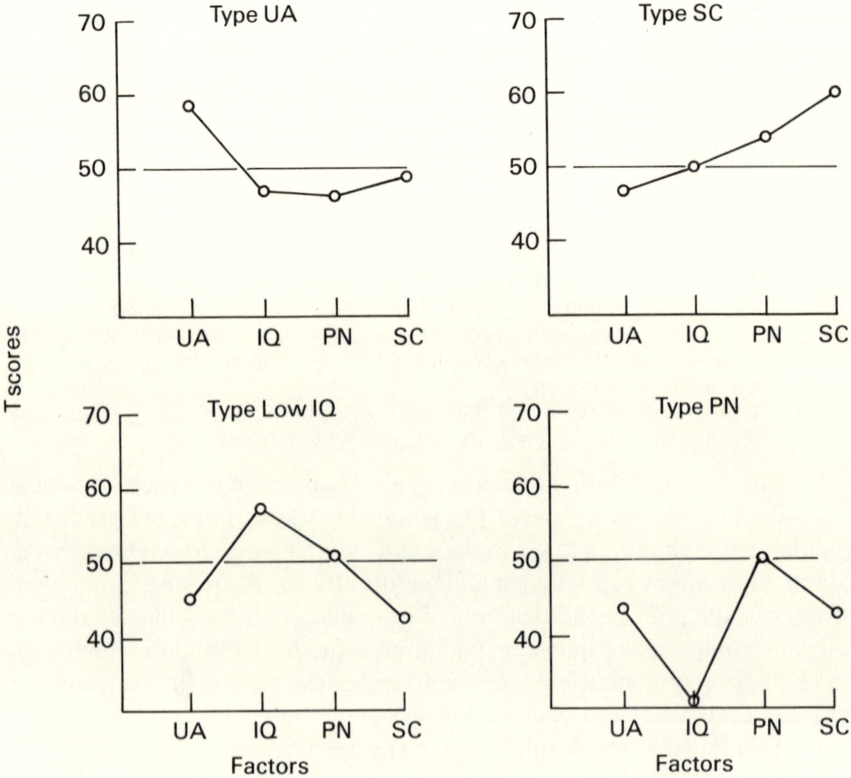

Figure 7.5. Mean factor scores for four factors for the revised childhood types.

aggression and low intelligence led us to analyze the relation of these two variables more closely.

The sample was dichotomized by median splits of the aggression factor score and IQ into groups of low and high aggressiveness, and below- and above-average IQ (median = 94.0). For each of these four subsamples (high and low aggression and high and low IQ), correlations were calculated between consensus outcome and both the schizoid childhood factor and whichever childhood factor (aggression or low IQ) had not been used to make the median split for that particular subsample. The relation of aggression to better outcome was significant only for the subsample with below-average IQ. Likewise, low IQ was related to poorer outcome only for the subsample with below-average unsocialized aggression factor scores. The schizoid factor, on the other hand, was significantly related

Table 7.4. *Dichotomized outcome group, neurological scores, and percentage never married for the revised types*

	Low IQ (N = 15)	UA (N = 17)	SC (N = 10)	PN (N = 3)	Total
Outcome – Good: Poor	4:11	13:4	2:8	3:0	22:23
Mean neurological scale score	3.4	.7	1.7	1.2	1.9
% never married	73	35	70	33	59

Note: IQ = Low IQ Type; UA = Unsocialized Aggression Type; SC = Schizoid Type; PN = Neurotic Type.

to poorer outcome across all four subsamples. The details of this analysis are described elsewhere (J. D. Roff & Knight, 1980). This analysis clearly indicates that in this sample low IQ and unsocialized aggression acted as moderators. Low IQ and lack of aggressiveness together were strongly related to unfavorable outcome, whereas one without the other was not.

Because our sample is small, these results must be considered tentative. Yet it is instructive to consider the possibility that if such moderating effects are not sample-specific, straightforward statements about IQ and aggressive symptoms as predictor variables may be misleading, unless the level of the other relevant variable is taken into account. Moreover, the probability that our findings of the predictive power of aggressiveness will be replicated might be primarily a function of the proportion of low IQ preschizophrenics included in the replication sample.

These findings suggested that the moderation of aggression might have masked the predictive validity of the Low IQ Type. We therefore revised our original types. Through the simple reassignment of those cases with significant secondary high loadings on the unsocialized aggression factor within the Low IQ–Poor Achievement Type to the Aggression Type, the Low IQ Type changed from a neutral to an unfavorable relation with outcome. We also included the Neurotic/Low IQ Type (Type 4) within the new Low IQ Type, because the major difference between the two types was neurotic symptoms, which did not prove to be prognostically significant. Figure 7.5 depicts the profiles of the four revised types. It is interesting to note that this change has resulted in types in which each of the original factors is the prime elevation on a single type, and therefore defines that type. Table 7.4 presents the ratio of favorable to unfavorable outcome and the percentage never married for each type. Two types, Low IQ and the Schizoid Type, were related to poor outcome, and two, the Unsocialized Aggression Type and the Neurotic Type, were related to good outcome. Table 7.4 also presents the means of each type on a five-item neurological scale that includes birth complications, poor attention, speech problems, poor motor coordination, and developmental lag in speech. The revised Low IQ Type was significantly higher than the other groups on this scale.

Discussion

From this sample of preschizophrenics, two revised types related to poor prognosis emerged. One type was best characterized by the presence of a schizoid syndrome during childhood. This syndrome was more common in older adolescent cases in this sample. These cases were seen as more disturbed when evaluated by clinics. Their disturbance was relatively independent of IQ level and aggressiveness, and possibly of mild neurological impairment and social class. The hallmark of this type was an affective deficit that had its roots in a schizoid childhood adaptation and was a relatively stable aspect of the person's clinical history. At outcome this syndrome was significantly related to both high levels of psychotic thinking and poor affect and social competence.

Low IQ and lack of aggressive symptoms interacted to produce what might be a different pathway to process schizophrenia. The combination of low IQ, learning difficulties, passivity, possible mild neurological impairment, and social maladjustment indicated that this type had a low level of social competence in childhood. These children tended to be younger and were not viewed as being as disturbed as the schizoid type by the clinic staff, and their adjustment difficulties were considered primarily a function of low or borderline IQ. Only as they reached adulthood did their adjustment difficulties become attributed to schizophrenia. Although the path analyses did not directly test the types, their causal links were consistent with a particular developmental history of this type. The path analysis of the scales suggests that during young adulthood these subjects were less likely to manifest florid psychotic thought symptoms and were perhaps more concrete. The path analysis of the clinical judgments suggests that during adulthood these subjects tended to become more withdrawn until, at outcome, they were not easily distinguishable from other chronic schizophrenics.

The isolation of the Low IQ Type is very important in light of a commonly accepted strategy in longitudinal studies of controlling for intelligence by establishing a minimum criterion (cf. Chapter 1 in this book). Our data suggest that such a strategy would systematically overlook this type and in so doing possibly eliminate those subjects with the greatest number of the neurological prodromal symptoms.

These types were generated by the application of several multivariate techniques to a relatively small sample. In addition, a number of complex interactions have emerged in our data analyses; for example, neurotic symptoms seemed to be related to good outcome only when accompanied by the absence of other symptoms; IQ and level of aggressiveness were reciprocal moderators; psychotic thought may be predictive only when associated with deficient affect. Such complex predictor–outcome relationships may go unnoticed if one conservatively sticks to the statistical analyses that are dictated by the limitations of small samples. Though we are aware of the dangers that lurk in dark corridors of error variance, and agree that it would be ideal to combat Type I error with the frugal analyses of large *N*s, we believe that a conservative strategy would miss the important interactions we uncovered in our data. In the present state of our science, it is better to uncover what might be sample-specific interactions and to test these by replication and cross-validation. Overanalysis seems a better strategy than underanalysis.

The bidirectionality of the analyses used to generate the revised types illustrates how such an approach can help to clarify relations that would be inextricably entwined if either a prospective or a retrospective analysis was applied without the other. Because the ultimate outcome of the two poor-prognosis childhood types was quite similar, a simple retrospective analysis of the childhood symptoms on the basis of adult outcome could not differentiate these two developmental paths. The prospective analysis generated specific types, but without the restructuring of these types using the touchstone of outcome, the moderation of intelligence and aggression would have gone unnoticed, and the types would have remained somewhat confounded. The bidirectional analysis clarified the relations within this sample and improved the predictive validity of the types. The generalizability of these types to other samples requires, of course, cross-validation.

In the present study there was abundant support for Strauss and Carpenter's (1978) contention that a multidimensional view of prognosis and diagnosis in schizophrenia must be adopted if our understanding the processes of the disorder is to be enhanced. As we have seen, not all outcome measures were predicted by the same variables or to the same degree, and not all predictors carried equal predictive clout. It is only by including measures of multiple domains at initial assessment and outcome that the plexus of relations in schizophrenia will be unraveled.

In contrast to Strauss and Carpenter's multiaxial approach to diagnosis, several recent investigators (e.g., Astrachan et al., 1972; Spitzer, Endicott, & Robins, 1975), in their attempts to devise more reliable diagnostic criteria for schizophrenia, have shunned the assessment of affectivity and social competence and have focused their schemes on more easily diagnosed thought disorder symptoms. Our data suggest that such a strategy will indeed achieve improved reliability, but at the very high cost of predictive validity.

As we indicated earlier, we used the overinclusive criteria of hospital diagnosis and of the broad *DSM*-II definition of schizophrenia in our sample selection. As it turned out, this was a felicitous decision, because had we employed the more stringent research diagnostic criteria cited earlier, we would have excluded some of the extremely schizoid, but much less florid, psychotics who had some of the worst outcomes.

It is interesting to note that among the more favorable outcomes – that is, those who were not process schizophrenics – what we called outcome 3 tended to be paranoid psychoses in passive aggressive or emotionally unstable personalities. Outcome 2 cases seem from a longitudinal perspective to have experienced episodic paranoid psychoses, but to be more accurately classified as affective psychotics with long-standing personality problems than as schizophrenics.

Our data strongly support the necessity of multitemporal follow-up. Prediction was clearly time-dependent. For instance, as evidenced especially by the fact that the childhood factors predicted middle adulthood better than they predicted young adulthood, distal stages tended to be better predicted than were proximal stages. As we indicated previously, because in the developmental literature short-term predictions are usually superior to long-term predictions (e.g., Olweus, 1979), such a finding requires an explanation. It seems reasonable to hypothesize that it would be more difficult to predict the symptoms of an acute break under the relatively stressful conditions of army life (young adulthood) than to predict long-term outcome. The initial diversity of early types may conceivably dissipate in an acute psychosis, resulting in a less-differentiated clinical picture. As seems to be the case in the present study, the long-term adaptation after such a break seems to be more related than the acute symptoms to a subject's premorbid characteristics.

Not only were there changes in prediction level, it was also found that the same set of symptoms was predicted by different variables at different times. For example, higher intelligence and lack of aggressive symptoms in childhood predicted psychotic thinking at the onset of the psychosis in young adulthood, whereas only the schizoid childhood factor predicted the same psychotic thinking symptoms at middle adult outcome (see Tables 7.2 and 7.3). In a multitemporal longitudinal framework one can make sense of these results. The young adult predictions may be explained by two factors. First, the sample contained a number of Low IQ Types (N = 15) who were characteristically concrete, but lacked the symptoms of florid psychotic thinking. Their presence helps explain why higher intelligence predicted the presence of young adult thought disorder symptoms (the thought scale). The second predictor, lack of aggressive symptoms, initially seems somewhat more difficult to explain, because the revised Low IQ Type was also low on aggressive symptoms. It should be remembered, however, that over the entire sample aggression and IQ were not correlated and that the Low IQ represented only one subset of subjects. The relation of low aggression to young adult psychotic thinking becomes more understandable if we remember that all subjects were in the service at their initial break, and were most often hospitalized because their symptoms called the attention of their superiors to their coping difficulties. It seems reasonable to speculate that a less severe thought problem was more evident in a more aggressive person and that less aggressive people had to be more severely thought disordered before their problems were noticed. Thus the relation might be an artifact of this sampling bias. The fact that the unsocialized aggression factor predicted the judgment (severity) and not the scale (presence or absence) supports this interpretation. The relation of the schizoid factor to middle, but not to young, adult thought disorder suggests that continued seclusion, poor social contact, and possibly continued deterioration led to increasing cognitive disorganization in the more schizoid individuals.

Both these temporal patternings and the many other interactions among variables that we have found underline the complexity of the disorder we are studying. Once again we are struck with the importance of striving to make our methods adequate to the difficult task of unraveling the tangled interrelations of the variables that predict schizophrenia.

Notes

1 Because all correlations reported in this chapter have 43 degrees of freedom, we will omit the degrees of freedom subscript from all subsequent correlations.

2 In our case, $D^2 = \Sigma\,(T_{ij} - T_{ij'})^2$, where T_{ij} = the T factor score for the jth subject on factor i, and $T_{ij'}$ = the T factor score for any other subject on the same factor. Cf. Tryon and Bailey (1970), p. 153.

3 In Knight et al., 1979, six additional subjects (all with consensus outcome ratings of 2) were included. These subjects had adequate service information, but very little postservice contact with the VA. This lack of contact was inferred to mean recovery, and they were added to the adult analyses because of the increased reliability they gave to the factor analyses of the service data. Because they had not been included in the original analyses

of childhood data, they are excluded here for consistency. The results of the adult data are equivalent with and without these subjects.

4 If a coefficient was both significant and part of a significant multiple regression, it was represented by a solid line.

5 The careful reader will notice that the beta values reflect this general summary rule somewhat less well than the total correlations. This does not invalidate the summary statement. The higher correlations between the childhood factors and the clinical judgments and among the clinical judgments themselves had the effect of increasing some indirect effects, and thereby reducing certain beta levels. Thus the decrease of some of the beta levels in the clinical judgments analyses can be accounted for by the overall higher correlations within this analysis.

6 A careful scrutiny of the decomposition tables will reveal that three additional correlations deviated from this general rule. The correlation between low IQ and young adult affect deficit for the clinical judgment was slightly lower than the same correlation for the scales, but both correlations were in the same direction and were small and inconsequential. The correlation of unsocialized aggression with middle adult thought disorder was negative for the judgments, $r_{UA,T_2} = -.02$, and positive for the scales, $r_{UA,T_2} = .09$, but both of these correlations were not significant, and their partitioned direct and indirect effects more closely followed the general rule. Finally, the correlation of young adult thought disorder with outcome was negative for the scales, $r_{T_1,O} = -.13$, and positive for the judgments, $r_{T_1,O} = .28$, $p = .06$. We did not include a discussion of this deviation because most of the variance in both correlations was noncausal. When this spurious portion of the relation was partitioned out, the betas followed the general rule.

References

Achenbach, T. M. The classification of children's psychiatric symptoms: A factor analytic study. *Psychological Monographs*, 1966, *80*(7, Whole No. 615).

Astrachan, B. M., Harrow, M., Alder, D., Brauer, L., Schwartz, A., Schwartz, C., & Tucker, G. A checklist for the diagnosis of schizophrenia. *British Journal of Psychiatry*, 1972, *121*, 529–539.

Astrup, C., & Noreik, K. *Functional psychoses: Diagnostic and prognostic models*. Springfield, Ill.: Thomas, 1966.

Campbell, D. T. From description to experimentation: Interpreting trends as quasi-experiments. In C. W. Harris (Ed.), *Problems in measuring change*. Madison: University of Wisconsin Press, 1963.

Garmezy, N. Process and reactive schizophrenia: Some conceptions and issues. *Schizophrenia Bulletin*, 1970, *2*, 30–74.

Hautaluoma, J. Symptoms, antecedents, and outcomes of psychosis: A cluster-analytic study. *Journal of Consulting and Clinical Psychology*, 1971, *37*, 332–344.

Kenny, D. A. Cross-lagged panel correlation: A test for spuriousness. *Psychological Bulletin*, 1975, *82*, 887–903.

Kim, J., & Kohout, F. J. Special topics in general linear models. In N. H. Nie, C. H. Hull, J. G. Jenkins, K. Steinbrenner, & D. H. Bent (Eds.), *Statistical package for the social sciences*. New York: McGraw-Hill, 1975.

Knight, R. A., Roff, J. D., Barrnett, J., & Moss, J. L. The concurrent and predictive validity of thought disorder and affectivity: A 22 year follow-up of acute schizophrenics. *Journal of Abnormal Psychology*, 1979, *88*, 1–12.

Lorr, M., & Jenkins, R. L. Patterns of maladjustment in children. *Journal of Clinical Psychology*, 1953, *9*, 16–19.

Olweus, D. Stability of aggressive reaction patterns in males: A review. *Psychological Bulletin*, 1979, *86*, 852–875.
Peters, C. C., & Van Voorhis, W. R. *Statistical procedures and the mathematical bases*. New York: McGraw-Hill, 1940.
Ricks, D. F., & Berry, J. Family and symptom patterns that precede schizophrenia. In M. Roff & D. F. Ricks (Eds.), *Life history research in psychopathology*. Minneapolis: University of Minnesota Press, 1970.
Robins, L. N. *Deviant children grown up*. Baltimore: Williams & Wilkins, 1966.
Roff, J. D., & Knight, R. Young adult schizophrenics: Prediction of outcome and antecedent childhood factors. *Journal of Consulting and Clinical Psychology*, 1978, *46*, 947–952.
Roff, J. D., & Knight, R. Preschizophrenics: Low IQ and aggressive symptoms as predictors of adult outcome and marital status. *Journal of Nervous and Mental Disease*, 1980, *168*, 129–132.
Roff, J. D., Knight, R., & Wertheim, E. Disturbed preschizophrenics: Childhood symptoms in relation to adult outcome. *Journal of Nervous and Mental Disease*, 1976, *162*, 274–281.
Roff, J. D., Knight, R., & Wertheim, E. A factor-analytic study of childhood symptoms antecedent to schizophrenia. *Journal of Abnormal Psychology*, 1976, *85*, 543–549.
Roff, M. Some life history factors in relation to various types of adult maladjustment. In M. Roff & D. F. Ricks (Eds.), *Life history research in psychopathology*. Minneapolis: University of Minnesota Press, 1970.
Spaeth, J. L. Path analysis. In D. J. Amick & H. J. Walberg (Eds.), *Introductory multivariate analysis*. Berkeley: McCutchan Publishing Corp. 1975.
Spitzer, R., Endicott, J., & Robins, E. *Research diagnostic criteria*. Unpublished manuscript, 1975. (Available from Biometrics Research, New York State Psychiatric Institute, 722 West 168th Street, New York, N.Y. 10032.)
Stephens, J. H. Long-term prognosis and follow-up in schizophrenia. *Schizophrenia Bulletin*, 1978, *4*, 25–47.
Strauss, J. S., & Carpenter, W. T. The prognosis of schizophrenia: Rationale for a multidimensional concept. *Schizophrenia Bulletin*, 1978, *4*, 56–67.
Tryon, R. C., & Bailey, D. E. *Cluster analysis*. New York: McGraw-Hill, 1970.
Vaillant, G. E. Prognosis and the course of schizophrenia. *Schizophrenia Bulletin*, 1978, *4*, 20–24.

8 The application of confirmatory factor analysis to longitudinal data: reciprocal effects of occupational conditions and intellectual functioning

Carmi Schooler

It is somewhat disconcerting that throughout the years scant attention has been paid during meetings of a society dedicated to investigating the relationships between life history and psychopathology to the increasingly sophisticated techniques for the analysis of longitudinal data and the making of causal inferences in nonexperimental research. Among the landmarks in the development of these, by now almost revolutionary, techniques is the seminal work by Simon (1957), the book by Blalock (1964) on causal inferences in nonexperimental research, Duncan's (1967) innovative use of path analysis to study the problem of status attainment, and the use by various investigators in the late 1960s and early 1970s of two- and three-stage least squares to examine reciprocal causal patterns (Blalock, 1971; Mason & Halter, 1968). Perhaps the most important of all these techniques is the development by Jöreskog and his associates of LISREL, "a general computer program for estimating a linear structural equation system involving multiple indicators of unmeasured variables." (See Jöreskog, 1969, 1970, 1973a, 1973b; Jöreskog, Gruvaeus, & van Thillo, 1970; Jöreskog & Sörbom, 1976a, and 1976b; Jöreskog & van Thillo, 1972; Werts, Jöreskog, & Linn, 1973; Werts, Linn, & Jöreskog, 1971). This program uses confirmatory factor analysis as a means of separating measurement error from the underlying concepts, while also making possible the examination and statistical evaluation of complex causal models.

The neglect of these developments by researchers unconcerned with the estimation of causal effects is understandable. However, it is another

As is readily apparent, this paper is the direct result of my long and close working relationship with Melvin L. Kohn, all of the analyses and substantive conclusions reported being the result of our collaborative efforts. Less evident are the debts I owe to Duane Alwin and Ronald Schoenberg, each of whom was an invaluable guide during different stages of the LISREL learning process.

matter to disregard a method such as confirmatory factor analysis, which makes it possible to eliminate the effects of measurement error.

Benign neglect of the problem of measurement error might even be defensible for researchers whose studies involve (1) experimental designs in which subjects are randomly assigned to undergo a precisely determined experimental condition (e.g., given a carefully measured amount of a particular drug) while other subjects are randomly assigned to a control group; (2) comparisons of differences in outcome among classes into which subjects can be categorized without error; (3) measurement of variables, particularly independent variables, that are error free; (4) phenomena so powerful or data analyses so compelling that the results are convincing despite the systematically attenuated results that occur because of measurement error.

All of this may seem querulous and academic. The problem of measurement error can be shown to be real, however, by citing two numbers – .59 and .93. Both numbers are estimates of the over-time correlation of ideational flexibility; both are based on exactly the same measures of the same individuals, over the same 10-year time span. But .59 is the over-time correlation of ideational flexibility factor scores based on principal component factor analyses of the data from the first and second stages of our longitudinal study, whereas the over-time correlation shorn of measurement error by the use of confirmatory factor analysis is .93.

Problems of measurement error should be of great concern in longitudinal analyses because measurement error of independent variables (which initial measures surely are) is particularly troublesome. This is so because the magnitude of the slope of the dependent variable on the independent variable (e.g., the path from the initial to the later measure) will be underestimated in direct proportion to the amount of error in the measurement of the independent variable.

In order to remove measurement error and separate unreliability from change, LISREL requires multiple indicators (i.e., measures) for each concept. With such information it is possible to construct models for the various concepts, which divide the variance of the indicators into two parts – one part reflecting the concepts to which they are connected, the second part reflecting anything else, which for measurement purposes is considered error. The program reduces these models to a series of simultaneous equations, which it solves using iterative function minimization procedures. The information needed to solve these equations is provided by the redundancy inherent in the fact that the number of parameters that have to be estimated in the model is smaller than the number of interrelationships among indicators about which information is contained in the basic empirical data input to the program – the covariation matrix of indicators.

The test of our success in differentiating "true scores" on the underlying concept from errors in the indicators in how well the variance–covariance matrix of indicators implied by the hypothesized model reproduces the original variance–covariance matrix of the indicators. χ^2 is used to make this evaluation. Because it is a function of the discrepancies between the actual variance–covariance matrix and the variance–covariance matrix implied by the measurement model, the better the fit the smaller the χ^2 per degree of freedom.

The most efficient way of using LISREL is in a two-stage process. In the first stage the technique is used to develop measurement models that provide estimates of the relevant constructs shorn of measurement error, whereas in the second stage it is used to model and evaluate the causal relationships among the constructs developed in the first stage. Several versions of the program exist, all modifications and extensions of the original Jöreskog and van Thillo (1972) program.[1] In order to use LISREL it is necessary to provide the variance–covariance matrix of the indicators of the "unmeasured variables" (i.e., concepts, constructs, factors), as well as a series of pattern matrices describing which relationships are fixed and which are to be estimated, together with matrices containing initial start values for all parameters. Insight into what the program can do can be gained by examining the nature of the matrices involved. Table 8.1 provides a verbal description of these matrices, and Figure 8.1 shows which part of the full-information model each of the matrices represents.

In LISREL analysis there are two types of constructs – exogenous constructs (XC in Figure 8.1) and endogenous constructs (YC in Figure 8.1). Exogenous constructs are those which are causally unaffected by the other constructs in the model, whereas endogenous constructs are postulated to be at least in part causally determined by other elements in the model. Both types of constructs are measured by indicators; exogenous indicators are labeled x_1 and so on, and endogenous indicators are labeled y_1 and so on. Each of these indicators is presumed to have two components: that part which reflects the underlying construct and that part which does not. The critical matrices for the development of measurement models are the lambda and theta matrices. The lambda X and lambda Y matrices determine the structure of the endogenous and exogenous constructs, respectively, by postulating which indicators are truly related to which constructs. The theta epsilon and theta delta matrices describe error – the variance of each indicator that is not determined by the constructs in the model. The theta epsilon matrix also describes the

Table 8.1. *Verbal description of LISREL matrices*

Lambda Y (structure endogenous)	
row = endogenous indicators	
col. = endogenous constructs	
Lambda X (structure exogenous)	
row = exogenous indicators	
col. = exogenous constructs	
Beta (effects among endogenous constructs) (columns affect rows)	
row = endogenous constructs	
col. = endogenous constructs	
Gamma (effects of exogenous constructs on endogenous constructs)	
row = endogenous constructs	
col. = exogenous constructs	
Phi (covariance of exogenous constructs, variances on diagonal)	
row = exogenous constructs	
col. = exogenous constructs	
Psi (covariance of residuals of endogenous constructs, unexplained variance on diagonal)	
row = endogenous constructs	
col. = endogenous constructs	
Theta epsilon (covariance of residuals of endogenous indicators, unexplained variance on diagonal)	
row = endogenous indicators	
col. = endogenous indicators	
Theta delta (covariance of residuals of exogenous indicators, unexplained variance on diagonal)	
row = exogenous indicators	
col. = exogenous indicators	
Theta epsi-delta[a] (covariance of residuals of endogenous and exogenous indicators)	
row = exogenous indicators	
col. = endogenous indicators	

[a] This matrix appears only in the MILS program.

covariation of the error among the endogenous indicators, the theta delta matrix the covariation of the error among the exogenous indicators, and the theta epsi-delta (available in the MILS program [Schoenberg, 1982]) the covariation between error of the endogenous and exogenous indicators.

For the development of causal models the gamma and beta matrices

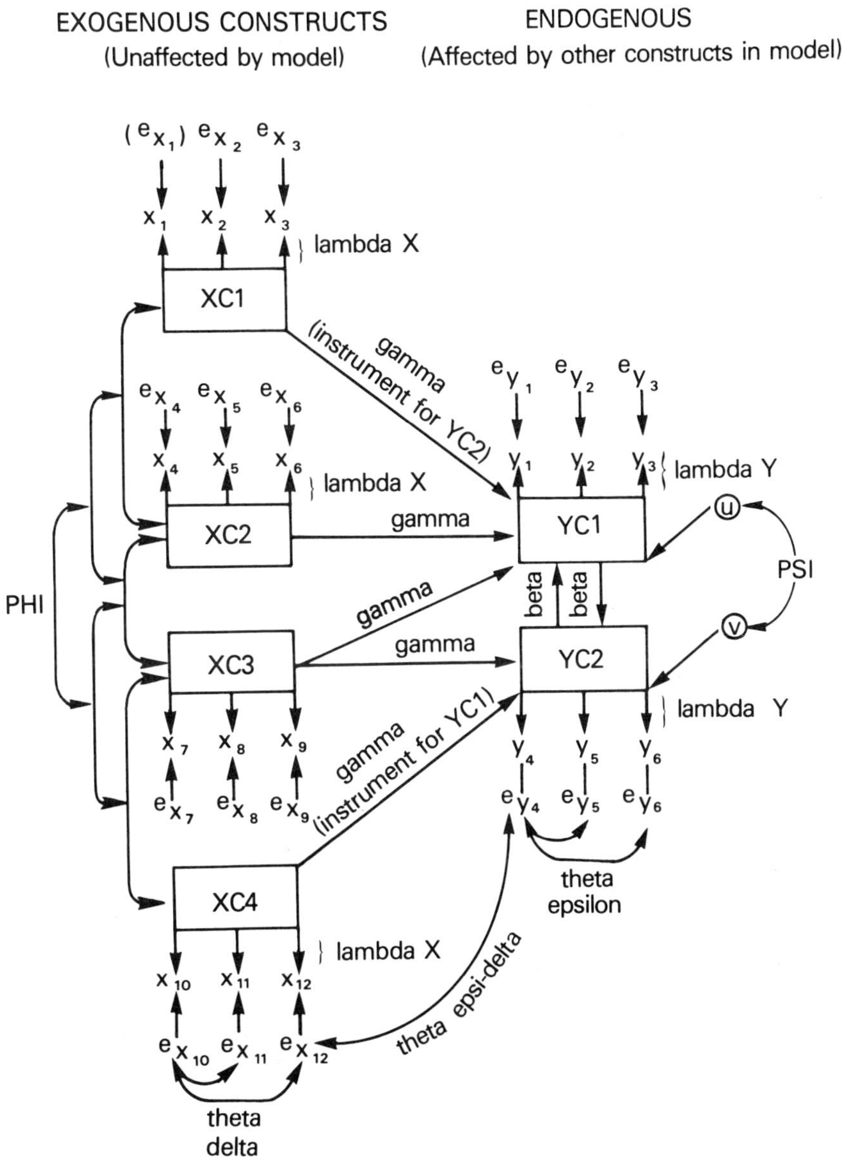

Figure 8.1. Components of the LISREL model.

are central. The gamma matrix is used to postulate which exogenous constructs affect which endogenous ones, and the beta matrix postulates the causal interrelationships among the endogenous constructs. The two final matrices, the phi and the psi, describe the nature of the covariance of the constructs. The phi matrix, which deals with constructs unaffected by the model, contains information about the variance and covariance of the exogenous constructs, and the psi matrix, which is concerned with constructs causally affected by the model, describes the residuals and covariance of the residuals of the endogenous constructs.

In sum, measurement models must specify the relationships of indicators to concepts (in the lambda matrices), take into account unreliability (or "measurement error") in all the items that measure a concept at a given time (in the theta epsilon and theta delta matrices), and allow for the possibility that measurement errors are correlated in repeated measurements of the same phenomena (in the theta epsi-delta matrix). In addition, causal models must specify the effects of the exogenous concepts on the endogenous ones (in the gamma matrix), the causal interrelationships among the endogenous concepts (in the beta matrix), the variance and covariance of the exogenous concepts (in the phi matrix), and the residuals and covariances of the residuals of the endogenous concepts (in the psi matrix).

In order to illustrate the utility of LISREL I will describe the procedure used by my collaborator, Melvin Kohn, and me, both to develop measurement error–free concepts and to model the concepts in complex yet statistically assessable ways (for a more complete account of the study see Kohn & Schooler, 1978, upon which the analysis to be described is based; for further extensions see Kohn & Schooler, 1982).

The general research question we faced was the nature and direction of effects in the relationship between occupational conditions and psychological functioning. The specific problem with which we were concerned in this analysis was the assessment of the reciprocal relationship between one pivotal dimension of occupational structure, the substantive complexity of work, and one pivotal dimension of psychological functioning, intellectual flexibility.

In earlier analyses of a cross-sectional survey carried out in 1964, we used the method of two-stage least squares to make provisional assessments of the reciprocal relationship between the substantive complexity of work and many facets of psychological functioning, including intellectual flexibility (Kohn, 1976; Kohn & Schooler, 1973). Although the results of these analyses provide prima facie evidence that the substantive complexity of men's work does affect their psychological functioning, cross-sectional data cannot provide definitive evidence of causality; only analysis of longitudinal data, measuring real change in real people, can be definitive.

In order to gather such longitudinal data we conducted a 10-year follow-up survey of 687 men, who constituted a representative portion of our original sample of 3,101 men, representative of all men employed in civilian occupations in the United States. Having collected the follow-up data, we faced the core technical problem in longitudinal analysis – how to separate unreliability of measurement from real change in the phenomena studied. The solution was to develop measurement models for our major concepts, substantive complexity of work and intellectual flexibility, before attempting to develop our causal model.

A measurement model for substantive complexity

By the substantive complexity of work we mean the degree to which the work requires thought and independent judgment. Substantively complex work, by its very nature, requires making many decisions that must take into account ill-defined or apparently conflicting contingencies. Although in general, work with data or with people is likely to be more complex than work with things, this is not always the case, and an index of the overall complexity of the work should reflect the degree of complexity in each of these three types of activity. Work with things can vary in complexity from ditch digging to sculpturing; similarly, work with people can vary in complexity from receiving simple directions or orders to giving legal advice; and work with data can vary from reading instructions to synthesizing abstract conceptual systems.

Our information about the substantive complexity of men's work is derived from detailed questioning of each respondent about his work with things, with data or ideas, and with people. The men's answers to these detailed questions provided the basis for seven ratings: appraisals of the complexity of each man's work with things, with data, and with people; an appraisal of the overall complexity of his work, regardless of its content; and estimates of the amount of time spent by each man working at each type of activity. We treat all seven ratings of the 1964 job as "indicators" of the underlying but not directly measured construct – the substantive complexity of that job (see Figure 8.2). Each indicator is conceived to reflect the underlying construct, which it measures only imperfectly, together with some degree of "error" in measurement.

The follow-up survey asks the same questions and makes the same seven ratings. Again, we treat these ratings as indicators of the underlying construct, in this instance the substantive complexity of the job held at the time of the 1974 interview. As before, we conceive of each indicator as reflecting the underlying construct, together with some degree of measurement error. We also allow for the possibility that errors of measure-

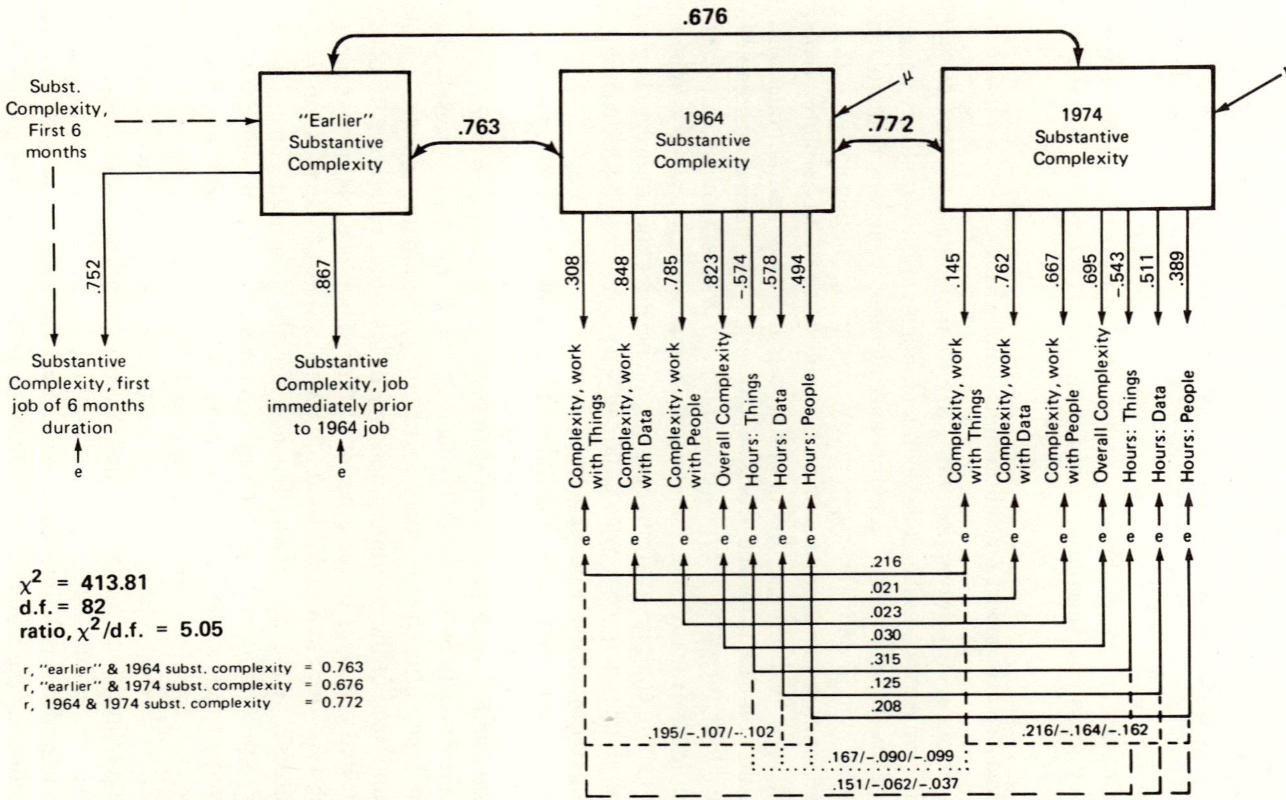

Figure 8.2. Measurement model for substantive complexity (figures shown are standardized).

ment are correlated over time – that whatever errors there may be in the measurement of complexity of work with things in the 1964 job, for example, may be correlated with errors in the measurement of complexity of work with things in the 1974 job. The fit of the model to data can be improved by taking into account other correlated errors of measurement – notably, between the complexity of each man's work with things and the amount of time he spends working with things, with data, and with people. The overall fit of this model to the data as estimated by χ^2 is 413, with 82 degrees of freedom, for a ratio of 5.05, which is quite good.[2] The most interesting information provided by this measurement model is that the overall stability in job complexity, from 1964 to 1974, is rather high: The correlation between the two measures of complexity, stripped of measurement error, is .77.

A measurement model for intellectual flexibility

Our index of intellectual flexibility is meant to reflect men's actual intellectual performance in the interview situation. In thc 1964 interview, we sampled a variety of indicators, including the men's answers to seemingly simple but highly revealing cognitive problems involving well-known issues, their handling of perceptual and projective tests, their propensity to "agree" when asked agree–disagree questions, and the impression they made on the interviewer during a long session that required a great deal of thought and reflection.

We claim neither that this index measures "innate" intellectual ability nor that intellectual flexibility evidenced in the interview situation is necessarily identical to intellectual flexibility as it might be manifested in other situations. We do claim that our index reflects men's actual intellectual functioning in a nonwork situation that seemed to elicit considerable intellectual effort from nearly all the respondents.

In the follow-up study, we secured entirely comparable data, after elaborate pretesting to be certain that the cognitive problems had the same meaning in 1974 as in 1964. The measurement model we now employ for intellectual flexibility is similar to that for substantive complexity in most respects, with one major exception: In the measurement model for intellectual flexibility, we posit that there are two factors underlying the several indicators, perceptual and ideational flexibility. Judging by the goodness-of-fit test, such a two-factor model provides an excellent approximation of the actual variance–covariance matrix of the indicators, for the χ^2 is 67, with 58 degrees of freedom, for a ratio of 1.17 – exceptionally low for a measurement model based on this many cases (see Figure 8.3).

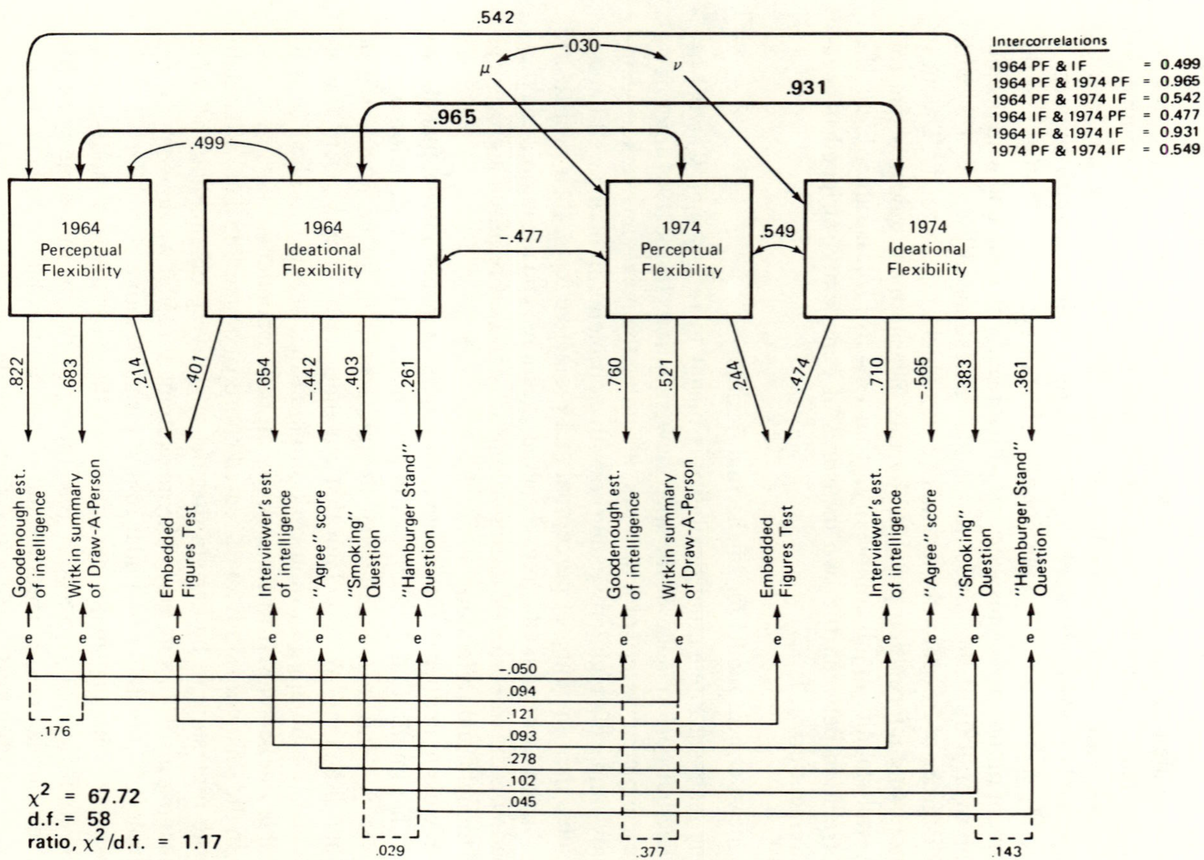

Figure 8.3. Measurement model for intellectual flexibility (figures shown are standardized).

From this model, we learn that the correlation between men's levels of ideational flexibility in 1964 and their levels of ideational flexibility in 1974, shorn of measurement error, is the previously mentioned .93. We conclude that there has been very great stability in men's levels of ideational flexibility over the 10-year period.

Causal analysis: the reciprocal effects of substantive complexity and intellectual flexibility

The question for the second stage of our LISREL analysis, causal analysis, was whether despite the overall stability within substantive job complexity and intellectual flexibility there had been enough individual change for job conditions to have had much of an effect.

To do structural equation causal analyses, we computed the variances and the (unstandardized) covariances between the true scores for job complexity at the various stages of the respondent's career, his intellectual flexibility in 1964 and in 1974, and all the other variables that will enter into the analyses.[3] These variances and covariances are the data on which the causal models of the reciprocal relationship between substantive complexity and intellectual flexibility are based.

A reciprocal relationship can occur contemporaneously (albeit not necessarily instantaneously) or more gradually over time. Our earlier analyses, using cross-sectional data, could consider only contemporaneous effects. But there is no reason in principle why substantive complexity and intellectual flexibility might not affect each other both contemporaneously and more gradually over time. We therefore assessed causal models that allow the possibility of both contemporaneous and "lagged" reciprocal effects (see Figure 8.4). Because our concern in these analyses is the ideational component of intellectual flexibility, we shall henceforth limit the analyses to ideational flexibility and use the terms *ideational flexibility* and *intellectual flexibility* interchangeably.

The model depicted in Figure 8.5 includes, as potentially pertinent exogenous variables, all social characteristics that prior research literature and our own earlier analyses give any reason to believe might affect either substantive complexity or intellectual flexibility. We thus include in the model the respondent's own age and level of education; his mother's and his father's levels of education; his father's occupational level; his maternal and paternal grandfathers' occupational levels; his race, national background, and religious background; the urbanicity and region of the country of the principal place where he was raised; and even the number of his siblings. We also include as exogenous variables the respondent's

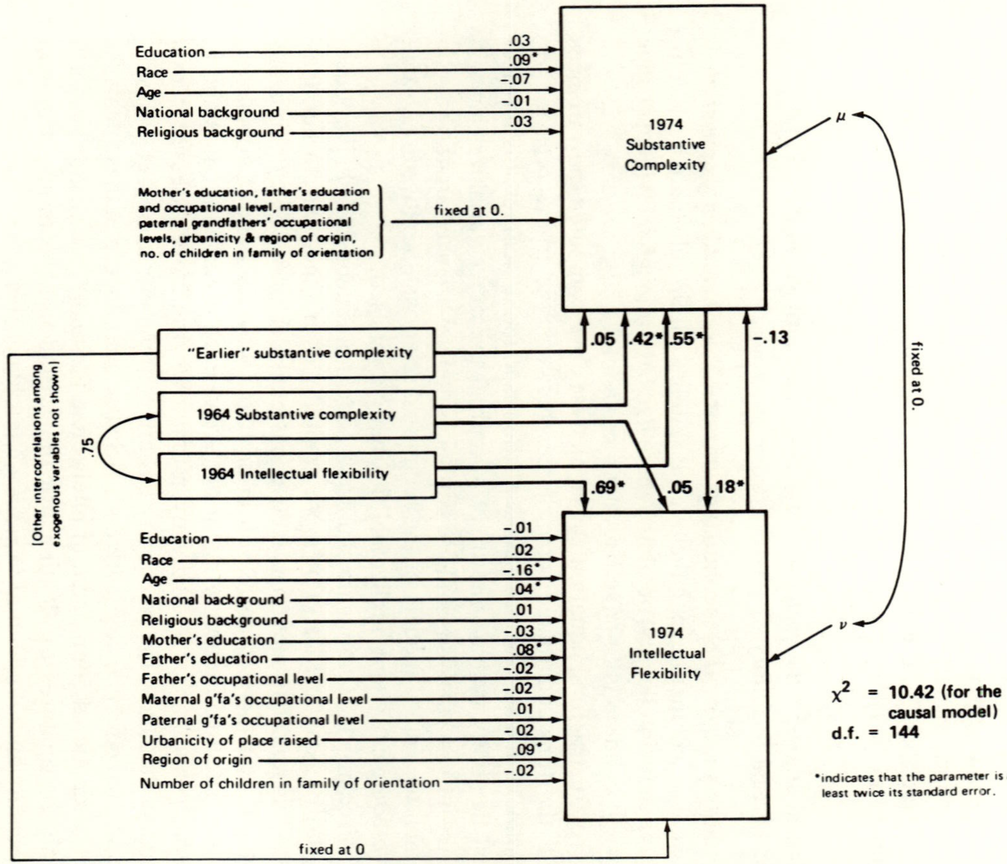

Figure 8.4. The reciprocal effects of substantive complexity and intellectual flexibility: full model (figures shown are standardized).

1964 levels of substantive complexity and intellectual flexibility, as well as the substantive complexity of his "earlier" (pre-1964) jobs.

Because in contemporaneous effects models the number of parameters to be estimated will be greater than the amount of information provided by the intercorrelations among the variables, some assumptions must be imposed on the model, usually by setting some path(s) to zero. For the model we are examining to be adequately identified (i.e., reducible to solvable equations), we must set to zero the direct effects on 1974 intellectual flexibility of one or more exogenous constructs that have a path to 1974 substantive complexity and at least a moderate correlation with 1974 intellectual flexibility. The constructs for which this assumption is made are known as the instruments for intellectual flexibility. Similarly, the direct effects of one or more exogenous constructs on 1974 substantive complexity must also be assumed to be zero; otherwise there will be too little empirical information for the equations to be solved unequivocally. Therefore we posit that background characteristics that would not be interpreted as job credentials by employers (even by discriminatory employers) – for example, region of origin – do not directly affect the substantive complexity of the 1974 job; these variables are thus used as "instruments" to identify the equation. The rationale is that by the time men are at least 10 years into their careers, these variables should no longer have any direct effect on the substantive complexity of their jobs, certainly not when the substantive complexity of their "earlier" and 1964 jobs is statistically controlled. Similarly, we posit that the substantive complexity of "earlier" jobs should have no direct effect on the men's intellectual flexibility in 1974, when the substantive complexity of their 1964 and 1974 jobs is statistically controlled.

The results of such an analysis demonstrate that the significant effect of substantive complexity on intellectual flexibility is contemporaneous and approximately one-fourth as great as the effect of men's 10-year-earlier levels of intellectual flexibility. The significant effect of intellectual flexibility on substantive complexity is also impressive, surpassing the effect of substantive complexity of the 1964 job on the substantive complexity of the 1974 job. This effect is lagged; that is, it is the men's intellectual flexibility in 1964, not contemporaneously, that significantly affects the substantive complexity of their 1974 jobs. The longitudinal analysis thus demonstrates something that no cross-sectional analysis could show – that the effect of substantive complexity on intellectual flexibility is rapid: Current job demands affect current thinking processes, whereas intellectual flexibility, by contrast, has a lagged effect on substantive complexity, the individual's earlier intellectual flexibility affecting the substantive complexity of his present job.

The one anomaly in the model shown in Figure 8.5 is that the path from 1974 intellectual flexibility to 1974 substantive complexity is not just statistically nonsignificant, it is negative. Despite its statistical nonsignificance, the existence of such a negative path suggests a problem of multicollinearity. Multicollinearity occurs when the correlations among the determinants of a dependent variable are much higher than the correlations between the dependent variable and the determinants (Heise, 1975). Under such conditions, slope estimates will be increasingly sensitive to sampling and measurement errors (Blalock, 1963; Farrar & Glauber, 1967; Gordon, 1968). In the present case the multicollinearity probably results from the very high correlation ($r = 0.92$) between 1964 and 1974 intellectual flexibility. A proper assessment of the effect of intellectual flexibility on substantive complexity requires our dropping the statistically nonsignificant contemporaneous path from the model. Similarly, a proper assessment of the effect of substantive complexity on intellectual flexibility requires our dropping the statistically nonsignificant lagged path from the model. Therefore, in Figure 8.5 we delete these (and all other) nonsignificant paths and reestimate the model. This, we believe, represents the most accurate assessment that can be made of the overall effects of substantive complexity and intellectual flexibility on each other. As can be seen from an examination of Figure 8.5, the significant paths remain virtually unchanged both in magnitude and in direction.

Both of our causal models indicate that substantive complexity of work both affects and is affected by intellectual flexibility, substantive complexity's effect on intellectual functioning being relatively immediate and intellectual flexibility's effect on substantive complexity taking place over time. Thus we have used confirmatory factor analysis first to develop measurement error–free indexes of our central concepts of substantive complexity and intellectual flexibility and then to examine their causal interrelationships over time.

Instead of using this two-stage process to estimate our model, we could also have begun by attempting to develop a full-information model in which both measurement and causal parameters are estimated simultaneously. However, although it is theoretically possible to begin by attempting to estimate all of the parameters at once, doing so is likely to be such a complex task that serious errors in specifying the model are almost certain to occur. Furthermore, because the model's parameters are estimated through an iterative minimization procedure, the better the initial start values, the lower the computer costs. Estimating a large model when little is known about the probable values of the parameters is likely to be very costly. However, once we had the solutions from our separately

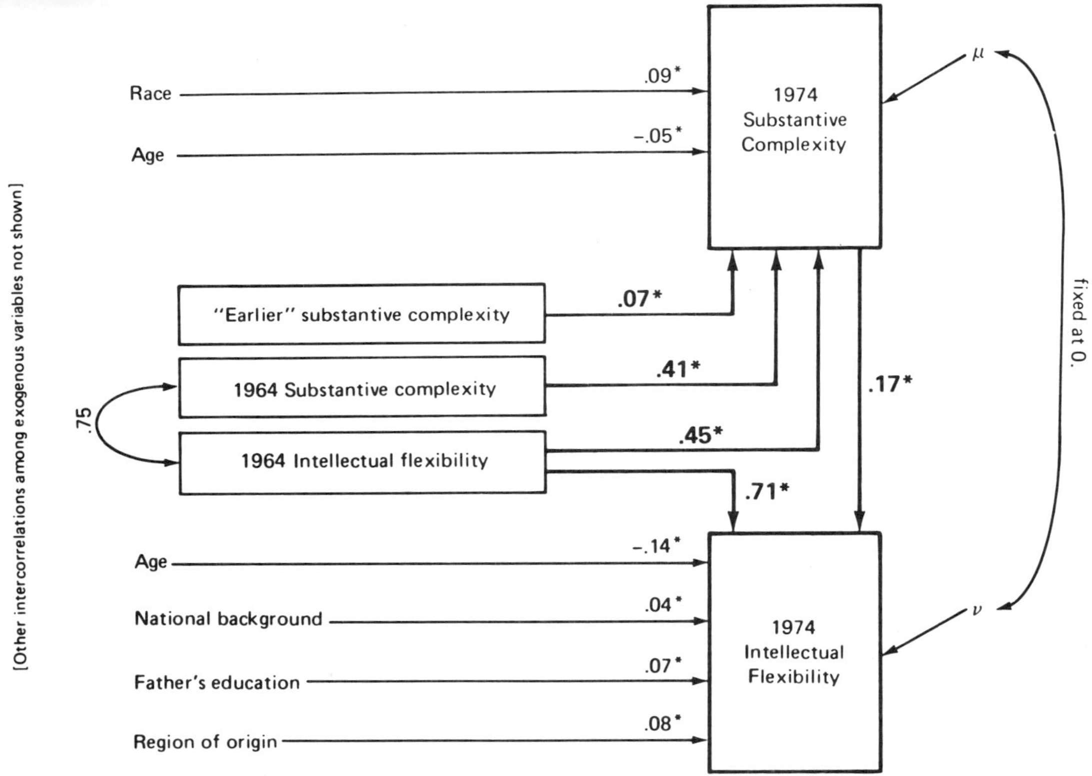

χ^2 = **11.45 (for the causal model)**
d.f. = 42

*indicates that the parameter is at least twice its standard error.

Figure 8.5. The reciprocal effects of substantive complexity and intellectual flexibility: significant paths only (figures shown are standardized).

estimated causal and measurement models, we developed a full-information model in which both measurement and causal parameters are estimated simultaneously. We did this to ensure that our findings did not result from our having fixed the values of the measurement models before estimating the causal model. When this was done all of the parameter estimates of the measurement models for both substantive complexity and intellectual flexibility proved to be very close to those obtained when the measurement models were estimated independently; the causal part of the model also remained essentially unchanged.

The use of confirmatory factor analysis on our longitudinal data thus permits us to demonstrate, beyond reasonable doubt, what heretofore could be stated as only a plausible thesis buttressed by presumptive evidence – that the substantive complexity of men's work both considerably affects and is considerably affected by their intellectual flexibility. I realize that this is a forceful conclusion, but it is one based on longitudinal data and LISREL analysis.

Notes

1 Several modifications and extensions of the original Jöreskog and van Thillo program exist. Of these, the two most comprehensive and easy to use are LISREL IV by Jöreskog and Sörbom (1978) of the University of Uppsala and MILS, an advanced version of LISREL developed by Ronald Schoenberg (1982).

2 Because of our theoretical interests, all men who do not work with things were excluded from the computation of the correlations involving substantive complexity of work. However, if such men are scored in the lowest category of the complexity-of-work-with-things indicator, and the analyses redone, the results are essentially the same (see Kohn & Schooler, 1978).

3 Two methods are presently available for obtaining the covariance between true scores derived from different measurement models or between true scores and other indexes. One procedure involves the development of models combining the principal features of two or more measurement models and possibly including as concepts nonmeasurement model derived indexes, the covariance among concepts being provided by the output. The second way such covariances can be obtained is made possible by the MILS program, which not only provides factor scores for the concepts, but also makes possible an accurate estimate of their reliability by producing their correlations with the true scores. Correlations between these factor scores and other variables can then be computed and corrected for unreliability.

References

Blalock, H. M., Jr. Correlated independent variables: The problem of multicollinearity. *Social Forces*, 1963, *42*, 233–237.

Blalock, H. M., Jr. *Causal inferences in nonexperimental research*. Chapel Hill: University of North Carolina Press, 1964.

Blalock, H. M., Jr. *Causal models in the social sciences*. Chicago: Aldine-Atherton, 1971.

Duncan, O. D. Some linear models for two-wave, two-variable panel analysis. *Psychological Bulletin*, 1967, *72*, 177–182.

Farrar, D. E., & Glauber, R. R. Multicollinearity in regression analysis: The problem revisited. *Review of Economics and Statistics*, 1967, *49*, 92–107.

Gordon, R. A. Issues in multiple regression. *American Journal of Sociology*, 1968, *73*, 592–616.

Heise, D. R. *Causal analysis*. New York: Wiley, 1975.

Jöreskog, K. G. A general approach to confirmatory maximum likelihood factor analysis. *Psychometrika*, 1969, *34*, 183–202.

Jöreskog, K. G. A general method for analysis of covariance structures. *Biometrika*, 1970, *57*(2), 239–251.

Jöreskog, K. G. Analysis of covariance structures. In P. R. Krishnaiah (Ed.), *Multivariate Analysis-III*. New York: Academic Press, 1973. (a)

Jöreskog, K. G. A general method for estimating a linear structural equation system. In A. S. Goldberger & O. D. Duncan (Eds.), *Structural equation models in the social sciences*. New York: Seminar Press, 1973. (b)

Jöreskog, K. G., Gruvaeus, G. T., & van Thillo, M. *ACOVS: A general computer program for analysis of covariance structures* (Research Bulletin 70-15). Princeton, N.J.: Educational Testing Service, 1970.

Jöreskog, K. G., & Sörbom, D. Statistical models and methods for analysis of longitudinal data. In D. J. Aigner & A. S. Goldberger (Eds.), *Latent variables in socioeconomic models*. Amsterdam: North-Holland, 1976. (a)

Jöreskog, K. G., & Sörbom, D. Statistical models and methods for test–retest situations. In D. N. M. deGruijter, L. J. Th. van der Kamp, & H. F. Crombag (Eds.), *Advances in psychological and educational measurement*. New York: Wiley, 1976. (b)

Jöreskog, K. G., & Sörbom, D. *LISREL IV – Analysis of linear structural relationships by the method of maximum likelihood*. Chicago: National Educational Resources, 1978.

Jöreskog, K. G., & van Thillo, M. *LISREL: A general computer program for estimating a linear structural equation system involving multiple indicators of unmeasured variables* (Research Bulletin 72-56). Princeton, N.J.: Educational Testing Service, 1972.

Kohn, M. L. Occupational structure and alienation. *American Journal of Sociology*, 1976, *82*, 111–130.

Kohn, M. L., & Schooler, C. Occupational experience and psychological functioning: An assessment of reciprocal effects. *American Sociological Review*, 1973, *38*, 97–118.

Kohn, M. L., & Schooler, C. The reciprocal effects of the substantive complexity of work and intellectual flexibility: A longitudinal assessment. *American Journal of Sociology*, 1978, *84*, 24–52.

Kohn, M. L., & Schooler, C. Job conditions and personality: A longitudinal assessment of their reciprocal effects. *American Journal of Sociology*, 1982, *87*, 1257–86.

Mason, R., & Halter, A. N. The application of a system of simultaneous equations to an innovation diffusion model. *Social Forces*, 1968, *47*, 182–195.

Schoenberg, R. *MILS – An advanced form of LISREL*. Unpublished manuscript, 1982. (Available free of charge from the author, Laboratory of Socio-Environmental Studies, NIMH, NIH, Bethesda, Md. 20205.)

Simon, H. A. *Models of man: Social and rational* (H. A. Simon, Ed.). New York: Wiley, 1957.

Werts, C. E., Jöreskog, K. G., & Linn, R. L. Identification and estimation in path analysis with unmeasured variables. *American Journal of Sociology*, 1978, *78*, 1469–1484.

Werts, C. E., Linn, R. L., & Jöreskog, K. G. Estimating the parameters of path models involving unmeasured variables. In H. M. Blalock, Jr. (Ed.), *Causal models in the social sciences*. New York: Aldine-Atherton, 1971.

Part IV

Legal and ethical questions

9 The consequences of the recommendations of the U.S. Privacy Protection Study Commission for longitudinal studies

Lee N. Robins

Records are useful to many kinds of social research, but to the longitudinal study, their availability in individually identifiable form is crucial. Longitudinal studies use such record data for four main purposes: sampling, locating subjects for interview and locating additional records about them, verifying interview data, and finally and most obviously, obtaining data for their own sake.

With respect to sampling, the access to records allows choosing the sample from rosters that were established before the outcome of interest could have occurred. The great advantage of choosing samples from records created before the period of risk is that such samples are unbiased with respect to that outcome – that is, the outcome cannot have affected the chances of an individual's appearance in the sample. This is not true of samples selected during or after the period of risk, such as samples collected in household surveys of adults. Sources like birth records, school records, armed service records, selective service records, and records of children's clinics afford access to appropriate samples of the general population or of populations with special problems. If virtually complete recovery of the selected samples is achieved at follow-up, an unbiased sample is achieved.

A second important use for identifiable records in follow-up studies is location of individuals for interview and use of identifiers found in one set of records to locate other records. Records may provide current addresses or may mention names and addresses of employers or relatives who know current addresses. Further, new addresses found in a record file that includes complete identifiers, such as birth date or social security number, may make possible a positive identification of a research subject in other records that lack complete identifiers.

A third use for records is verification of information obtained by in-

This work was supported by U.S.P.H.S. grants DA 00013, MH 18864, and AA 03539.

terview. This may be particularly important when the outcome variables of interest are likely to be concealed in an interview because they are considered disgraceful or in any case not redounding to the credit of the individual called upon to report them. Access to records in which the reported information can be confirmed or disconfirmed not only can test the respondents' veracity with respect to verifiable items but also, when verifiable discreditable information is found to be freely acknowledged, can enhance confidence in the accuracy of other items that cannot be directly verified.

Records are also very important sources of outcome data that cannot be achieved by interview alone. Some data of interest may be unknown to the subject. For instance, if a physician has made a diagnosis of anxiety neurosis but has not told the subject the diagnosis, the subject cannot report it. Similarly, it is not possible to learn from a parent how well an adopted-away child succeeded in school, if the parent has lost contact with the adopted child, but school records can provide that information. Further, data available in records may be more accurate than those a respondent can supply, no matter how willing he or she may be to report accurately. For instance, the research may require knowing whether truancy typically predates or postdates the first juvenile arrest. A respondent may be able to say that he was both truant and arrested, but he may be unable to remember which came first.

Records may have an advantage over interviews even when information is equally available from either source, because record searches avoid invading the individual's privacy or interfering with his life. One can, for instance, learn from local police records whether an individual has ever been arrested during the follow-up interval. If that is the only outcome of interest, it will not be necessary to recontact the subject for a second interview. Similarly, if the outcome of concern is the school achievement of the index subject's adult offspring, school records for those offspring can provide that information without requiring the researcher to enlist the cooperation of persons who had not participated in the initial phase of the study and may not be motivated to participate as secondary subjects.

Finally, data available from records is protected against bias both of the subject and of the interviewer. For example, interviews investigating the transmission of behavior between generations may tend to exaggerate the similarity between the parent's and child's behavior because either the respondent or the interviewer believes that behavior in parents often forecasts the same behavior in the child. Where the parent's and child's behaviors are obtained from independently constructed records, that is, records made by separate persons who had no knowledge of the existence of the other records, such bias is avoided.

For all six reasons – improved sampling, easier location, verification of interviews, provision of otherwise unavailable data, avoidance of unnecessary intrusion into the lives of subjects and their families, and avoidance of biased information – personally identifiable records can play an important role in follow-up studies. However, since the passage of two recent laws in 1974, the Privacy Act of 1974 and the Educational Rights Act of 1974, access to records in the United States without permissions obtained directly from subjects has become very difficult and often illegal. These laws were not designed with research in mind, and their effect on longitudinal research is a largely unforeseen side effect. The laws were intended to assure that record information could not be used against persons without their knowledge, a commendable goal. Unfortunately, they failed to distinguish the utilization of records for research and statistical purposes from their use for administrative or clinical reasons.

The Privacy Protection Study Commission was set up by the U.S. Congress in 1975 to review the whole question of federal regulation with respect to privacy. The main goal of this commission was not to discuss the problems that existing laws created for research enterprises, but the commission members did indeed recognize such problems for research and devoted a chapter to these issues in their report, published in July of 1977. In preparation for writing the report, the commission heard from more than 300 witnesses and received written statements from many (including the author). The report represents the commission's efforts to resolve the tensions between those who did and those who did not judge it important that research be carried out and that records be used in the process. The commission has made some excellent suggestions about ways of repairing some of the damage done by the 1974 laws. One of its most important contributions is to underscore the vital distinction between administrative uses and statistical and research uses of records. Administrative use is defined as use that is interested in and can have consequences for the subject as an individual. Statistical and research users are interested in the subject only as a representative of a class of individuals and assure that any information collected will not affect his or her status as an individual.

This chapter is a commentary on the report of the Privacy Protection Study Commission and its recommendations as they would affect access to personally identifiable records in longitudinal research. As already pointed out, the essence of longitudinal research is that it links information about individuals collected independently at two or more points in time.

Those who disapprove of allowing researchers access to personally identifiable records have argued that one can make do by studying the same population longitudinally without providing these individual links. There is ample evidence that this is not the case. To take one example, turnover tables of alcohol abuse show that the level of problem drinking in the population is quite constant over time, but that *different* people are involved at different points. We cannot learn what makes for remission or for late onset if we have only rates of alcoholism in the population as a whole.

Although following the recommendations of the commission would certainly improve access to records for longitudinal research, these recommendations would not by any means solve all the problems. I will argue for specific revisions of the commission's recommendations that I think would again make it possible to do excellent longitudinal research without breaching confidentiality. And a breach of confidentiality is, I believe, the only threat to research subjects from most longitudinal studies. My assertion that a breach of confidentiality can be avoided even when access to individually identifiable records is allowed applies to research that selects its sample from a large population and to research conducted by persons with no administrative responsibility for members of that sample. The problems of research on small populations, such as one town or U.S. congressmen, and of research done in-house by a treatment agency are ticklish ones with respect to confidentiality, whether the research is longitudinal or cross-sectional. When the population is small or is made up of well-known people, it becomes virtually impossible to hide identities. If the research is in-house, it becomes very difficult to assure the research subject that what he or she tells the interviewer can never be obtained by someone who has responsibility for making decisions about that subject's future. What I am speaking about, then, is the easiest case in which to preserve confidentiality, that is, the collection of information over time about sample members from a large population by an academic or commercial research team that has no connection with or responsibility for any actions concerning the subjects' future.

The commission notes that longitudinal research has a greater risk of breach of confidentiality than cross-sectional research:

> The Commission recognizes that identifiers must be retained in some kinds of research, most notably longitudinal and panel survey studies which refer to the same respondents from time to time, but retention should be the exception, not the rule. The decision to retain identifiers should not be left solely to the discretion of researchers . . . . Furthermore, the retention of identifiers should trigger special precautions, such as maintaining face-sheet information separate from the survey instrument, or recording personal identifiers in a separate file that is cross referenced to the rest of the data.[P. 584]

I would agree that there are special problems in maintaining confidentiality in longitudinal studies, but it is important to recognize that the precautions outlined in the quoted paragraph, along with other available techniques, have successfully maintained confidentiality of files kept over many years.

Aside from the dangers of breach of confidentiality, the privacy commission deals with one other type of threat, the threat of oversurveying, particularly in captive populations such as schoolchildren. This is a legitimate concern for certain populations, but in noncaptive populations or when such unobtrusive research techniques as record reviews are being used, it does not seem to be a problem, particularly given the current low funding levels for research. The chances that a member of the general public will be oversurveyed seem rather remote at present.

I would like to discuss six of the recommendations of the commission. These recommendations concern which records are to be available to researchers, when permissions should expire, the principle of limited disclosure, agency responsibility for judging the merit of the research, restrictions on redisclosure, and the prompt destruction of identifiers in research records.

First, the commission recommends opening to research certain agency records – including medical records, school records, records of most federal agencies except those that are now restricted by law, and records of social agencies – without requiring individually signed permission forms. The argument in favor of opening medical records appears on page 309 of the report:

> Although a researcher's obligation to obtain an individual's informed consent to participate in any study that may expose him to physical or psychological harm is widely recognized, the researcher's obligation to obtain the patient's permission to use information in records about him has always seemed less compelling. For one thing, the practical difficulties are considerable. Patients are difficult to locate, and if asked for an authorization might refuse, thereby skewing the results of the study in unknown ways. Insistence on patient authorization would make many important studies impossible. The recent search for the cause of the "Legionnaires' Disease," for example, would have been doomed at the start if the researchers had had to obtain authorizations before reviewing medical records.

Though research would certainly benefit from having the records listed by the commission reopened to research without requiring individual permissions, other records are also of great value, and to some of these the commission is strongly in favor of restricting access. Credit and employment records are among those to which the commission would severely curtail access, apparently without recognizing the role these records can play in health research. The commission fails to recognize that the government's interest in health, which it presents as a major reason for opening medical records, applies not only after a disorder comes to treatment and appears in a medical record, but also to indicators of risk for morbidity and mortality, indicators that play an important role in preventive medicine. Simultaneous appearance in some combination of police records, poor credit ratings, applications for unemployment compensation, poor work-attendance records, and discipline problems in the military is an excellent early indicator of alcoholism or drug abuse, and thus prognosticates the associated physical illnesses of tuberculosis, pneumonia, cirrhosis, hepatitis, and cancers of the mouth, esophagus, and cervix. These records can also serve as excellent measures of treatment effectiveness, much better measures for some disorders than is a return visit to a physician. If drug treatment is followed by no further arrest, no employment or absenteeism, and no failure to pay back loans, this is much better evidence of "success" than is the absence of morphine in the urine. Unfortunately, rather than recognizing the usefulness of police, credit, and employment records for research purposes, the commission applauds the narrowest definition of access to credit and employment records. On page 87 the commission recommends "that the Federal Fair Credit Reporting Act be amended to provide that information concerning an individual maintained by a credit bureau may be used only for credit-related purposes, unless otherwise directed or authorized by the individual." Similarly, page 272 recommends

> that each employer be considered to owe a duty of confidentiality to any individual employee . . . and that, therefore, no employer or consumer-reporting agency . . . should disclose, or be required to disclose, in individually identifiable form, any information about any individual applicant, employee, or former employee, without the explicit authorization of such individuals, unless the disclosure would be:
>
> (a) in response to a request to provide or verify information designated by the employer as directory information, which should not include more than:
> (i) the fact of past or present employment;
> (ii) dates of employment;
> (iii) title or position;
> (iv) wage or salary; and
> (v) location of job site;
>
> (b) an individual's dates of attendance at work and home address in response to a request by a properly identified law enforcement authority.

(The latter exception, which opens attendance records only to a law enforcement agency, is apparently intended to allow presence at work to serve as an alibi for an employee accused of a crime.)

I would like to see the recommendation of the commission that allows access to medical (p. 306), school (p. 441), social agency (p. 476), and federal agency (p. 602) records for research purposes generalized to include *all* records when the appropriate provisions for confidentiality are met. Not only might credit and employment records then become available, but so might those government agency records that by law or regulation may not now be disclosed in individually identifiable form: records of the Census Bureau, the Social Security Administration, and the Internal Revenue Service. These records would be valuable research resources for longitudinal studies.

Expiration dates. The commission recommends that when permissions are obtained from individuals for access to record information about them, the interval over which that permission remains effective should be as brief as possible. As one example, the commission recommends that when an employer has been granted permission to obtain record information about a prospective employee, the duration of that permission should not exceed 1 year. The commission does not discuss the impact of such restricted permission periods on longitudinal research.

If authorizations obtained by researchers remain in effect for so brief a period, it becomes extremely difficult to carry out longitudinal research. The only recourse for a researcher engaged in follow-up covering a number of years is to return to his subjects yearly to update their permissions, a procedure that leads to unnecessary intrusion into their lives and risks damaging the representativeness of the sample if they resent this repeated invasion and refuse. If the subjects are willing to grant the permissions for longer periods, why should they not be allowed to do so? I would like to see an exemption for longitudinal research in the recommendation for early expiration dates of permissions.

Limited disclosure. On page 313, the commission recommends "that any disclosure of medical-record information by a medical-care provider, with or without the authorization of the individual to whom it pertains, be limited only to information necessary to accomplish the purpose for which the disclosure is made." If this recommendation were to be taken literally, it would create havoc in all record research enterprises. The researcher never needs *all* the information in any medical record, for instance. A strict interpretation would mean that the staff of the medical facility would have to abstract the medical records for the researcher in order to keep him from seeing anything he did not need. This would severely reduce the quality of the data collected, because the clerk so assigned by the agency would be both uninterested in the research project and untrained for this purpose. It would also mean that medical records would seldom be available to research, because few medical agencies would have staff with sufficient time to do the abstracting. My suggestion would be simply to state that the agency should be permitted to disclose only those records that contain information necessary to the research.

Agency judgment of the merit of the research. Among the conditions under which the commission recommends that records be made available for research and statistical purposes without the consent of the individual to whom the record pertains is the provision that the entity (i.e., the agency that has control over the records). "determines that the research or statistical purpose for which any disclosure is to be made is of sufficient social benefit to warrant the increase in the risk to the individual of exposure to the record or information" (p. 602, Guideline 3[c]; this recommendation is repeated for each type of record the disclosure of which is advocated). To fulfill this requirement, the government agency that holds the record would have to decide on the scientific merit of the research. Clearly, poorly designed research is of no social benefit. This requirement seems excessive, because research projects for which records are sought will often be supported by federal grants and will thus have been judged to have scientific merit by the peer review process. I have heard informally that NIMH has already decided to accept grant approval as evidence of merit, rather than asking the record-holding agency to make this decision. It seems to me that it ought to be an official policy that a project which has been federally funded shall be considered of sufficient social benefit to merit the release of information from records. The necessity for formalizing this policy becomes clear when one realizes that research projects often need to link information from various agencies. If one of those agencies should decide that it is unable to judge the scientific merit of the project, the refusal of that one agency to grant access to its records might compromise a whole project. My suggestion would be that this guideline should read instead: "determines that the research has met tests of feasibility, scientific soundness, and ethicalness through peer review and institutional review procedures."

Restrictions on redisclosure. In addition to having to review the scientific merit of a proposal the agency in control of records must, according to the commission report's recommendations (Guideline 3[e], p. 602, is again one of several statements of this recommendation), "prohibits . . . any further use or redisclosure of the record or information in individually identifiable form without its express authorization." Enacting this recommendation would mean that once records had been obtained and the follow-up completed, no future follow-up would be possible without again getting permission from the same agency. This problem raises two important issues: First, a decision to do a second follow-up study might be made many years later, perhaps as much as 15 to 20 years after the original study. Examples of follow-up studies repeated long after the end of the initially planned final data collection can be found in Vaillant's reopening of the Grant study (1977), McCord's (1978) re-follow-up of the Cambridge-Somerville study, and Block's (1971) continuation of the Berkeley Guidance and Oakland Growth Study follow-ups. In the interval, the agency that provided the original records might well have been involved in a reorganization, making it very difficult to decide who now has the authority to give permission for further use of the records. Second, in the course of a follow-up study that begins with records obtained from a government agency, the researcher amplifies the identifiers obtained from those agency records. He may add telephone numbers, update addresses, and identify relatives who can help in location. It is difficult to see how the government agency that provided the original records could have the right to prevent the use at some future date of data the researcher had himself created during the study. Thus the restriction really seems unenforceable as well as undesirable.

Rather than requiring a return to the original agency to get permission to do a second follow-up, my recommendation would be that Guideline 3(e) be revised to state: "[The entity] prohibits further use or redisclosure unless the further use is for research that conforms to all the rules set for preserving confidentiality of the data and meets tests of feasibility, scientific soundness, and ethicalness as specified for the original study." This recommendation would ensure that standards applied in the first research use of the records would continue to apply in all subsequent uses.

Destruction of records. The commission strongly recommends that the identifiers on research records be destroyed as soon as the research is completed: "The Commission believes that the single most important procedure for maintaining the confidentiality of research and statistical data is the prompt removal and destruction of identifiers. . . . Ideally, identifiers should be removed or destroyed as soon as the data are collected and verified" (p. 584). With respect to applications to a school, there is a further specific recommendation, Recommendation 4(c), page 434: "that records created about an unsuccessful applicant be maintained by an educational agency or institution for 18 months after the close of the application process, after which time they must be destroyed." If these recommendations were followed, it would mean that no cross-sectional study could become the basis for a later follow-up unless the follow-up had been planned from the beginning. This would be a tragedy. One simply cannot predict ahead of time when it may be of great social value to follow up subjects from an earlier study. The discovery of the delayed adverse outcomes of exposure to radiation and to DES during pregnancy are among the many examples that come to mind. There would have been no way of anticipating 20 to 30 years earlier that identifiers for subjects in various drug trials should be saved for later follow-up. The Census Bureau saves its records for 72 years in the National Archives, at which point the records enter public domain. Although I would not suggest that all research records go to the National Archives, various methods can be used to keep identifiers safely separate from the research protocols for many years. A key linking the two can be maintained in a safety deposit box, for instance, so that the two could be reunited in the future, should there be a decision to do a longitudinal study. Destruction of identifiers loses that opportunity forever. I would recommend deleting the recommendations for destruction of identifiers and substituting the recommendation that identifiers be kept separate from research protocols and be secured in such a way that they cannot be linked to the protocols without permission from the principal investigator or his designated agent.

Some suggestions that might make these recommendations more acceptable. All the suggestions made so far have been for liberalizing researchers' access to records. Perhaps we should also add some new restrictions. One of the reasons that the commission is uneasy about researchers' use of data is that violations of confidentiality have indeed occurred in the past by inadequately trained researchers. The commission report describes this case:

> A researcher was doing a follow-up study of people who had been enrolled in a methadone maintenance program. . . . The contractor had the name and address of one particular individual who had been enrolled in the program several years previously, and the contractor went to the individual's residence. It was Saturday night, and the person was having a party and the contractor said, "Hi, I am so-and-so from such-and-such an organization, and we are doing a follow-up study of patients who have been enrolled in the methadone maintenance program."[P. 309]

Clearly such behavior is reprehensible, and competent researchers do not let it occur. However, it is notable that regulations aimed at preserving confidentiality have been more often addressed to protection of research records than to the conduct of the data-collection process. There is not to my knowledge a formal code designed to minimize the risks of breach of confidentiality during the data-collection period. The following items

(Robins & Smith, 1977) might be included in such a code:

1. In case-control studies, that is, studies in which affected and nonaffected individuals are selected for follow-up, the identity of the individual as case or control must be separated from other identifiers during the period of data collection, so that there will be no disclosure of the case or control status to agencies from which information is being sought, in case those agencies might have administrative interest in the subjects, or to subjects' relatives or acquaintances from whom help in locating them might be sought.
2. If no control subjects, that is, no subjects with "nonincriminating" identities, are to be included in the study, lists of subjects must be liberally salted with random names before they are submitted to agencies for acquisition of data or locating information, so that agencies from which further data are sought will have no assurance that any particular individual on the list is of administrative interest to them.
3. When record information other than identifiers is obtained before subjects are interviewed, interviewers must be kept ignorant of that record information so that there will be no danger of their disclosing such information to the subject or to anyone else.
4. Research studies on sensitive topics should be required to develop an innocuous description of the study and innocuous letterheads for contacting employers or relatives for help in locating subjects, so that mere participation as a study subject does not in itself give away any information that interested parties might not already have.

Following these strictures would prevent the kinds of unfortunate disclosures during collection of research data described in the examples presented to the commission. Once data are collected, separation of identifiers from protocols maintains confidentiality. The only remaining danger of disclosure then lies with the government itself, through the power of the courts.

The commission advocates protection of research records from subpoena: "The Commission has concluded that the individual's privacy interests as well as his right to refuse to testify against himself demand, albeit indirectly, that research and statistical records be generally immune to disclosure compelled by judicial order"(p. 579). The commission does not, however, recommend total immunity, but would allow disclosure in court if necessary to prosecute a researcher or research institution for violating the law. These seem reasonable limitations.

Until such time as there are laws exempting research records from subpoena, researchers are in a very difficult position. If a researcher has guaranteed confidentiality to a respondent, it seems to me that he or she has promised to destroy the list of identifiers in the face of subpoena, even if that meant having to go to jail. In our own research with veterans, we have hoped to avoid this risk by keeping the list pairing name identification numbers with protocol identification numbers outside the borders of the United States, so that the only remaining danger period is while the interview is still in the hands of the interviewer. We have told our interviewers that we expect them to honor their obligation to destroy the identifiers or the protocol should the interview be demanded by law enforcement officers before it has been mailed. Because none of us wants to go to jail, and because maintaining a "foreign connection" is onerous, we would ask for immunity of research records from subpoena.

Finally, we need to look at the problem of risks and benefits from the point of view of the agencies whose cooperation is necessary if we are to obtain records for longitudinal research. So far, our attention has been exclusively focused on the research subject's needs. Risks to the agency administration may be at least as great, and the agency usually has nothing to gain from letting its records be used in a research enterprise. One federal agency to whose records we needed access asked for an opinion from the Department of Justice about whether the records could legally be given to us. When this assurance of legality was obtained, we returned to talk to the head of the agency. He was still uneasy, and said, "I know now that I *can* let you have the records. But I *can* go out and stand in traffic too." We are grateful to him for having decided to take a chance on us and letting us have the records despite his feeling that he was taking grave risks on our behalf. We need to find ways in which the agency's risks – that is, "standing in traffic" – are better balanced by benefits to the agency. Those of us who do longitudinal research need the help of agencies that collect the records we use. We need to reduce the risks and increase the agency's rewards for helping us.

References

Block, J. *Lives through time*. Berkeley: Bancroft Books, 1971.

McCord, J. A thirty-year follow-up of treatment effects. *American Psychologist*, 1978, *33*(3), 284–298.

Privacy Protection Study Commission Report. *Personal privacy in an information society*. Washington, D.C.: U.S. Government Printing Office, 1977.

Robins, L., & Smith, J. E. Ethical considerations and confidentiality. In L. Johnston, D. N. Nurco, & L. N. Robins (Eds.), *Concluding follow-up research on drug treatment programs* (Treatment Program Monograph Series Number 2). Washington, D.C.: National Institute on Drug Abuse, 1977.

Vaillant, G. *Adaptation to life*. Boston: Little, Brown, 1977.

10 Issues of confidentiality in the development and maintenance of psychiatric case registers

Haroutun M. Babigian

Confidentiality is an issue that must be seriously considered in the development of any case register. In the instance of psychiatric registers, the protection of confidentiality is extremely important because of the stigma that is attached to mental illness. Even today, the mentally disabled continue to face discrimination, particularly when it comes to securing positions with high levels of responsibility.

Broadly speaking, a register is a longitudinal data file of all individuals with diagnosed or treated mental illness living in defined areas or communities. Baldwin (1968) characterizes registers as individual- rather than event-oriented, with systematic and standardized data collection from all agencies. Register data are prospective and cumulative rather than retrospective and point-related. Because of the individual orientation, identifying information such as name, address, birth date, sex, and race is needed for linkage purposes. It is this identifying information, which is kept on computer tape, that makes all computerized information systems vulnerable to criticism regarding the issues of privacy and confidentiality.

The Monroe County Psychiatric Case Register is operated and maintained by the Department of Psychiatry of the University of Rochester School of Medicine and Dentistry. It was established on January 1, 1960, and contains the psychiatric history of virtually all Monroe County residents entering the formal mental health care system. Reports to the register are received from all public and private psychiatric facilities and the majority of psychiatrists in private practice. The register's goals, operation, and functions are described in greater detail by Babigian (1972), and Gardner et al. (1963), and Liptzin and Babigian (1972).

The Monroe County register is strictly a research instrument. It has never been used as a record-keeping system to enhance the provision of patient care. Being a research instrument, it contains very little clinical information as compared to the hospital record. The same standardized information is reported by all agencies. It is important to note that registers are totally dependent on the cooperation of all agencies and individuals involved in the delivery of mental health care; without the full cooperation of hospitals, clinics and practitioners, a register would be impossible to maintain.

The major functions of a psychiatric case register are threefold: (1) to promote epidemiologic, clinical, and administrative studies; (2) to aid other studies, particularly early case detection and prevention projects, by adding meaningful follow-up information over a period of many years; and (3) to provide sampling bases for other studies, especially those that need the identification of high-risk cohorts and control groups.

Legally, the register is regulated by the State of New York under Part 60 of the New York State Commissioner of Education's regulations governing medicine, osteopathy, and physiotherapy. This regulation deals with

> the revealing of facts, data, or information obtained in a professional capacity relating to a patient or his records without first obtaining consent of the patient or his duly authorized representative, except if duly required by a court of competent jurisdiction or statute. Nothing in this Part shall prohibit a physician from making such facts, data or information available to a department of State government, providing that such department shall when requesting such facts, data, or information notify the physician in writing that such facts, data, or information shall be used only for research and study and that their confidential nature shall be maintained.

The register project was from the very beginning made part of the State Mental Hygiene Department so that it would be able to function under the jurisdiction of this regulation.

In the register's development phases, the ethical issues of reporting and concerns about confidentiality were fully discussed with all concerned parties. Some psychiatrists were afraid that reporting might interfere with the therapeutic process, and others questioned the legal implications of reporting without obtaining prior permission from every patient.

The ethical issues were handled differently by the individual physicians: Some chose to inform every patient about the reporting; others reported without informing their patients; and a few decided to report their patients by code without revealing their identity. As the project progressed, all concerned were impressed with the safeguards taken to protect the confidentiality of patients and continued their participation. During the 1960s reporting continued without any major questions.

With the proliferation of data banks in government, banking, and industry, concern was raised about the regulation of such systems to protect the right of privacy of citizens and to assure confidentiality. The United States, like many European nations, began considering guidelines and legislation to protect the rights of citizens. The deliberations and recommendations of the U.S. Department of Health, Education and Welfare Secretary's Advisory Committee on Automated Personal Data Systems are published in Records, Computers and the Rights of Citizens (1973). In the foreword of this document, then-Secretary of HEW Casper W. Weinberger summarizes the issues involved:

> Computers linked together through high-speed telecommunications networks are destined to become the principal medium for making, storing, and using records about people. Innovations now being discussed throughout government and private industry recognize that the computer-based record keeping system, if properly used, can be a powerful management tool. Its capacity for timely retrieval and analysis of complex bodies of data can be of invaluable assistance to hard-pressed decision makers. Its ability to handle masses of individual transactions in minutes and hours rather than in weeks or months, as was formerly the case, makes possible programs of service to people that would have been unthinkable in the manual record-keeping era. . . . Nonetheless, it is important to be aware, as we embrace this new technology, that the computer, like the automobile, the skyscraper, and the jet airplane, may have some consequences for American society that we would prefer not to have thrust upon us without warning. Not the least of these is the danger that some record-keeping applications of computers will appear in retrospect to have been oversimplified solutions to complex problems, and that their victims will be some of our most disadvantaged citizens.

In forming its recommendations, the committee reviewed the efforts of several European countries in developing guidelines and legislation for computerized data systems. One of these was Sweden, which in 1973 established an independent Date Inspectorate responsible for the execution and enforcement of the provisions of the Data Law, with the following key provisions:

> No automated data system containing personal data may be set up without a license from the Data Inspectorate.
>
> Data subjects have the right to be informed about all uses made of the data about them, and no new use of the data may be made without the consent of the subject.
>
> Data subjects have the right of access without charge to all data about them, and if the data are found to be incorrect, incomplete, or otherwise faulty, they must either be corrected to the subject's satisfaction, or a statement of rebuttal from the subject must be filed along with the data.
>
> The Data Inspectorate will act as ombudsman in all matters regarding automated personal data systems. [Cited in U.S. Department of Health, Education and Welfare, 1973, pp. 170–171]

In Great Britain, the Younger Committee (1972) studied the entire subject of privacy, emphasizing the private rather than the public sector. The proposed safeguards are clear and comprehensive:

> 1. Information should be regarded as held for a specific purpose and not to be used, without appropriate authorization, for other purposes.

2. Access to information should be confined to those authorized to have it for the purpose for which it was supplied.
3. The amount of information collected and held should be the minimum necessary for the achievement of the specified purpose.
4. In computerized systems handling information for statistical purposes, adequate provision should be made in their design and programs for separating identities from the rest of the data.
5. There should be arrangements whereby the subject could be told about the information held concerning him.
6. The level of security to be achieved by a system should be specified in advance by the user and should include precautions against the deliberate abuse or misuse of information.
7. A monitoring system should be provided to facilitate the detection of any violation of the security system.
8. In the design of information systems, periods should be specified beyond which the information should not be retained.
9. Data held should be accurate. There should be machinery for the correction of inaccuracy and the updating of information.
10. Care should be taken in coding value judgments. [Cited in U.S. Department of Health, Education and Welfare, 1973, pp. 173–174]

Public Law 93-579, also known as the privacy act, was passed by Congress in 1974. It basically follows the recommendations made by congressional committees and incorporates most of the safeguards adopted by other countries, including the establishment of a Protection Study Commission. This law affects all record systems maintained by governmental agencies. Even though it does not specifically apply to private systems, it does affect psychiatric registers indirectly, through the reporting of federally operated mental health facilities like Veterans Administration hospitals and clinics.

From the very beginning, the Monroe County Psychiatric Register developed and adopted many safeguards that were later adopted by legislation. Register information was kept to a minimum for reasons of both confidentiality and ease of reporting, especially by busy private practitioners. Two separate data files are kept, one for such identifying data as name, address, birth date, and serial number, and the other for the basic data preceded only by the serial number. Only the data tape is used for specific studies. The data are handled exclusively by our own programmers and staff, and the tapes are kept under lock at all times. Accuracy of information is maintained through rigorous manual checks and computer edit programs. The project has always been directed by a psychiatrist who is responsible for the conduct of all studies and the application of safeguards to protect confidentiality. Identifying data is never provided to other agencies, not even to the Department of Psychiatry. All employees are carefully screened and informed about the safeguards involved. They are also warned that, should a breach of confidentiality occur, they will lose their jobs, and that this information will be transmitted to all future potential employers who request a recommendation from us. In the case of follow-up studies where patients must be contacted, the physician is always consulted for approval first. No patients are seen if the physician refuses to grant permission. The register has not been used as a sampling base for follow-up studies since the early seventies because of the complexities involved and because of changes in reporting that make it impossible to identify specific patients. Because of these safeguards, the confidentiality of the Monroe County Psychiatric Case Register has never been seriously compromised in the nearly two decades of its operation.

Informed consent is another ethical issue involved in the maintenance of registers. Informed consent gives the patient the right to decide whether confidential information will be reported to the register. If the patient refuses, the loss of such information will result in an incomplete file that then provides an inaccurate picture of the services delivered to a specified population. Under these conditions, the impact of the missing data on the effectiveness of the register as an epidemiologic research instrument must be evaluated.

Clearly, when informed-consent rules are in effect, how the matter is presented is crucial in obtaining each patient's cooperation. Certain professionals, in presenting the issue, carefully emphasize the importance of the project and of the participation of every individual. Others may downgrade the project and indicate to the patient that he or she does not need to provide approval. Thus the obtaining of informed consent from every patient increases the register's vulnerability to the attitudes and feelings of the multiple care providers in the system who can easily act to lessen the value of the register for personal or other reasons.

The alternative to informed consent for registers is the acquisition of a system that can identify individuals for research purposes without revealing their identities. The method that has been chosen for the Monroe County Register is an allegory system previously used by the Tri County Psychiatric Case Register (Figure 10.1). Only a set of prespecified letters of each name and address are reported, so that it is possible to link records but impossible to identify specific patients by name and address for further possible contact. It is important to note that such a system will automatically restrict the use of the register as a sampling base for other studies. Despite this limitation, it is hoped that the allegory method will maintain the integrity of the register by reassuring psychiatrists and patients alike of the confidentiality of patient material.

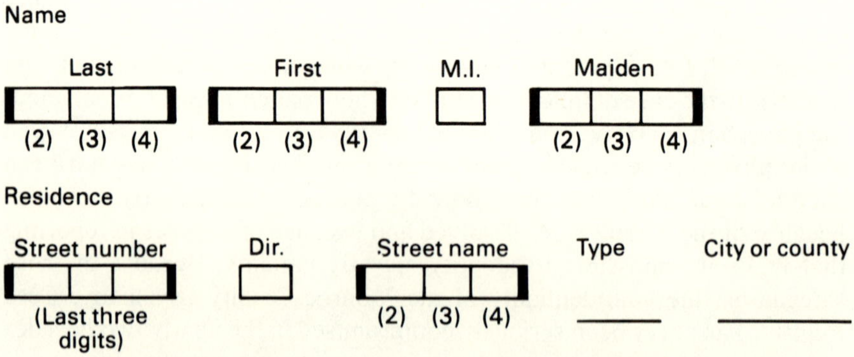

Figure 10.1. Allegory system used by the Tri County Psychiatric Case Register.

In summary, psychiatric case registers are invaluable research instruments with multiple potential uses and roles. Their primary characteristic as an individual-oriented longitudinal data file makes them highly vulnerable to the ethical and legal concerns of privacy and confidentiality. Legislation enacted in the United States during 1974 provides guidelines and safeguards for governmental data systems. One important characteristic of most of these data files is that the information collected is governmentally mandated. Most registers in the United States, on the other hand, are voluntary systems, built on mutual trust and belief in the advancement of knowledge. Voluntary participation and the necessity of collecting complete data make it impossible to obtain informed consent from every single patient receiving psychiatric care in the community. Based on the Monroe County data, approximately 3% of the county population, or 21,000 individuals, receive psychiatric care annually, and 1%, or 7,000 individuals, enter the psychiatric system for the first time in their lives. If the system required informed consent and 20% of the patients refused to grant consent, over 4,000 individuals would be lost to the register annually. It might still be possible to conduct some planning and utilization studies correcting for the error caused by such a loss of information, but even with corrections for error, these studies would be less credible than those based on complete and accurate data.

I strongly believe that psychiatric registers are essential for good planning, utilization and evaluation studies, clinical and epidemiologic investigation, and the generation of hypotheses. Several registers, strategically located in different areas of the United States, are needed to provide a solid data base for the planning and evaluation of mental health services. This venture, then, either should be legislatively mandated in each area or, if based on voluntary participation, should use an allegory system that will guarantee the privacy of all participants, yet provide accurate and complete information necessary for the conduct of quality research, and thereby justify expenditures required for the maintenance and use of registers.

In Monroe County we have chosen to adopt the allegory system and are waiting to see how well it will work. As to the question how long registers should continue operation, I have no good answer. I sometimes think that registers, like good red wine, become more valuable with age. At other times I feel that data spanning a generation (approximately 30 years) should be adequate. With the frequent changes in the mental health care delivery system, registers may be necessary at all times in selected communities in order to complement the event-oriented data collected by governmental agencies. In any event, responsible individuals and agencies should develop safeguards that will guarantee the confidentiality, the accuracy, and the completeness of the information gathered.

References

Babigian, H. M. The role of psychiatric case registers in the longitudinal study of psychopathology. In M. Roff, L. Robbins, & M. Pollack (Eds.), *Life history research in psychopathology*. Minnesota: University of Minnesota Press, 1972.

Baldwin, J. A. Evaluative function of a case register. In R. H. Williams & L. Ozarin (Eds.), *Community mental health*. San Francisco: Jossey-Bass, 1968.

Gardner, E. A., Miles, H. C., Iker, H. P., & Romano, J. A cumulative register of psychiatric services in a community. *American Journal of Public Health*, 1963, *35*, 1269–1277.

Great Britain, Home Office. *Report of the Committee on Privacy* (Rt. Hon. Kenneth Younger, Chairman). London: H.M. Stationary Office, 1972.

Liptzin, B., & Babigian, H. M. Ten years experience with a cumulative psychiatric patient register. *Methods of Information in Medicine*, 1972, *11*, 238–242.

Sweden, Justice Department. *Date och integritet [Data and privacy]* (Document SOU 1972:47). Stockholm: Almänna Förlaget, 1972.

U.S. Congress. *Privacy Act of 1974*. Public Law 93-579, December 31, 1974.

U.S. Department of Health, Education and Welfare. *Records, computers and the rights of citizens: Report of the Secretary's Advisory Committee on Automated Personal Data Systems*. Washington, D.C.: U.S. Government Printing Office, 1973.

11 Patient records: a lawyer-legislator's practical perspective on confidentiality

Stanley J. Aronoff

As governments get larger and larger and as the problems connected with delivery of services to people become more and more complicated, even medical and research professionals are going to have to look at the legal consequences of some of their acts.

Let us talk very simply before we get into more complicated issues of the ramifications of privacy. In its simplest form, privacy means just the right to be alone, the right to have a life of one's own. We need to start from the individual's point of view – the perspective of a person who merely gets up in the morning and gets into his or her automobile and starts off the day and is arrested for going 1 mile over the speed limit, or that of one who has been treated by a medical professional at some time in his life. Forget for the moment that you, the readers of this book, are psychiatrists, psychologists, sociologists, or other researchers. Just think of yourselves as citizens. Then mentally transport yourselves to Columbus, Ohio; observe the new office tower that rises above the state capitol; and realize that at least four of the floors are the computer network for record keeping in the state of Ohio. Plugging into 150 departments, agencies, or bureaus in that building are hundreds and hundreds of terminals throughout the state.

The state of Ohio keeps records on all of its residents from the moment they are born until the time they die. Each record is composed of all kinds of information. Birth, education, military service – the state has all the background. There is credit information. There is information on rankings from universities. There are records of what neighbors have reported. The State Medical Board keeps records on psychiatrists. The Department of Health keeps records on psychologists. The state has records of all arrests. (One shocking statistic is that 50% of young people under 25 already have a criminal record.) It has records on whether individuals are "slow pays" or "late pays" in respect to bills, and on how much they pay in state taxes. All these records can be cross-checked with welfare information.

There is incidence information on the treatment of patients. For example, every case of venereal disease is a public record in the state of Ohio by name of the person who is affected. Every abortion is a public record in Ohio. There it resides in the Department of Health, waiting for some eager lawyer to use his subpoena power.

This storehouse of information is voluminous and ever-growing. What would you as a citizen want to have protected, for yourself as an individual?

The Ohio Privacy Act states that there will be no secret record-keeping system in the state of Ohio. Until Watergate and the aftermath, and until the creation of the National Health, Education and Welfare Privacy Committee (of which I was a member), secret record-keeping systems were the rule – not only in Ohio, but in all of the other 49 states and the U.S. federal government. There was no way that a citizen could get an answer to the question, "Is there a record on me?"

That is not the case in Ohio now. Every governmental record-keeping system must file with the Department of Administrative Services a statement of its purpose, the kind of records that it keeps, and the name of a person in control. By calling the state information system, an individual can find out what departments have records on him or her. But that is only the beginning, because, unfortunately, there is no way that the individual can say, "Tell me all the bad stuff." Each person is going to have to seek that information directly. But if the citizen has a feeling that he or she has been rejected for too many jobs that seemed to be definite offers, then I would suggest that this person take a look at Item 2 of the Privacy Act. It says that people have a right to *see, amend*, and *correct* their records, so that if in fact someone did not flunk out of the University of Podunk, but in fact was Phi Beta Kappa, and was mixed up with the wrong John Jones, then he would have the right to go in and correct his record.

If a person presents credentials to correct a record and the record keeper disputes them, there is a mediating mechanism set out in the Ohio Privacy Act, providing for one of two possibilities. The person can mark the record; anyone who receives it realizes that something is incorrect, and can request the person's own version. Or, briefly, the person can give his or her version of what the record should be; when the record is disseminated to other people, the person's statement of fact is there, even though there is a dispute.

The Ohio Privacy Act also does something that directly affects the professions. It says that record keepers dealing with government data of any kind have certain obligations, called the Code of Fair Information Practices. The concepts of fairness and due process are involved. Those people in control of records have an obligation to the public to use records for the purpose intended. If you are doing data collection for statistical research, or if you are collecting sensitive information for a specific purpose, that and only that is the purpose for which records can be disseminated. And your statement of purpose has to be filed with the state of Ohio: This is the key.

I am not promoting business for lawyers, but I would suggest that this issue is the heart of the whole privacy question. It seems to me that scientists are very similar to lawyers and physicians. When you are in pursuit of something that you believe to be truth, or something that is going to benefit society, you sometimes come into contact with astonishingly personal information. It is one thing when you are putting that information to use in your own research program. It is something else, however, when you decide that Joe Smith, who is doing some research in a similar area, ought to have access to it. You have now disseminated the sensitive information to Source 2 without, perhaps, putting any restraints on Source 2. Source 2 now has it free, clear, and unencumbered, and what Source 2 does with the information is beyond your control.

This simple unwitting passing of information is the real danger to privacy. People do not mean to hurt other people; they just disseminate information without thinking. The clerks in the Department of Health or the clerks in the Department of Welfare probably do more harm in terms of record keeping *by mistake* on a daily basis than can be prevented by all of the privacy protections that we put into effect by way of law. The average person merely gives information out on request.

In the United States, tax information is not so protected as most people think – at either the federal level or the state level. Consider your own tax filings and judge just how much you feel should be made public. To reiterate, the only way to consider privacy is always to think of oneself.

The next part of the Privacy Act is the most controversial. I could not keep this section in the Ohio Privacy Act; no state has been able to keep it in, nor has the federal government. The original section in the bill said that when one deals with sensitive information (and *sensitive* is the key – the word is hard to define), one cannot disseminate that information without the consent of the subject of information. That seems to me to be the guts of privacy. But that part of the privacy bill, passed in 1977, was knocked out in the early part of 1978. The same pattern occurred at the federal government level; it is recurring elsewhere. Basically, government record-keeping systems do not want to be restricted. They do not want to have to get the consent of the individual. Even though I included exemptions through which trucks could be driven (e.g., the individual's consent did not have to be obtained if the information was within the nature and purpose of the system, if it was for statistical research, if it was for the good and welfare of the state, if it was a health issue), I still could not keep the consent section in the bill.

It was not researchers who were most concerned about the consent proviso. It was, especially, regulators. Crime departments, the Welfare Department (supposed to be entrusted with the delivery of service), the bureaucracy, and the administrators said no, and ultimately business did also, even though business was not directly implicated. Two hundred thirty-three corporations and labor unions said no. Why? They wanted access to all of this information. (Big business, labor, and the private market buy these records for their own uses.) Employment records are tremendously important: "Did a person have a psychiatric history at any time? I don't want to hire some nut and put him in charge of an important part of my business!" "I don't want to hire anybody who was a lousy student." "I don't want to hire anybody who is sickly. If he had a heart attack, he might have a heart attack on the job." That is why the consent doctrine did not stay in the bill.

So Ohio and every other state have essentially open records. There is a right to know, unless the legislature specifically closes a record by statute. Closing a record by statute entails identifying the exact kind of record and getting a bill through 99 members of the house, 33 members of the senate, and the governor. It is an enormous job, but one that falls squarely on the shoulders of researchers – because it seems to me that they are dealing with exactly the kinds of records that need some specific kind of regulation.

To provide several examples of the way that privacy rules are being used and misused in Ohio and by the U.S. federal government:

1. Cincinnatians were shocked when, in 1978, they read the front-page headline "Noted Psychiatrist Indicted for Corrupting TV Executive with Drugs." The prosecutor was Simon Leis. The psychiatrist was Dr. V. of the University of Cincinnati. The television executive was Mr. Z. The evidence was supplied by the drug-collecting agent of the federal government that works under federal grant with the prosecutorial office around the state. The defense was a motion to dismiss for violation of the doctor–patient confidentiality relationship.

2. Dr. Arnold Pembauer, a noted Cincinnati physician, had developed a huge Medicare/Medicaid workmen's compensation practice. The ques-

tions were, "Were any of the bills padded?" "Was there fraud?" and so forth. Ordered by the prosecutor to obtain patients' records, the police broke into his office with a search warrant. The defense was illegal search and seizure. Even though there was some complaints filed against the doctor, the Ohio Medical Association filed an amicus brief to intervene, asserting that this was the kind of case that must be won: If medical records are subject to search and seizure, then every doctor is in jeopardy.

3. The director of health of the state of Ohio faced an enterprising reporter from the "exotic" news media, who cited the Ohio Public Records Act and demanded to see alcohol records, abortion records, and venereal disease control records. The director of health refused to give the information. The *Akron Beacon Journal* and the *Dayton Daily News* intervened and said that all this was a matter of public record. The director said that it was highly sensitive information, the dissemination of which would be harmful to citizens. The reporter said, "I have a right to know."

4. In a hypothetical case, an emotionally unstable patient who has incurable cancer demands his records from the Department of Health, a state hospital, or a private physician. (Let us say the doctor works at a state hospital and has a private practice.) The doctor refuses. The patient brings a suit to compel. The doctor says that it is his record, and the hospital's record, and that it will do the patient harm if it is given to him. The doctor decides to spend the night in jail in order to test the constitutionality of the Privacy Act.

5. A proctologist who was making quite a bit of money decided to follow the ethics of his profession and donate 50% of his time to working in a public hospital. A woman who was tattooed from head to toe with various symbolic kinds of artwork needed a minor operation. After she came out of her anesthesia, even though the surgery was quite successful, she filed a complaint with the State Medical Board that the doctor had raped her. What were the doctor's protections?

Dr. V., the psychiatrist at the University of Cincinnati (Example 1), was granted his motion to dismiss. His refusal to divulge the medical records was upheld, and the matter was closed at the municipal court level. The agency decided not to appeal that particular case. But what about his reputation? Not only Dr. V.'s reputation but that of everyone involved suffered when the headlines screamed "Doctor Corrupts TV Executive" on the front page. Dr. V. said that he was interested in protecting the reputation of Mr. Z. Would Dr. V. have had a right to reveal the record if he was protecting himself? Could he, in effect, destroy another person's reputation in order to protect himself if Mr. Z. was in fact corrupted by drugs and did something terrible? I do not know the answer, but it is an interesting question. Are there any barriers that government should face in its laudable crusade against trafficking in drugs? Public sentiment would be likely to say that RENU should be able to get whatever it wants.

Dr. Pembauer's case (Example 2) is still in progress at this writing, and whoever loses will almost certainly appeal. The search and seizure question is one that goes back to the founding of the United States. The argument in the case is the one the British used when they were going to confiscate the arms of the colonists: "We have a right for the protection of society to find out if you are bearing arms against us." The prosecutor in the Pembauer case said that taxpayers' money was involved, and consequently the Medicare/Medicaid workmen's compensation records belonged to the state.

So far as the director of health (Example 3) is concerned, unless the law of Ohio is changed, or unless these medical records are specifically made private, they are open as incidence records and the Department of Health would not be able to withstand subpoena. In Akron Beacon Journal v. *Bureau of Motor Vehicles* and Dayton Daily News v. *City of Dayton*, the Ohio Supreme Court has already ruled that publicly held records – not only health, but also welfare, insurance, personal education, and in fact all agency records – must remain open. Accordingly, then, if the agency wanted to reveal how many times Psychiatrist X had been driving while intoxicated (DWI), the information would be there for public review. An interesting point is that records are compiled for statistical purposes. A newspaper reporter may not really be after an individual's story; he may just want to know how many DWIs there are in Hamilton County. That is a simple statistical record kept by the Bureau of Motor Vehicles. The record has, however, easily decipherable symbols referring to the component data on individuals. Furthermore, there are increasing numbers of studies done by alcohol units, which demand that government collect information on drunk drivers to find out whether alcohol arrests and their programs are having the desired deterrent effect. In New York City for a time, the name of every DWI was published in the *New York Times*.

To return to the incurable cancer patient (Example 4), the physician dealing with the person has a terrible decision to make because he really believes that if the patient receives the information, it may kill him. The doctor happens to be associated with the University of Cincinnati – a government agency. All records at the University of Cincinnati, because it is a state university, are governmental. Even if the physician is in private practice, if he takes anything that smacks of government money, his records become public. So if there is any Medicare/Medicaid money, any state money of any kind, or any government research money involved, the record becomes public.

> An agency shall upon request disclose medical, psychiatric, or psychological information to a person who is the subject of the information or to his legal guardian unless a physician, psychiatrist, or psychologist determines that the disclosure of the information is likely to have an adverse effect on the person, in which case the information shall be released to a physician, psychologist, or psychiatrist designated by the person or his legal guardian.

Now this does not mean that the information ultimately will not get to the patient, but it does mean that the issue can be ducked by the physician. He gives the information to someone who is qualified to analyze it and then to make the ultimate decision about whether the patient should be told. The problem is not fully solved: Suppose the psychiatrist to whom the physician gives the data does not think it should be given out, and the patient still wants to know and sues the psychiatrist? In my opinion divulgence would probably be ultimately necessary. A practitioner, according to Ohio law, has to give information to the qualified person if a government record is involved. The definition of *government record* is an expansive one, but if no government money is involved, in my view, the physician does not have to give out the information. The law has not been taken that final inch at this stage, although it is currently being tested.

There has been no change in Ohio. The Ohio Medical Association, the Ohio Psychiatric Association, the Ohio Psychological Association, and the Ohio Social Welfare Organization have all sued to claim that their records are their own. There is now a debate raging on the subject. My position is that information belongs to the individual, who ought not to be compelled to give it in order to obtain social services.

Finally, let us consider the tattooed lady (Example 5). She filed a complaint with the State Medical Board, and her complaint is a public record. Complaints filed by allegedly seduced women are all public in every state and subject to subpoena, true or not true. The physician in this incident settled for $1,000 because he had made a mistake: He had let anesthesia be administered without being present himself, and he had violated hospital procedure by failing to have his operation directly observed by a second person. So in effect, even though the story seemed to be a total fabrication, and even though the particular form of anesthesia used can cause hallucinations, his advice from legal counsel was to settle. The settlement was a great deal cheaper than the cost of front-page headlines.

I would like to close with a report on the status of the law, not only in

Ohio but in other states. When the Privacy Act of 1974 was passed, it was passed as a result of recommendations from the study commission of which I was a member, the Health, Education and Welfare Privacy Commission. This commission included a diverse array of experts, for example, the chairman of the MIT computer science department, the dean of the University of Michigan Law School, the first black woman to run a New York hospital, the head of the Oklahoma State Welfare Department, the head of the Savings and Loan League of California, and the head of the AFL-CIO Privacy Committee.

Watergate gave unexpected impetus to the work of the committee, which, after much initial groping in the dark, obtained a mass of information that astounded even midwestern conservatives like me. *Records, Computers, and the Rights of Citizens* (Secretary's Advisory Committee on Automated Personal Data Systems, 1973), the committee report, attracted a great deal of attention from the Watergate-scarred Congress and public. It was written by the varied group that constituted the committee for a general readership, in journalistic style. To my astonishment the Federal Privacy Act echoed the report faithfully, verbatim in some sections. Journalistic phrases were suddenly freighted with tremendous meaning and rushed into law. The act is being interpreted and refined in practice. But it is clear that, however its provisions may narrow with time, the climate for researchers will never be the same.

Reference

U.S. Department of Health, Education and Welfare. *Records, computers, and the rights of citizens: Report of the Secretary's Advisory Committee on Automated Personal Data Systems*. Washington, D.C.: U.S. Government Printing Office, 1973.

Part V

Prospect

12 Reflections on blame and responsibility for schizophrenia

Lyman C. Wynne

In looking back on schizophrenia research during my professional life history, I am dismayed, and intrigued, by the wild diversity of viewpoints that have been stoutly espoused. Despite my dedicated attention to the topic, I must confess that the morass of data and concepts has more than once suggested to me that a radically fresh approach may be needed; perhaps it would be easier to start over again with new observations and new concepts than to clean up the mess. Despite such impulses, I concede that it may be helpful to see if the conceptual swamp can be drained. A currently popular approach, as in *DSM*-III, is to try to identify something (if not somebody) that is small and clean and still can be named "schizophrenia." However, many would argue that the broader area of "psychosis" remains as messy as ever. Here I will step back to take a more historical view of certain issues that we often overlook in our examination of details, statistical and otherwise. I must trust in your forbearance if some of these comments appear to be overgeneralizations to the point of caricature.

Threaded through all cultures and eras of history is the issue of blame and responsibility for psychotic behavior and experience. In our scientific efforts to be objective and nonpejorative, we have redefined *blame* and encompassed it under the headings of etiology and pathogenesis. The etiologic question can be rephrased in lay terms as "Who, or what, is 'at fault' for producing the disorder?" The question of responsibility, a key issue in the realm of prevention and treatment, can be rephrased as "Who, if anybody, is expected to do something about the disorder and associated problems?" Notions of blame and responsibility are, in turn, intertwined with epistemological beliefs, as well as with concepts of the nature of madness, and whether it is expected to be transient or enduring, a self-limiting or a permanent handicap.

Historically, and cross-culturally, concepts of possession – for example, by demons and evil forces – have been central in one of the most common etiologic theories of mental disorder. In the rural Lebanese village in which I worked in 1963–1964, the evil eye of a specific person often was explicitly blamed; in other cultures, blame is ascribed to nonperson external forces that enter and possess the mind of the afflicted. Such theories are, of course, directly consonant with the delusions of control and experiences of passivity that we regard as the most nearly pathognomonic symptom of schizophrenia. What I especially wish to note here is that possession and witchcraft theories of etiology, as well as related concepts of soul loss, largely exonerate the patient from blame, which is then directed externally. At the most, the victims may be mildly criticized, in some settings, for letting themselves be exposed to the evil force or for not having taken precautionary measures.

The notion of possession is conceptually analogous to that of infection: An alien agent temporarily has entered the person and can, in principle, leave the person relatively unchanged. Although fear and disgust may lead to inhumane care during the acute "spell," there is no great expectation of chronic or residual secondary handicap following the episode. Furthermore, the responsibility for exorcism or other treatment does not fall on the patient but on an external person or event.

The concept of madness as basically episodic, transient, and curable, with blame externalized, involves fear and uncertainty, but it also carries a clear hope for full recovery. Most important, neither blame nor responsibility rests primarily with either the patient or the immediate family. It seems reasonable to regard the imputation of blame and responsibility as a stimulus burden; from the standpoint of present-day stimulus-overload formulations of schizophrenic onset and relapse, one can infer that demonic theories foretell a favorable outcome or at least an episodic course. Modern-day versions of such concepts are still common throughout the world, including this country, within numerous religious cults and subcultural groups. I find it fascinating to compare and contrast such concepts with the presumptively more scientific ideas of the last two centuries. Whether we like it or not, all of our concepts of etiology and treatment for schizophrenia and other mental disorders have the direct even if unintended consequences of implying who or what should take the blame and responsibility. Quite often the heat generated in allegedly scientific controversies has come from these ethical considerations and implications, and these in turn can easily becloud the objectivity of clinician and investigator alike.

Those "organic" theories that look for a schizophrenicoccus, exotoxins, or brain injury as the etiology of schizophrenia are, like demonic theories, still around, though now clothed in computer-age garb. As with demonic theories, their confirmation is reassuring to patients and families who are prone to speculate, even without professional instigation, that they may be at fault. But there is also a difference: These kinds of organic theories are embedded in the concept of the central nervous system as nonregenerative, so that there has been a widespread, though simplistic, belief that presumed organic damage or defect implies permanency, hence hopelessness, and, all too often, personal disengagement justifying inactive, custodial care.

Vaguely formulated "reasoning" along these lines pervaded much institutional care from 1850 to 1950. Still today, far more of the public than most professionals realize suspect fearfully that any serious mental illness is a permanent and largely untreatable handicap. In carrying out educational meetings and workshops with families of schizophrenics, I have been amazed how often such notions are still held even by persons who are otherwise well informed. Again, we see how anxiety can snuff out comprehension. The situation is not unlike that for cancer, where the word itself implies hopelessness (my own father left untreated a skin cancer and prepared to die because of the fright and despair this diagnosis induced).

Genetic theories, too, have been widely known and widely misinterpreted. Only gradually, during the last 30 years, have the complex formulations of sophisticated geneticists begun to be understood by psychiatrists on the patient firing line. Much denial of genetic evidence has been based on the erroneous but persistent belief that if schizophrenia is "genetic" (implying total causality, to most people, and not a factor contributing to predisposition), then "blame" resides exclusively in the genes. Because our genes stay with us throughout life, it is understandable that this interpretation all too often has been translated to mean that nothing very significant can be done, and that patient responsibility is limited to the taking of maintenance medication in order to suppress the permanent disorder.

With respect to blame, professionals often assume that a genetic view of schizophrenia at least relieves the burden of self-blame that relatives are prone to assume. To the contrary, I have been impressed by how often parents, who may not have a personal history of schizophrenia but who have been convinced by the lay press in the last decade that mental illness is genetic, blame themselves guiltily as the cause of their offspring's illness. Sounding much like parents who accidentally let a child be injured, these parents wistfully and sorrowfully ask: "How can I 'make up' to my son or daughter for this fate?" It is psychologically simpleminded for us to expect families to understand causation in the objective, impersonal terms of the professional. Far more professional and public education is needed to clarify the fundamental distinction between vulnerability and symptomatic illness (Wynne, 1978), and to correct the widespread, erroneous belief that a "genetic factor" means a permanent, fixed handicap.

Although misunderstandings and controversies have been common concerning the biological aspects of schizophrenia, surely they have been even greater concerning the experiential and psychosocial components. Here too, as with biological theories, the evolving concepts and hypotheses of the last 30 years have been quite poorly differentiated and inadequately understood by nonspecialists, even within psychiatry.

When I was a student and trainee in Boston in the 1940s, many psychoanalysts were still using a purified *intrapsychic* concept of psychological health and disorder. The implications for the issues of blame and responsibility arising from an intrapsychic formulation should be explicitly recognized. First, as in the "organic" theories of toxins and genes, the patient, in classical psychoanalytic theory, is assigned no personal blame for causing the illness. Rather, the etiology is unidirectionally determined by unconscious forces that are external to the ego. In psychoanalytic theory prior to Hartmann's revisions in the 1940s, the ego was viewed as struggling to integrate the conflicting demands of id and superego intrapsychically. In 1897, Freud concluded that his earlier hypothesis about the importance of seduction and other traumatic experiences was in error; thereafter in psychoanalytic theory, unconscious fantasies *within* the mind reigned supreme as developmentally formative. In psychoses, ego functioning was viewed as so impaired that an analytic treatment alliance was classically regarded as impossible and outside the realm of patient responsibility as well as blame. Nevertheless, in the classical model of psychoanalytic treatment, the burden of responsibility for recovery, and blame for failure, rests with the patient and the analyst–patient dyad to an extraordinary degree; other-than-intrapsychic pathways to change become superficial or adjunctive, and the real, current family can and should be ignored.

I find it both amusing and astonishing to recall the intense passions that were aroused in discussions of 1945–1955, when Lindemann in Boston and Sullivan and Fromm-Reichmann in Washington insisted on the importance of the nonfantasied social orbit and interpersonal context of psychiatric patients, even of schizophrenics. One of the points that was viewed as truly heretical was the suggestion that some of the precursors of, and responsibility for, schizophrenic illness might be identified outside the patient. This deviation was not only regarded as conceptually unorthodox and hence erroneous, but also as disastrously diluting the responsibility for treatment, which was thought to rest necessarily with the patient alone, beginning with payment of fees and ending (more or less) with the production of free associations.

Nowadays, there often is a considerable blurring of history when Frieda Fromm-Reichmann is thought of as a psychoanalyst. She wanted to broaden psychoanalysis, but she was bitterly denounced for calling her work with schizophrenics "psychoanalytic." In fact, what she and her colleagues did, and thought, *was* different, fundamentally so, as is dramatized in Fromm-Reichmann's 1948 concept that looked beyond the patient to the "schizophrenogenic" mother. This concept is now regarded as incorrect and unfortunate, but at the time it was more immediately and more crucially a reaction against the rigidities of classical psychoanalytic theory. In my contacts with Fromm-Reichmann, I regarded her as a very sweet lady (in some ways too sweet to cope with the nastiness of schizophrenics) who wanted the individual eccentricities of schizophrenics to be more tolerated. She thought that psychiatrists expected too much of schizophrenics, who needed more elbow room and less of a burden of responsibility for becoming autonomous (as the traditional psychoanalytic treatment model implied). She, and Sullivan, believed that schizophrenics might indeed be enduringly eccentric (a degree of permanent handicap!), but if their therapists, their families, and the community made reasonable allowances for such individual differences, many schizophrenics could adapt most of the time without being incapacitated or incarcerated. I believe that current views of schizophrenics have now become far more congruent with these basic premises of Fromm-Reichmann and Sullivan than is generally appreciated.

Unfortunately, Fromm-Reichmann ran afoul of later theorists with her inflammatory term *schizophrenogenic mother*. This term was resented because of the attribution of blame, but historically it had a number of reverberations with both negative and positive consequences. First, it overfocused on mothers (more in summaries and critiques by others than in Fromm-Reichmann's own writing); but this focus did help draw attention to the rest of the family. Second, taken out of context from other hypotheses by Fromm-Reichmann, the term suggested *uni*directional causality, a conceptual error held in common with many other formulations, even though the imputed causes have varied. Third, attention to the quality of mothering stimulated later, broadened interest in a developmental, life history approach to schizophrenia. Fourth, the attribution of blame to mothers aroused a lively and useful controversy because it stood in contrast to both prevailing alternatives – no blame or responsibility for anyone (biological hypotheses), or total responsibility on the patient (psychoanalytic implications).

In my view, another approach to psychosocial issues, neither Freudian psychoanalytic nor Sullivanian interpersonal, was needed to begin the task of achieving a more comprehensive and reconciliatory perspective. The beginnings of this approach can be found in the family studies of schizophrenia in the mid-1950s; the full ramifications are still being worked out. I had begun working intensively with families of schizophrenics in 1953, but only in 1956 did I become aware that others were exploring similar issues. Ted Lidz was placed on the same program at the 1956 American Psychiatric Association meeting, and we discovered some overlap in our thinking at that time, particularly an attention to fathers and to the whole family as a small social system, going beyond the mother–patient dyad of Fromm-Reichmann. Later that same year, the paper on the double bind by Bateson et al. (1956) was published.

The first version of that formulation unfortunately included several sentences that subsequently have been regarded as an extension of Fromm-Reichmann's blaming stance toward mothers. Specifically, Bateson et al. referred to the schizophrenic as a "victim" in the double-binding situation. Within a few years, these authors retracted and corrected that component of their hypothesis; they subsequently emphasized the multidirectionality in family systems, the inaccuracy of concepts of victims and victimizers, and the developmental unfolding of "circular," feed-back processes, as opposed to models of linear etiology. My own formulations have followed the same general lines. In such a framework, nobody, and certainly not the parents, is scapegoated as blameworthy. But catchy terms like *schizophrenogenic mother* appear difficult if not impossible to take out of circulation, even though this particular concept has not been advocated by anyone, so far as I am aware, for at least 20 years. Nevertheless, for some psychophobes, it is still fashionable to add a layer to the blaming and scapegoating – to blame the theorists who allegedly blamed the parents who allegedly blamed the schizophrenics.

With respect to the double-bind idea, it was pointed out long ago by Bateson that this formulation was primarily part of his epistemology, a way of thinking about relationships and communication, and should never have been considered an empirically specific, testable hypothesis about schizophrenia. Additionally, except for axe-grinding critics, everyone has long recognized that double binding is a phenomenon that is highly significant in many familial, psychotherapeutic, and other relationships, but that it has no unique function in schizophrenia. (For two collections of articles that updated the 1956 double-bind articles, see Sluzki & Ransom, 1976; Berger, 1978. Double binding is associated not only with other psychopathologic states, but also, as I suggested in 1969 (Wynne, 1976), with creativity. In a program with Gregory Bateson, I recommended standing the double bind on its head to improve its circulation. I proposed that double binds are an important ingredient in normal development and may be a valuable stimulus to creative versus crazy solutions to impasse (Wynne, 1976). Quite delightfully, Bateson described how he had come to exactly the same conclusions through his experiments in putting dolphins into double binds, a proceeding that led them to behave in an entirely novel, creative manner (Bateson, 1976).

Such observations have been part of a broad trend, both in family studies and in psychiatry more generally, to give increasing attention to the positive and healthy resources that exist side by side with dysfunction and symptoms. Since the early 1960s, Margaret Singer and I have emphasized in our research findings that the balance of input from all family members must be considered (e.g., Singer & Wynne, 1965). For example, if a parent is individually quite chaotic, it is important to consider whether the other parent is also disorganized, individually clear but passively collusive, or corrective and counterbalancing. And the active input of the offspring is obviously crucial. However, the results of longitudinal, developmental studies are still awaited to document empirically how child characteristics modify family life and, in turn, adult outcomes. Relatively invulnerable or stress-resistant children in dysfunctional settings have been observed clinically for many years, but only quite recently has study of their identifying characteristics begun.

The question of responsibility is also highly relevant to the evaluation of assets and resources. In our Rochester family studies, we are now creating scoring manuals for healthy communication as well as for communication deviance; preliminary indications are that these measures of family health are highly predictive of child functioning in the school setting. Therapeutically, attention to strengthening those family assets that are already present is efficacious in establishing an alliance even with seemingly very disorganized families. After all, there are both positive and negative components to any behavior. For example, emotional overinvolvement can be seen as including dedication and caring. Ordinarily, however, families become discouraged and doubtful that they have anything constructive to offer, and hospital and office practices that are exclusionary toward families only confirm their own negative view of themselves. Correctively, a family systems viewpoint includes attention to the social support network beyond the family and to the integration and linkage of family system and therapeutic team system.

The result, then, is a concept of shared or joint responsibility, evolving over time, with emphasis on what can be done positively by each participant – patient, family members, social network members, and treatment team members. If such an approach deals with manageable problems one at a time, then the taking of responsibility is a welcome opportunity, not a burden to be avoided. All too often, I fear, our treatment approaches of the past have followed the same sequence as those found in the beleaguered family: We are so impressed by distress and disability that we assume total responsibility for a while but, when this becomes impossibly burdensome, flipflop to total abdication of responsibility. This sequence has taken place historically, with the shift from placing schizophrenics in custodial institutions to dumping them, unsupported, into the community.

It is to be hoped that we are reaching a point where sophisticated biological hypotheses and psychosocial variables can be considered within a comprehensive framework. One unifying concept that was vigorously brought forward in the Second Rochester International Conference on Schizophrenia in 1976 is *attention* (Wynne, Cromwell, & Matthysse, 1978). This concept has both biological components and psychosocial ones, especially in the sharing of focuses of attention in communication (Wynne, 1968). Additionally, attention can be studied empirically and systematically, both cross-sectionally in time and developmentally.

Another key integrating concept is *vulnerability*. The distinction between vulnerable and symptomatic states has even been incorporated into *DSM*-III in the diagnostic category of Schizotypal Personality Disorder, basically characterizing those who have features that may underlie or lead to schizophrenia, but do not have the active florid symptoms. As I see it, there still needs to be a good deal of work done to clarify the notion of acquired vulnerability (Wynne, 1978). I would argue that if we think of vulnerability as merely genetic, we are going to misread the data and misunderstand the variations that are found in our research samples. This makes, to be sure, certain problems for a simple concept of specific etiology. But I am quite happy to shift to a developmental frame of reference in which "specificity" becomes a rather dubious notion. Perhaps the specific aspect of etiology should refer only to what Gottesman and Shields (1976) call endophenotypes. Most of the measures that look promising as potential endophenotypes actually are quite variable across groups and may also in themselves be polygenetic or even genetically heterogeneous. I am referring to such measures as platelet MAO levels, eye-tracking, and augmenting–reducing in cortical evoked responses. There is also the need to study acquired vulnerability from a biological standpoint, to consider how biological measures with a genetic component are modified during development, both during pregnancy and later.

I believe that it may be useful to amplify the concept of "intermediate" variables (Wynne et al., 1977). Not just "ultimate" origins but also the whole sequence of modifiers and potentiators needs investigation if, as seems likely, only a small fraction of those with genetic vulnerability eventually become symptomatically schizophrenic, and an even smaller percentage become chronically ill.

Such considerations point again to an educational task in which both researchers and therapists need to join with lay groups that have taken the initiative. This also returns us to the notion of shared responsibility, as we examine such concepts as vulnerability and the multidirectionality of impact in families and therapeutic systems. These matters now can be examined, I believe, within a more comprehensive conceptual and therapeutic framework.

References

Bateson, G. Double bind, 1969. In C. E. Sluzki & D. C. Ransom (Eds.), *Double bind: The foundation of the communicational approach to the family*. New York: Grune & Stratton, 1976.

Bateson, G., Jackson, D. D., Haley, J., & Weakland, J. Toward a theory of schizophrenia. *Behaviorial Science*, 1956, *1*, 251–264.

Berger, M. M. (Ed.). *Beyond the double bind*. New York: Brunner/Mazel, 1978.

Fromm-Reichmann, F. Notes on the development of treatment of schizophrenics by psychoanalytic psychotherapy. *Psychiatry*, 1948, *11*, 263–273.

Gottesman, L. L., & Shields, J. A critical review of recent adoption, twin, and family studies of schizophrenia: Behavioral genetics perspectives. *Schizophrenia Bulletins* 1976, *2*, 360–398.

Singer, M. T., & Wynne, L. C. Thought disorder and family relations of schizophrenics: III. Methodology using projective techniques. *Archives of General Psychiatry*, 1965, *12*, 187–200.

Sluzki, C. E., & Ransom, D. C. (Eds.). *Double bind: The foundation of the communicational approach to the family*. New York: Grune & Stratton, 1976.

Wynne, L. C. Methodologic and conceptual issues in the study of schizophrenics and their families. *Journal of Psychiatric Research*, 1968, *6*(Suppl.), 185–199.

Wynne, L. C. From symptoms to vulnerability and beyond: An overview. In L. C. Wynne, R. L. Cromwell, & S. Matthysse (Eds.), *The nature of schizophrenia: New approaches to research and treatment*. New York: Wiley, 1978.

Wynne, L. C., Cromwell, R. L., & Matthysse, S. (Eds.). *The nature of schizophrenia: New approaches to research and treatment*. New York: Wiley, 1978.

Wynne, L. C., Singer, M. T., Bartko, J. J., & Toohey, M. L. Schizophrenics and their families: Recent research on parental communication. In J. M. Tanner (Ed.), *Developments in psychiatric research*. London: Hodden & Stoughton, 1977.

13 A social competence model meets an early intervention program: description and evaluation of Cincinnati's Social Skills Development Program

Daniel S. Kirschenbaum, JoAnne L. Pedro-Carroll, and Joyce B. DeVoge

Psychologists are currently undertaking the most painful form of self-scrutiny. We are beginning to explore the nature of our own failures by examining the impact of our therapies over time. The methods of such analyses are also becoming increasingly sophisticated. Use of multimodal assessment criteria and sophisticated controls have slowly appeared in long-term follow-up studies in such areas as weight control (Wilson, 1978), smoking reduction (McFall, 1978), prevention of juvenile delinquency (Davidson & Seidman, 1974), and modification of behaviors of chronic mental patients (Anthony et al., 1972; Kazdin, 1977). Although definitive studies remain elusive, the evidence to date pertaining to therapeutic efficacy generally supports the conclusions reached by the founders of the community mental health movement more than 2 decades ago (Albee, 1959; Joint Commission on Mental Illness and Health, 1961). Traditional (and even nontraditional) tertiary or remedial therapeutic efforts offer generally inadequate help to inadequate numbers of people (see Eysenck, 1966; Garfield & Bergin, 1978; Levitt, 1971; Lorion, 1973; President's Commission on Mental Health, 1978, Rotter, 1973).

Rather than wallowing in the depressing implications of this failure in remedial therapies, clinicians and researchers have taken appropriate action. One of these steps involves studying the active ingredients in the maintenance of adaptive behavior change (e.g., Ashby & Wilson, 1977; Kirschenbaum & Karoly, 1977). Another research direction is investigation of childhood predictors of adult dysfunctioning, well illustrated by

Funding both for the SSDP project and for preparation of this chapter was provided in part by Community Development Fund #63090 (HUD) and EPSDT (HEW, #11-90468/01). Sincere thanks are also extended to Addy Kochanowski and Flora Golding. The work described was completed while Daniel S. Kirschenbaum was Research Director, Social Skills Development Program, Cincinnati Health Department. He is now at the Department of Psychology, University of Wisconsin, 1202 W. Johnson St., Madison, Wis. 53706.

several chapters in this book and by previous research (e.g., Cowen, Pederson, Babigian, Izzo, & Trost, 1973; Robins, 1966; Watt & Lubensky, 1976; Zax et al., 1968). Finally, at a greatly accelerated rate during the last several years, mental health professionals have used findings showing that early identification of children at "high risk" is possible – and even fairly simple (see Cowen, Door, Clarfield, Kreling, McWilliams, Pokracki, Pratt, Terrell, & Wilson, 1973; Kirschenbaum, Marsh, & DeVoge, 1977) – as the foundation to the development of a rich variety of preventively oriented early intervention programs (Cowen, Davidson & Gesten, 1980).

In this chapter we describe one of the largest and most thoroughly evaluated of these preventive programs, the Social Skills Development Program (SSDP) of Cincinnati, Ohio (cf. Cowen et al., 1980). SSDP is unique because it is the only large-scale inner-city program that incorporates a social competence model in its philosophy, intervention, consultation, and evaluation (see Kirschenbaum, 1979; Kirschenbaum et al., 1976; Kirschenbaum et al., 1979).[1] Another of SSDP's key features is its use, for the most part, of validated and published instruments for its evaluation research (cf. Kellam et al., 1975). Our description of SSDP includes a brief historical sketch, a rationale for the use of the social competence model, a presentation of SSDP's methods of operation, two illustrative case reports, and, finally, a summary of the first 3 years of evaluation studies that examine the efficacy of this approach.

Historical and financial perspectives

The historical roots of SSDP can be traced to a well-established secondary prevention program in Rochester, New York. Over a period of more than 20 years, Rochester's Primary Mental Health Project (PMHP) grew, with dedicated nurturance from Emory Cowen and his associates, from a training opportunity for psychology students to the national prototype for early intervention (see Cowen et al., 1975). PMHP is now coordinating services for approximately 11% of the primary grade population within 17 schools in the greater Rochester area. And as the National Training Center for the National Institute for Mental Health since 1972, PMHP has facilitated the development of more than 30 similar programs serving over 200 schools that house upward of 120,000 pupils (Cowen et al., 1980). Most recently, PMHP, via NIHM findings, has helped establish the first two Regional Training Centers for early intervention programs (SSDP became the Midwest Regional Training Center as of July 1978). Primary Mental

Health Program stalwarts provide assistance for such developmental efforts by means of nearly 150 published articles and books, annual national workshops, the sharing of evaluation instruments, and direct consultation.

After reading several articles by Emory Cowen and his co-workers, the first assistant commissioner of mental health for the City of Cincinnati Health Department, David Sanders, decided that Cincinnati would benefit from a PMHP of its own. He developed a program based upon the four major elements of the PMHP model: (a) the delivery of school-based services; (b) the use of systematic mass screening procedures for children in primary grades (K–3); (c) the implementation of new, supervisory/consultant, roles for mental health professionals; and (d) the use of paraprofessional staff as primary care-givers. Sanders proceeded to obtain grass-roots approvals for initial program implementation. That is, he asked the principal and PTA members of the school his children attended if they would be interested in having such a program in their school. When they eagerly agreed to house the pilot project, Sanders set up a bootstrap organization, with four Health Department staff members on a part-time basis. These staff members began providing intervention and consultation services to 20 "target" children and their teachers and parents in the 1973–1974 school year.

The informality of approvals and staffing greatly accelerated project development but proved problematic when expansion to other schools and legitimization of staffing was planned. Since that time, administrative approval within the Health Department has been firmly secured, and effective liaison has been established with the Cincinnati Public Schools through the school's enthusiastic associate director for psychological services, Michael Landwehr. The significant point here is that the program became operational in part because of the commitment of several imaginative people, without any special staff funding. The original SSDP, then called the School Mental Health Program, required only $200 to purchase equipment (e.g., punching bags, clay, games) to begin what is now a well-established program.

During the first full pilot year, 1973–1974, the school community clearly supported the School Mental Health Program services. The following year this initial support helped to secure additional dollars from Cincinnati general funds to expand the project to two additional schools. The efforts of a tireless supporter of mental health services, Addy Kochanowski, sparked significant growth during the 1974–1975 year. Kochanowski, the third author, and others secured a grant of more than $150,000 from locally controlled community development funds (Housing and Urban Development money). At this point the program ceased being a pilot project, as it expanded to four additional schools, making a total of seven, with support from its new program director and research director.

The School Mental Health Program evolved into the Social Skills Development Program during the 1975–1976 year. The program became a variation on the PMHP model through its emphasis on children's social competencies and the use of small structured groups as a primary means of enhancing these strengths. An elaborate evaluation research project was planned and implemented. Additional energies were directed toward obtaining financial security, refining staff selection and training strategies, and solidifying local and regional support.

The following sections describe the fruits of these labors first by elucidating the rationale and operations of the present (i.e., 1978) program model and then by examining its outcomes. Table 13.1 shows a summary of costs for the average SSDP school for the 1976–1977 school year.[1] These data present SSDP as an intensive, but relatively costly, service compared to other PMHP-like efforts (Cowen et al., 1980). However, the price tag, in terms of money and wasted human potential, of instructional and other forms of remedial care, balances against tens of thousands of dollars per year per child. Looked at in this context, SSDP and similar programs may well be one of the last remaining genuine bargains for consumers in this country (Dorr, 1972).

Rationale for the social competence approach to early intervention

Interpretation of the terms *social competence* and *social skills* varies widely (Anderson & Messick, 1974). In SSDP, we have used the following definition of social competence or skills: *those coordinated sets of behaviors that help people adapt effectively within the context of their social environments and that can be enhanced through experience.* Following Anderson and Messick, these skills include differentiation of feelings, interpersonal problem solving, social cognition, self-management, and self-esteem. A variety of studies have demonstrated that each of these social skills meets the most important and practical parts of our definition: They can be enhanced through experience and they help people adapt.

Differentiation of feelings and social cognition are skills that can be enhanced through training. Instruction, modeling, and contingency management have been shown to produce gains in empathy, differentiation of feelings, social cognition, or ability to recognize feelings in oneself and others (Chandler, 1973; Fry, 1966, 1969; Gottman, Gonso, & Rasmussen,

Table 13.1. *Input variables describing the average 1976–1977 SSDP school*

Cost = $43,000 (includes staff salaries plus fringe benefits, equipment expenses, and 1/7th of administrative costs, e.g., salaries of 3 program administrators, 2 secretaries, office rentals, travel)
Service staff = 1 MA mental health professional (full time), 1 paraprofessional (full time), 4 part-time students (8–20 hours/week)
No. of children screened for high-risk behaviors = 300
No. of children who received individual therapy = 6 (mean no. sessions = 30)
No. of children who received individual and group therapy = 2 (mean no. sessions = 30)
No. of children who received group therapy = 27 (mean no. sessions = 27)
No. of children who received indirect services (consultation with teachers and parents but no therapy) = 25
No. of teachers consulted = 18 (mean no. of consultations = 12)
No. of parents who received consultation = 40 (mean no. of consultations = 4)

1975; Seymour & Stokes, 1976; Shantz & Wilson, 1972; Staub, 1971; Stokes, Fowler, & Baer, 1977; Walker & Hops, 1973). Spivack and Shure (1974; Spivack, Platt, & Shure, 1976; Shure & Spivack, 1978) and others (e.g., Allen et al., 1976; Blechman & Olson, 1975; Gesten et al., 1978) have consistently demonstrated that such interpersonal problem-solving skills as alternative and means–end thinking can be improved in children and adults via structured feedback, specific game playing, and other techniques. Children's self-management skills can be increased through self-instruction (Finch et al., 1975; Kendall & Finch, 1976, 1978; Meichenbaum & Goodman, 1971), forced delay (Heider, 1971; Kagan, Pearson, & Welch, 1966), modeling (Debus, 1970; Denney, 1972; Robin, Schneider, & Dolnick, 1976), external contingency management (O'Leary & O'Leary, 1972), and self-regulated contingency management (e.g., Brownell et al., 1977; Drabman, Spitalnik, & O'Leary, 1973; Glynn, 1970; Humphrey, Karoly, & Kirschenbaum, 1978). In a similar vein, studies have demonstrated a variety of means of improving positive self-reactions or self-esteem and other important personal beliefs (Lefcourt, 1976).

Not only can these skills be improved by a variety of strategies, but studies that produce gains in such skills concurrently demonstrate how to assess children's social skills. In all of the previously cited studies on training in social skills, assessment devices were required to determine the effects of the training. There are, therefore, published tests to measure global social competencies (e.g., Butler, 1975; Gesten, 1976; Gottman et al., 1975; Pekarik et al., 1976), empathy (e.g., Borke, 1971; Urberg & Docherty, 1976), interpersonal problem solving (e.g., Shure & Spivack, 1972, 1974), self-esteem (e.g., Coopersmith, 1967), and related personal beliefs (Mischel & Zeiss, 1974; Nowicki & Duke, 1974; Nowicki & Strickland, 1973).

Methods to improve children's social skills exist, as do methods to assess social skill development. Most important, evidence supports the logical assertion that developing good social skills improves adjustment (for reviews, see Shantz, 1975; Spivack et al., 1976). Deficits in social skills – that is, social isolation and overly aggressive social behaviors – have serious consequences for children's later lives, and for their communities' well-being. Such deficits should not be ignored. Poor social skills generally predict who will appear on community-wide psychiatric registers (Cowen, Pederson, Babigian, Izzo, & Trost, 1973); who will receive bad conduct discharges from the armed forces (Roff, 1961); who will develop serious behavioral dysfunctioning, such as schizophrenia or manic depressive behavior in adulthood (Kohn & Clausen, 1955; Robins, 1966; Watt & Lubensky, 1976); who will attempt to commit suicide (Seiden, 1966; Stengel, 1971); and who will evidence a variety of maladjusted behaviors in adolescence (Roff, Sells, & Golden, 1972). These findings present a cogent argument for the proliferation of programs that "inoculate" or train children in social skills.

In SSDP, the impetus for actualizing a social competence model to replace the more traditional "mental health/illness" model was derived in part from the logic and evidence outlined in the last several paragraphs. Another factor leading to SSDP's use of a social competence model was our frustration with the popular connotations of the traditional model. For too many teachers, parents, and school staff members, selecting a child to participate in the School Mental Health Program implied that the child was not "mentally healthy." As long as this program title was used, staff time and energy was expended to change negative attitudes toward it. Furthermore, studies by Farina and his associates (Farina et al., 1978; Fisher & Farina, 1979) show that advocating a social learning model, compared to supporting more traditional medical models, leads to more active problem solving (see also Reppucci & Saunders, 1974; Saunders & Reppucci, 1978). Accordingly, we believe the program's transformation in name, philosophy, and methodology, from the original School Mental Health Program to the Social Skills Development Program, has facilitated active and optimistic collaboration among many significant adults, thereby improving the quality of the preventive intervention for many children.

Methods of operation

Staffing

The 1976–1977 SSDP staff were directed by three administrative supervisors who were all clinical psychologists: a PhD program director, a PhD research director, and an MA program coordinator. Each administrator conducted staff training programs and weekly or biweekly supervisory meetings at two or three schools. Each school team consisted of a full-time MA-level mental health professional team leader (e.g., MA clinical psychologist or special education teacher), a full-time paraprofessional (three had BAs in psychology or social work; four were community people who had experience with children), and three to five part-time students and/or volunteers.

All staff were selected through a series of interviews to identify those individuals who evidenced desirable "therapist" characteristics, such as warmth and empathy, in addition to a commitment to children and community service (see Cowen, Dorr, & Pokracki, 1972; Sandler, 1972). Among the service staff, 80% were women and 20% men; 55% were black and 45% white; the mean age was 31, with a range of 22–38.

Although much of the staff's training was acquired on the job, more than 50 hours of workshops and seminars were used to train students and paraprofessional staff. Other mechanisms of staff development included weekly or biweekly supervision sessions with the assigned administrative supervisor, biweekly team leader meetings, biweekly full staff meetings, monthly case conferences, and attendance at local, regional, and national meetings on such topics as PMHP, black mental health, parent training, and family therapy.

Facilities in the schools

The relationship between SSDP and the Cincinnati Public Schools has always been cooperative. In 1976–1977, on behalf of the City of Cincinnati's Health Department, SSDP provided mental health services; in turn, the Cincinnati public schools provided for each SSDP school a classroom; an office; an array of desks, blackboards, and chairs; and no charges for rent or utilities. Most important was their official blessing and encouragement, which promoted a collaborative relationship between school staff and SSDP staff.

The office sometimes served as an individual session or testing room. The group room consisted of five distinct areas, as illustrated in Figure 13.1: arts and crafts, family living, gross motor skills, group discussion,

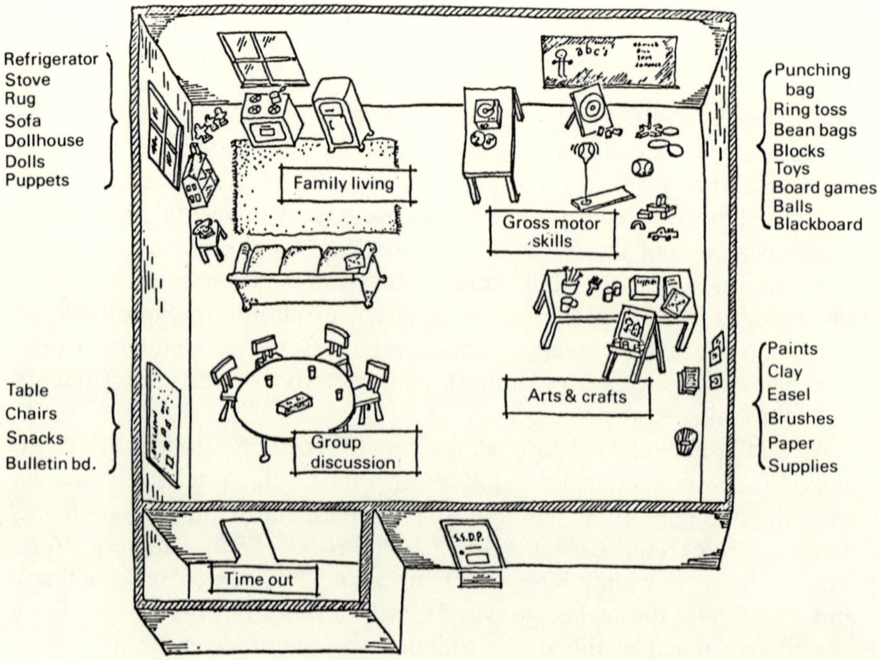

Figure 13.1. Social Skills Development Program's playroom (group counseling room).

and "time out." Each area contained appropriate materials, as shown, except that in some schools the time-out area was merely a designated part of the group room, rather than a separate enclosure. Dividing the large room into small areas seemed to maximize the likelihood that children would be able to communicate comfortably, and also tended to reduce the chances that they would be overstimulated.

Screening and assessment

A behaviorally oriented social competence model emphasizes specific goals. SSDP followed PMHP's lead in designing a mass screening and individual assessment system. That assessment was used to formulate highly specific behaviorally oriented goals for each selected target child. The assessment process selects the 15%–25% of the primary grade children in each school who evidence behaviors – including excessive acting out, extreme moodiness and withdrawal, and difficulties with learning – that predict adult dysfunctioning (see Cowen, Pederson, Babigian, Izzo, & Trost, 1973; Wood & Zabel, 1978).

In SSDP, the following 10-step process was developed to systematize and standardize mass screening and selection of target children across all SSDP schools:

1. *Gathering referrals*. SSDP teams conduct an orientation session for teachers and again for parents during the first few weeks of school. During these meetings the teams provide examples of the kinds of behaviors that show deficits in social skills (e.g., excessive withdrawal) and, conversely, the behaviors indicative of high levels of social competence. Referral forms are then distributed that ask for ratings of frequencies of key behaviors, using the AML developed by Cowen, Dorr, and associates (1973).[2] Pamphlets describing SSDP and listing appropriate phone numbers and school room numbers are given to parents and teachers, along with a request to use those phone numbers whenever they believe it is appropriate – to ask questions, to request help, and so on.

2. *Conducting mass screening interviews with teachers*. A full-time SSDP staff member interviews each primary grade teacher, using an interview schedule. First, the interviewer shares definitions of high and low social competence from the interview schedule:

Characteristics of Highly Competent Children: good student, gutsy (assertive), friendly, follows rules, tolerates frustration.

Characteristics of Less Competent Children: acts-out (is disruptive, restless), appears moody-withdrawn (immature, friendless, unhappy), has difficulty learning (doesn't complete work, trouble following directions).

Second, the interviewer asks the teacher to review his or her class list and identify and then rank order three to six highly competent children. This process allows the teacher to understand the changes SSDP hopes to achieve for children who initially appear less socially competent.

Third, the teacher identifies and then rank orders six or more children exhibiting deficits in social skills. Finally, the team member asks the teacher to identify children who have experienced significant life crises during the past year (Felner, Stolberg, & Cowen, 1975). Specifically, the teacher notes which children have experienced within the year the death of a close family member, divorce, hospitalization, or the birth of a new sibling.

3. *Obtaining classroom and free play observations*. All SSDP staff members become involved in observing children referred to them or identified by teachers as low in social competence. This process includes utilization of a recently developed observational system that requires observers to rate 28 aspects of a child's behavior in the classroom and in a free play situation (i.e., playground or lunchroom or classroom free play). This system affords data gathering about key behaviors within two social contexts. Preliminary analyses of the system's validity show that it dis-

criminated among three groups of children whom teachers rated differently in social competence, $F(2,294) = 2.87$, $p < .05$.

4. *Having teachers complete ratings of referred and low-competence children.* At this juncture, the team leader usually eliminates several children from consideration as target children on the basis of observations and discussions with school staff. Usually the children who are eliminated evidence considerable social skills but deficits in particular academic subjects. The remaining children are then rated by teachers on two other teacher rating forms. In SSDP, we have always found quite useful both a global social competency–oriented form (e.g., the Health Resources Inventory, or HRI [Gesten, 1976]), and a problem-oriented questionnaire (e.g., the AML [Cowen, Dorr, and associates, 1973]; the Classroom Activity Rating Scale, or CARS [Lorion, Cowen, & Caldwell, 1975]; see also Clarfield, 1974).

5. *Selecting target children.* After charting information obtained at this point (i.e., from referrals, mass screening teacher interviews, observations, and teacher ratings), SSDP teams, in consultation with their administrative supervisor, decide the total number of children to be seen in individual and/or group therapy in the forthcoming school year, and determine which of the children presently known to the teams should receive these services. Usually this process requires assigning a priority number to each child and thereby narrowing a pool of 70–90 children down to 50–60. This selection process does not form a group of children whose names are carved in stone. Designed in the selection process is a 10%–15% margin for early termination of some children and the flexibility to accept new referrals throughout the year. Years of experience in managing this program have taught that it is essential for the teams to feel free to accept new referrals and to terminate services before the end of the school year. This flexibility produces benefits for the children involved (i.e., it reduces unnecessary dependence for those ready for early termination), and it maintains SSDP's credibility in the eyes of the school staff (i.e., SSDP is seen as responsive to teachers' requests).

6. *Conducting child-specific teacher interviews.* After likely high-risk children have been identified, a second interview is conducted. Detailed questions are asked to obtain additional information about each child from the teacher's perspective. The staff use a "Structured Teacher Interview" schedule that includes:

1. Academic performance (e.g., What is the child's attitude toward work?)
2. Special skills, interests (e.g., What is the child's favorite activity?)
3. Peer relationships (e.g., Can the child ask or accept help from others?)
4. Physical health (e.g., Does the child have frequent bruises, cuts, sores?)

5. Classroom management (e.g., What is the child's response to instructions?)
6. Family information (e.g., What do you know about the child's family? Mention source of information.)

This interview can be a seminal influence in establishing collaborative working relationships with the individual teachers.

7. *Initial home visits.* A prerequisite to any child's participation in the program is a home visit. During the first home visit written parental consent is obtained. More than 98% of parents interviewed give their written consent. During this visit, the SSDP staff person assesses the home environment, describes the philosophy and goals of the program, and obtains information about the child's social and developmental history. This initial consultation is frequently instrumental in opening channels for dialogue – the foundation for later consultation. Parental cooperation and permission is one of the key assets presented to the school by a program like SSDP: SSDP can serve as an effective liaison between the school and the home, facilitating the development of a functional school community (see letters from parents in Kirschenbaum, 1977).

8. *Reviewing school records.* The parental consent form allows parents to give SSDP staff permission to review the child's cumulative school record confidentially. The staff reviews these records to determine in more detail the child's school history.

9. *Conducting individual child assessment interviews.* An SSDP staff member interviews each target child individually to assess the following areas: perceptual/motor skills; affective responses about him- or herself, peers, family, and school; range of affective responses; sensory preferences; favorite activities; daily activities; interpersonal problem solving; and several other aspects of childhood functioning.

10. *Establishing initial behavioral goals for each child.* Approximately 80% of the target children selected to participate in SSDP's program are assigned to groups. The remaining 20% receive individual or individual plus group intervention (for details on the intervention processes see Kirschenbaum et al., 1976; Kirschenbaum, 1979; Kirschenbaum et al., 1980; Kirschenbaum, Pedro, & DeVoge, 1977; in addition, illustrative cases reported later in this chapter present an outline of intervention strategies for two children). Children are assigned to individual sessions when their behaviors seem either too unusual or too primitive for them to function effectively in a small group (four to five children with two adults). Before the twice-weekly group sessions or following the first few group sessions, the SSDP team formulates specific behavioral goals for each child, selecting from among 85 specific goal statements, grouped in 10 broad goal

categories, listed in the SSDP *Handbook for Helping* (Kirschenbaum et al., 1976). After choosing the appropriate goals for a child, the team completes a Goals Information Sheet for that child. For example, Kirschenbaum et al. (1979) presented a sample Goals Information Sheet that included this entry: "To Improve Positive Self-Image: (a broad goal category) – increase Raymond's frequency of making positive statements about himself" (p. 262). This sheet is then distributed to principals, teachers, and parents (with an explanatory phone call or meeting) to promote communication and cooperation.

This assessment process is a long and difficult one, generally requiring 2–4 months to complete. We studied the effectiveness of an earlier version of this process, because we feared that we might have been wasting too much precious time. We obtained evidence that SSDP screening is effective (Kirschenbaum, Marsh, & DeVoge, 1977). Children referred to SSDP and children screened following the initial referrals were subsequently rated by teachers as extremely maladjusted; in fact, they were rated significantly less well adapted than children referred to Rochester's PMHP (p s $< .001$). Additional validation of the efficacy of the screening process was provided by team leaders at three SSDP schools. Following the screening process, but before they had access to the ratings made by teachers on the CARS, each of these team leaders predicted the teacher ratings for each referred target child. Their predictions did not differ significantly from the actual teacher ratings.

Although abbreviating the assessment process is a continual project in SSDP, careful assessment remains a high priority. This is consonant with assessment's recognized status as one of the crucial elements in effective therapy (see, e.g., Cone & Hawkins, 1977; Kanfer and Saslow, 1969; Karoly, 1977). As such it deserves a great deal of attention, coupled with sensitivity to such issues as the dangerous possibility of stigmatization (Rosenthal & Jacobson, 1968). In the assessment process just outlined, *no labels* are applied that could be harmful to children. Throughout assessment, emphasis is placed on the skills children possess and ideas about how to improve upon those skills. We consider this a child advocacy assessment system.

Illustrative cases

Perhaps the best way to breathe life into this description of SSDP's approach to assessment and direct intervention is to present examples of how it works. In this section we describe two cases, both involving young children who exhibited poor self-regulatory skills but who also evidenced cleverness and creativity.

"Janie"

During the 1975–1976 school year, SSDP staff at one of SSDP's most economically disadvantaged inner-city schools began working with Janie, a 6-year-old first grader. One of six children from an impoverished family, she showed evidence of physical abuse and neglect. She was referred by her classroom teacher, "Ms. Smith." Ms. Smith, during one of several teacher interviews early in the fall, appeared frustrated when describing Janie's disruptive effect on the entire class. The specific low-competence behaviors that she identified as targets for change were Janie's inattentiveness to directions, frequent meanderings around the room, and excessive attention seeking. Ms. Smith particularly disliked Janie's oft-heard shouts, "I gotta go pee!"

The initial referral and interviews with the teacher were followed by several observations of Janie's in-class and out-of-class behaviors. SSDP staff members noticed that Ms. Smith referred to Janie in very negative terms. She often called Janie names and used physical punishment in a futile attempt to modify Janie's behavior.

Home interviews revealed a similar pattern of chastisement for Janie in a very different setting. After many home visits, Janie's parents slowly began acknowledging her role as the family scapegoat. Even the initial visit provided evidence of the kind of message consistently being communicated to Janie: "You are worthless and troublesome."

Inspection of Janie's cumulative record revealed a report from a school psychologist during her kindergarten year. Her excessive activity level and deficit of quiet on-task behavior were already apparent at that point. Although her performance on a Slosson IQ test and Bender-Gestalt were in the low average range, the school psychologist noted that "her concentration is far below average – she looks at visual stimuli very quickly and draws conclusions too quickly to maintain control." Reports of physical exams showed her to be in good health.

After the first of Janie's biweekly group sessions began in November 1975, behavioral goals were formulated:

1. To improve positive self-image: to decrease frequency of negative self-statements; increase frequency of positive self-statements.
2. To improve self-controls: to increase frequency of quiet on-task behaviors in class and in group; to reduce frequency of meanderings around the classroom and around the group room.

During the first group sessions, the staff recognized a consistent behavior pattern. Janie denigrated herself as inadequate. She was certain that she would fail at any new attempt and therefore was very reluctant to try new games or exercises.

The staff also recognized many strengths in Janie's behavioral repertoire. She showed cooperative, affectionate, and helpful behaviors quite often. Group leaders reinforced these behaviors and encouraged her to try new experiences (e.g., new games, communication exercises). She was, to her surprise, rather successful in her new endeavors. With continual practice, she began replacing her usual "I can't" statements with positive "I" statements. She also acquired an important role in the group as a "friendly helper" – a significant and most welcome departure from her role in the classroom and at home as a scapegoat.

Unfortunately, the process observed in the group did not generalize to the classroom. Ms. Smith remained unconvinced that Janie's behavior was modifiable in the classroom and repeated her desire to have Janie removed from class as frequently as possible.

The SSDP team leader then presented Ms. Smith with a clear summary of the frequency of 11 categories of Janie's task-relevant, task-irrelevant, and prosocial behaviors (see Kirschenbaum, 1978; Kirschenbaum, Steffen, & D'Orta, 1978). Janie exhibited a mean frequency of 55.67% disruptive behavior across 6 time-sampled 10-minute observation periods. This level of disruptiveness was considerably higher than the 35% mean level recorded for five other students in Janie's class (three of whom were SSDP target children). The team leader at Ms. Smith's school was pleasantly surprised to discover that Ms. Smith was reassured by the data indicating that her own assessment seemed accurate. After reviewing the observational data, Ms. Smith was ready to accept the team leader's classroom-management suggestions. These suggestions included having the teacher provide material and social rewards contingent upon Janie's exhibiting gradual improvements in task-relevant and prosocial behaviors (see Homme, 1970; Kirschenbaum & Pedro-Carroll, 1979).

Figure 13.2 shows the dramatic change in Janie's behavior that followed this intervention. In addition, Ms. Smith developed a distinctly positive and even caring attitude toward her. In fact, the day after beginning her change strategy, Ms. Smith bought Janie a much-needed new pair of shoes! She was pleased to notice a sharp decline in Janie's disruptiveness in the classroom, hallmarked by a virtual cessation of requests to "go pee." The change in Janie's classroom behavior was also accompanied by continued improvements in positive self-statements in the group.

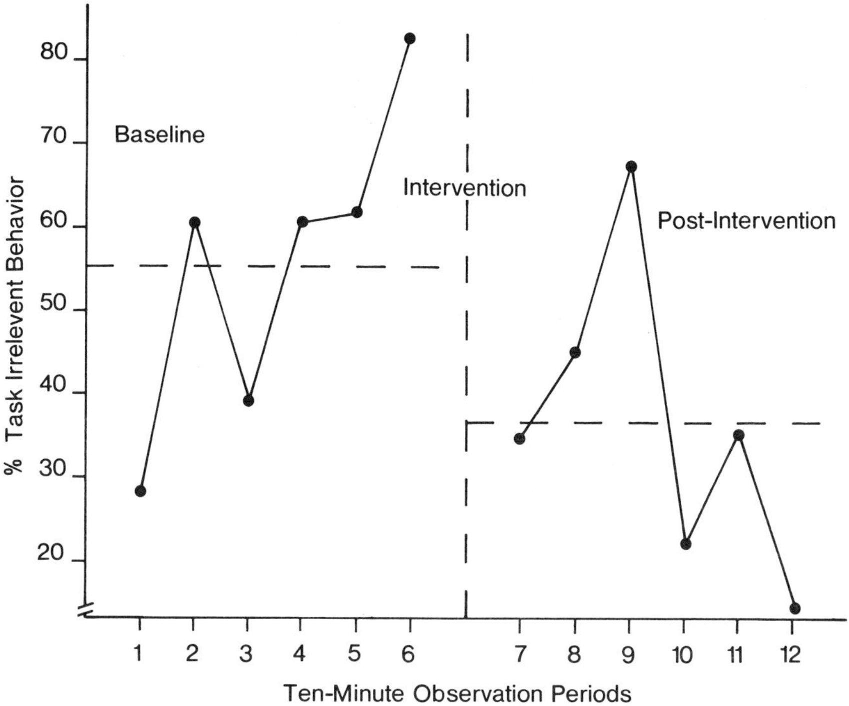

Figure 13.2. Janie's percentage of task-irrelevant behaviors during baseline and postintervention assessments.

"Joey"

During the 1977–1978 school year, SSDP staff at another school, one similar in poverty level, worked with a kindergarten 5-year-old named Joey. The assessment system described earlier yielded a very consistent behavior pattern, perhaps the most disruptive and dramatically dysfunctional of any noted in SSDP's history.

Nearly everyone around Joey – teachers, parent, school staff, and day care center staff – referred to him as a "monster." His routine *daily* activities consisted of attacking other children, attacking teachers, kicking, screaming, biting, pinching, growling, tearing up nearly every other child's work, and lying on his back and sliding around the room. Data gathered in a classroom observation corroborated Joey's excessive acting-out behaviors. Not surprisingly, in the self-portrait drawn by Joey during the child assessment interview, he portrayed himself as a Dracula-like

Figure 13.3. Joey's preintervention self-portrait.

monster and labeled the picture accordingly (Figure 13.3). It also became evident during this interview that Joey had many fears and anxieties, mostly relating to interacting with other people. He completed the phrase "I would really like . . ." with the words "to be left alone."

A highly skilled team leader[3] worked with Joey in individual sessions (two to seven times per week) for 6 months after developing the following goals:

to increase the frequency of Joey's making realistic positive statements about himself;

to increase the frequency of Joey's ability to accurately express how situations affect other children;

to do classwork and play cooperatively for longer periods of time with decreased external reinforcement;

to decrease the frequency of Joey's aggressive acting-out, fighting, screaming, throwing things.

In designing an approach to assist Joey, the team leader relied heavily on information accumulated about Joey's strengths. He was an attractive, very bright child, full of energy, very likable ("a real character"), and he loved to read. The team leader consulted with Joey's classroom teacher and his day care center teachers, who were eager to try almost anything to help this appealing child.

In both the classroom and the day care center, it was found that the teachers were willing to establish a special "reward corner." In this corner children spent time alone doing things of interest to them. The contingency was that the children had to earn the privilege of spending time there. For Joey, this earning process included the use of a fairly elaborate token economy. Joey earned tokens (smiling faces) by working at his school work for gradually increased durations, starting from 1 minute and getting to 30 minutes after several months. Joey also earned tokens during individual sessions. In these sessions Joey learned very basic communication skills: to maintain eye contact while talking, to regulate his voice more effectively, and to express himself more fully. He received tokens, exchangeable for quiet reading time in class, and he earned the right to play his favorite games with the team leader in the SSDP room.

The success of this token system led to the development of other structured classroom-management procedures. For example, the day care center staff found that all the children loved back rubs with talcum powder. They used this potent reinforcer during nap time. The child who remained most quiet got the longest back rub. Because all of the children tried to be the quietest one (including Joey), they too earned back rubs. Nap time became a quiet, peaceful rest period for the first time all year after the teachers instituted this structured approach.

Information obtained at the end of the school year suggests that direct intervention and consultation led to some important gains for Joey (and for his teachers). One teacher reported that he no longer destroyed other children's work, and he finished work that he would not have attempted at the beginning of the year. She also related a marked decrease in his acting-out behavior: "It is greatly reduced from constant to once or twice a day. . . . He used to have wide mood swings but is now generally a happy child." If you compare the self-portrait completed by Joey at the end of the school year (Figure 13.4) with the one he drew earlier (Figure 13.3), you will find additional (albeit *very* anectodal) support for the teacher's claims of improvement.

Evaluation studies

As thought-provoking and heartening as illustrative cases can be, they should not serve as evaluative instruments. Uncontrolled case studies highlight techniques employed and a philosophical approach to helping. They do not demonstrate efficacy because they do not control for the many extraneous factors that influence outcomes of intervention. In SSDP during the past several years we have conducted a variety of evaluation studies to allow us to scrutinize the effects of our intervention more closely than is possible with a case-by-case analysis.

Before describing SSDP's evaluation findings to date, it is important to emphasize a cautionary note. As Cowen (1978) warned, communities' "extraordinary complexity, omnipresent flux, action-service orientation, and susceptibility to day-to-day pressures, present real and formidable barriers to Mr. Clean program evaluation studies" (p. 803). These very real factors mitigating against evaluation research all played a role in SSDP's research program over the years. They contributed to our use of both nonexperimental and experimental designs, and they limited the scope of some of our investigations. Yet, through it all, data emerged. The weight of the evidence yields a favorable gestalt, albeit far from perfectly consistent or overwhelmingly positive.

Nonexperimental studies

We conducted a nonexperimental investigation of program effectiveness "(a) to provide additional evidence of SSDP's effectiveness or worth to local (e.g., City Council; Board of Health) and national (e.g., HUD; HEW) funding personnel, and (b) to improve program functioning" (Kirschenbaum et al., 1979). These goals reveal that our intention with this evaluation modality was *not* to demonstrate that SSDP facilitated social competence relative to appropriate control or comparison groups or comparative methods. Rather, we used a simpler level of analysis to show

Figure 13.4. Joey's postintervention self-portrait.

that people who worked as SSDP staff members and teachers who worked with those staff members valued the program. We have found through our own experience and the experience of others that funding agents and the population at large respond favorably to the opinions of people who know a program well (Meyers, 1975). These responses often lead to continued program funding; secondarily, this level of analysis provides suggestions about the efficacy of a program and useful inputs about how to improve program functioning.

SSDP staff ratings. In June 1977, 27 staff members rated each child with whom they had worked (N = 223). Most of the children were rated by 2 staff members (independently) because most children were seen in groups led by 2 staff members. Using a slightly modified version of the Child Behavior Change Scale (Dorr & Cowen, 1973), the staff compared the way the children seemed at the end of the year with the way they seemed at the beginning of the year. They used Likert ratings from 1 to 5 (from "considerably less often" to "considerably more often") to rate children's behaviors (a rating of 3 indicated "no change"). Items included (a) eight "positive" adjectives (e.g., calm, expressive), (b) eight "negative" adjectives (e.g., angry, frightened), and (c) three global items (behavioral, educational, and overall change, rated from 1 = very much worse to 7 = very much improved; 4 = no change).

There was substantial agreement in ratings of 70 children whose pairs of ratings were randomly selected for comparison across raters, $r = .64$. Average correlations within the seven school teams showed considerable agreement within each SSDP team about the changes noted in children. The range in correlations within school teams was from $r = .52$ to $r = .70$.

Relative to the appropriate no-change standard, SSDP staff rated children as significantly and favorably changed on all 19 dimensions (all ps $< .0005$, one-tailed t tests). The staff also indicated that the children changed more in the eight ratings of positive characteristics than in the eight ratings of negative characteristics, $t(7) = 4.97$, $p < .005$.

Although these findings are not very surprising, they are remarkably consistent relative to the two previous evaluative uses of this Child Behavior Change Scale (Dorr & Cowen, 1973; Durlak, 1977). The present ratings appear more consistent and more dramatically positive than those in the previous studies. Also, although previous investigations did not examine staff agreement on these kinds of ratings, the present results document an adequate level of consensual validation among raters. The staff's more favorable ratings on the positive adjectives could testify to their increased sensitivity or bias toward more positive characteristics, or toward social competence rather than problem-oriented characteristics, in accord with SSDP's operational philosophy.

Certainly these results cannot stand alone as evidence of SSDP's effectiveness. Yet they do show that the people conducting the intervention view it as leading to substantial gains for many children. If their ratings were not favorable, there would be some cause for consternation about the efficacy of the program.

Teachers' overall evaluations. At the end of the 1977 school year, 93% of the 76 teachers who received SSDP consultation completed a brief, anonymous questionnaire concerning the effectiveness of SSDP's direct intervention and consultation services. The questionnaire requested ratings and comments about teachers' impressions of SSDP's effects on children's classroom behavior, expression of feelings, and academic skills, as well as effects of SSDP consultation on the teacher's own understanding of children, classroom management, and feelings of emotional support. The final item asked teachers to list aspects of SSDP that should be either kept the same or changed.

Table 13.2 summarizes the teachers' generally very supportive ratings and comments. None of the 420 ratings offered by the 71 teachers were in the category "more harmful than helpful." Over 92% were in the "somewhat helpful" to "very helpful" range. The most favorable ratings and comments pertained to overall impressions of SSDP and to the emotional support provided by SSDP consultation. Changes in children's academic skills and changes in teachers' classroom management skills received the least favorable reactions. Teachers also commented that they would like most aspects of SSDP kept the same and that they would like more feedback about SSDP's specific goals and methods.

Specific examples of teachers' comments showed that teachers at every SSDP school viewed the program as very important in one way or another. For example:

> It was successful with 80% of the children in my class who benefited either from therapy or consultation. The consultations were about the only thing that got me through the year.
>
> [The SSDP staff at my school] are a great help when you get down. They are terrific listeners. They really stress positive points, never condemn. They give constructive criticism.

Ratings and comments like these were indeed gratifying. Not only did they serve as a morale booster to SSDP staff but they led to very positive comments from funding agents and also sparked a modification in SSDP's methods of operation. These comments, however, supply only slightly more rigorous evidence of the efficacy of SSDP than do the staff ratings. They show that people who work closely with SSDP indicate, in response to a questionnaire, that it is helpful. Even the extreme consistency of the

Table 13.2. *Teachers' overall evaluation ratings of the Social Skills Development Program, 1976–1977*

Item	No. of responses	Average rating[a]	Most frequent comments (no. of teachers commenting)
1. Overall, what is your reaction to this year's Social Skills Program (SSP?)	70	4.06	1. saw improvement in children (11) 2. due to strike/weather, children did not have enough time in program (4)
2. Did SSP help some children from your class behave more cooperatively and appropriately in class?	68	3.74	1. saw improvement in children (5) 2. saw improvement in children's behavior and cooperation (5)
3. Did SSP help some children from your class become better able to express their feelings?	66	3.61	1. saw positive changes in children (7) 2. particularly helpful for quiet children (4)
4. As a result of SSP, did some children from your class improve their academic skills?	58	3.24	1. along with self-concept and behavior, academics improved (5) 2. attentiveness improved (3) 3. unsure if improvement due to SSDP or other sources (3)
5a. Did SSP consultation with you help you to understand children better?	53	3.72	1. helped me to understand children better (4) 2. emotional support very helpful (2)
5b. Did SSP consultation with you help you manage the behavior of your class more effectively?	48	3.25	
5c. Did SSP consultation with you help you to feel more emotionally supported in what you do?	57	3.86	
6. List the aspects of the Social Skills Program you would like to see: (a) kept the same and (b) changed.	60		*Kept the same* 1. keep everything the same (14) 2. many small groups (6) *Changed* 1. see more children (9) 2. more feedback to teachers (6)

[a] Rating scale: 5, very helpful; 4, quite helpful; 3, somewhat helpful; 2, not at all helpful; 1, more harmful than helpful; NA, not applicable.
Reprinted with permission from D. S. Kirschenbaum, R. G. Klei, J. E. Brown III, & J. B. DeVoge. A non-experimental, but useful, evaluation of a therapy/consultation early intervention program, in G. Landsberg, W. Neigher, R. Hammer, C. Windle, & R. Woy (Eds.), *Evaluation in practice: A sourcebook of program evaluation studies from mental health care systems in the United States* (Washington, D.C.: U.S. Government Printing Office, 1979).

teacher's favorable ratings and comments does not alter the very real possibility of a Hawthorne effect: Any change, in inner-city school systems especially, could produce some benefits. In addition, the teachers could easily be responding to obvious demand characteristics. Despite the many built-in methodological flaws of this study, it does show that teachers did not rate the program negatively. These nonnegative ratings provide additional "soft" evidence suggesting that SSDP provided useful services.

Experimental studies

To afford a more rigorous analysis of the effects of SSDP, several experimental studies were conducted. These studies examined the impact of SSDP on the lives of hundreds of children over 1 year (for more details see Kirschenbaum, 1979; Kirschenbaum et al., 1980). They do not provide evidence of the value of SSDP's social skills "inoculation" as a preventive approach in the long run: We believe it is necessary to show that the approach has some measurable value over a relatively short period of time, and then to take steps to maximize this impact, before undertaking costly analysis of program effects over a period of several years.

Teachers' ratings of children's behaviors. Between November 1975 and February 1976, and then again between May and June 1976, teachers completed pre- and postintervention ratings, respectively, on target and control children. They used two previously validated teacher rating forms, Gesten's (1976) Health Resources Inventory (HRI) and the Classroom Activity Rating Scale (CARS) developed by Lorion and his colleagues (1975). The HRI is a 54-item social competency–oriented 5-point Likert rating form that yields five factor scores (Good Student, Gutsy, Peer Sociability, Rule Following, and Frustration Tolerance) and an Overall Competency summary score. The CARS consists of 41 items, also rated on 5-point Likert scales, that describe problem behaviors within three factors (Acting-Out, Moody-Withdrawn, and Learning Difficulty), in addition to an overall maladjustment summary score.

Complete pre- and postintervention ratings were available on 338 children, 280 target children and 58 controls. The target children at each SSDP school formed three different groups: Direct Intervention I, Direct Intervention II, and Consultation. Direct Intervention I children were those 10–20 children selected by SSDP staff as definitely in need of both direct intervention and consultation services. The remainder of the target children at each school were randomly assigned to either Direct Intervention

II, receiving both direct intervention and consultation services, or to Consultation, receiving only consultation, no direct intervention services. The control children were those children selected by teachers as potential target children at two schools that were demographically similar.

Comparisons of the four groups (Direct Intervention I, Direct Intervention II, Consultation, Control) with respect to sex, age, and grade revealed no significant differences. Overall, 58.5% were boys and 41.5% girls; the mean age was 7.35 years (SD = 1.3); the modal grade was second. Although socioeconomic comparisons showed that all nine school communities were equivalent and very low in income level, with a 1975 median family income of $8,200, there were more Appalachian white children and fewer black children in the SSDP groups than in the control group. SSDP groups were 58.1% black and 41.9% white, whereas the control group was 80.28% black and 19.72% white, χ^2 (3) = 18.13, $p <$ .001. Thus race was employed as a covariate in analyses involving this control group.

Table 13.3 presents the major significant results obtained from this study. With race and preintervention ratings as covariates, teachers rated children in both SSDP-Direct Intervention and Consultation groups as significantly improved over Controls in social competence. In addition, children who functioned more effectively prior to SSDP intervention, those in Direct Intervention II and Consultation, benefited more than their less competent peers (Direct Intervention I) on several dimensions of social competence, *p*s < .01. No group differences emerged in the analyses of the problem-oriented CARS.[4]

These findings provide additional evidence for the efficacy of SSDP interventions. Improvements relative to controls indicate that both direct-services and consultation may be active change agents. Of course, a Hawthorne effect cannot be eliminated as a possible artifact in this study, because Control children were taken from non-SSDP schools. In addition, the fact that Direct Intervention children improved only to the same degree as Consultation children suggests that direct intervention may be less potent than originally expected. Additional studies, described shortly, involving school record data, observers' frequency counts of classroom behaviors, and tests of social skills, provide a more refined comparison of direct intervention and consultation services.

Teachers' ratings on the problem-oriented CARS are another stimulus for further analysis of the impact of SSDP interventions. Perhaps the teachers were unusually aware of children's strengths because of SSDP's emphasis on the importance of that kind of positive viewpoint. Thus the CARS may have lost its sensitivity for this population of teachers. Evi-

Table 13.3. *Summary of analyses of covariance* F *ratios on teachers' ratings with preintervention ratings and race as covariates*

		Health Resources Inventory						Classroom Activity Rating Scale			
Source of variance	*df*	Good Student	Gutsy	Peer Sociability	Rule Following	Frustration Tolerance	Overall Competence (HRI SUM)	Acting-Out	Moody-Withdrawn	Learning Difficulty	Overall Problems (CARS SUM)
Group (G)	3	4.84**	4.34**	3.26*	2.41	1.62	4.46**	1.50	1.89	1.91	.64
Sex (S)	1	1.24	.37	.48	6.26*	3.59	1.61	15.60***	.04	.21	3.43
Age (A)	2	.39	.48	.12	.14	1.08	.57	.17	1.01	2.07	.94
G × S	3	.46	2.12	.56	1.04	.18	.95	.61	.56	.31	.15
G × A	6	1.17	.32	.62	.86	.19	.66	1.16	.42	2.02	.88
S × A	2	.78	.51	.55	.73	.92	.86	2.00	5.44**	.11	2.45
G × S × A	6	.18	.87	1.10	.85	.49	.62	1.70	.50	1.65	.78
Error = 311											

* $p < .05$. ** $p < .01$. *** $p < .001$.

Reprinted with permission from D. S. Kirschenbaum. Social competence intervention and evaluation in the inner city: Cincinnati's Social Skills Development Program, *Journal of Consulting and Clinical Psychology*, 1979, *47*, 778–780. © American Psychological Association.

dence obtained in the study using observers in the classrooms, described later on, supports this explanation.

Data available from school records. Because parental permission was required for inspection of school records, data were not available from Control children's cumulative records. Thus analysis of school records afforded comparison of Direct Intervention and Consultation components only. Differences between SSDP groups were examined on measures of lateness, absenteeism, grades, and standardized achievement-test performance.

Analyses of covariance showed that the groups did not differ on lateness or absenteeism. Whereas all groups improved in grades from the fall to the spring quarters, children in Consultation improved their grades more than children in either Direct Intervention I or Direct Intervention II, $F(2,210) = 4.42$, $p < .04$.

In view of previous studies showing at least moderate relationships between adjustment and grades (e.g., Bower, 1960; Stringer, 1959), the Consultation group's relative improvement in grades made consultation appear more cost-effective than direct intervention. This conclusion must be qualified slightly by one contrary trend in math achievement-test results (see Kirschenbaum et al., 1980). A more detailed comparison is provided by the results of the studies reported next, using behavioral observation data and social skills tests.

Observers' frequency counts of classroom behaviors. In one kindergarten, two first-grade, and two second-grade classrooms, we assessed the overt classroom behaviors of 22 children, pre- and postintervention. Two Intervention, 2 Consultation, and 2 randomly selected Comparison children were originally chosen for participation from the five classes. For various reasons, such as children moving, 8 of the original 30 children were eliminated, leaving children in the following groupings: 8 in Direct-Intervention, 7 in Consultation, and 7 in the Comparison condition.

We trained observers to assess these children's classroom behaviors using the Social Competence Classroom Behavioral Observation System (Kirschenbaum, 1978; Kirschenbaum et al., 1978). This study consists of five task-irrelevant behaviors (Physical Aggression, Disturbing Others, Gross Motor, Vocalization, and Inappropriate Quiet), three task-relevant behaviors (Appropriate Solitary, Peer Cooperation, and Teacher Cooperation), and three prosocial behaviors (Affection, Assertion, Smiling/Laughing). Two pairs of observers assigned to each of the five classrooms reliably observed children's behaviors with 92% agreement using the most stringent reliability assessment. These observational data correlated significantly and in expected directions with teachers' HRI ratings but not with their CARS ratings.[5]

The two significant findings pertaining to group assignment concerned the Teacher Cooperation and Appropriate Solitary behavioral categories. Direct Intervention children improved their cooperative interactions with teachers (by 128%), whereas Consultation and Comparison groups decreased the frequencies of their cooperative interactions, Group × Time $F(2, 19) = 5.04, p < .02$. On the other hand, Comparison children improved their Appropriate Solitary behaviors slightly but significantly (7%); they were, however, the only group to increase the frequency of this type of quiet academic behavior, Group × Time $F(2,19) = 3.65, p < .05$. Consultation children decreased their frequency of Appropriate Solitary behaviors (−13%) significantly more than did Direct Intervention children (−6%) (Newman-Kuels, $ps < .05$).

These data suggest that greater benefits accrued to children in skills training than to those in consultation. The small sample size limits external validity. However, we can cautiously assert that improvements in cooperative interactions with teachers and lesser decrements in quiet academic work favoring Direct Intervention children over Consultation children are not incidental or meaningless differences. The significant correlations between teacher ratings and this observational system lend additional credence to this statement.

The lack of correlations between CARS ratings and observed behaviors supports our earlier guess about teachers' CARS ratings. We posited that one reason teachers did not rate SSDP children as improved in problem behaviors was that these teachers may have learned to think in terms of competencies rather than in terms of problems. The fact that the validity of the CARS has been demonstrated repeatedly (Clarfield, 1974; Durlak, 1977; Jason & Ferone, 1978; Lorion et al., 1975) gives additional support to this interpretation.

Tests of social skills. Further comparison of direct intervention and consultation services is possible by examining the results of our study of children's social skills (Kirschenbaum et al., 1980). We tested a sample of Direct Intervention II children and a sample of Consultation children in the following areas: empathy, interpersonal problem solving, and internal–external locus of control. As described earlier in this chapter, empathy and interpersonal problem solving are examples of key social skills (cf. Shantz, 1975; Spivack, et al., 1976). Internal–external local of control is a personal belief or generalized expectancy of importance in social intercourse (see Lefcourt, 1976; Nowicki & Strickland, 1973). We expected that direct intervention would lead to greater gains in these social skills than consultation. The operational translation of this hypothesis was that direct intervention (relative to consultation) should lead to improved empathy scores, improved interpersonal problem-solving scores, and greater internality in locus of control (cf. Gilbert, 1976; Joe, 1971).

A Solomon four-group design afforded examination of interactions between testing itself and our experimental manipulations (Campbell & Stanley, 1963). Accordingly, we randomly assigned half of the Direct Intervention II participants and half of the Consultation participants in this study to receive both pre- and posttesting. The other halves of each experimental group received only posttesting. With posttest scores as dependent variables, this becomes a 2 Group (Direct Intervention II vs. Consultation) × 2 Testing (pre- and posttested vs. posttested only) between-subjects factorial design. If Direct Intervention II leads to the predicted gains, relative to Consultation, main effects for Group should emerge unqualified by Testing × Group interactions.

The results of this study included significant differences between Direct Intervention II and Consultation on the measures of empathy and internal–external locus of control. Children in Direct Intervention II improved more than their peers in Consultation on their ability to correctly identify faces depicting various emotions (Borke's Empathy Test, 1971), $F(1, 91) = 4.03$, $p < .05$. This finding was not qualified by a Group × Testing interaction.

Children in Direct Intervention II, contrary to expectations, became more external in locus of control on the Nowicki–Duke Test (1974) than Consultation children, $F(1, 91) = 5.00$, $p < .05$. This result was also unqualified by a Group × Testing interaction. However, additional findings involving this measure suggest that an external locus of control in this population may be a more adaptive generalized expectancy than originally anticipated. First, older children (mean age = 8.51 years) produced significantly more external scores than younger children (mean age = 6.31 years), $F(1, 91) = 6.00$, $p < .05$. Second, examination of correlations between I–E (internal–external) scores and all other indexes of adjustment revealed a surprisingly consistent pattern positively associating externality with adjustment. Externality correlated positively with age, empathy scores, teacher ratings on the HRI Good Student factor, and report card grades (all *p*s < .06, two-tailed). Internality was not significantly associated with any of the indexes of adjustment.

These tests of social skills supplied additional information allowing comparison of direct intervention with consultation. Recall that teachers' ratings of children's behaviors did not differentiate these treatment modalities; report card grades favored consultation; a nearly significant trend in a standardized math test favored direct intervention; and behavioral observation data showed some benefits accrued to direct intervention children. In the social skills tests, direct intervention improved empathy scores and increased externality.

Previous studies showing consistent relationships between empathy or role perspective taking and a variety of indexes of adjustment (Shantz, 1975) suggest that improvements in empathy may serve the direct intervention children well in their social interactions. Increased externality may be the kind of generalized expectancy that is most adaptive for these young children. Previous evidence provides at least tangential support for this post hoc analysis of the I–E finding. The relationship between I–E and age may be curvilinear, with very young children normatively increasing in externality until they reach about 8 or 9 years of age (cf. Nowicki & Duke, 1974; Nowicki & Strickland, 1973; Phares, 1973). It may have been important for the primary graders in the present study to learn to expect others to influence them. Perhaps, for maladapting young children especially, expecting others' influence to be very important leads to improved responsiveness to adults and to related improvements in self-perceptions (cf. Tolor, Tolor, & Blumin, 1977). Further studies are needed to clarify the relationship between I–E and adjustment, particularly for young children (Lefcourt, 1976). However, the present speculations seem parsimonious and again show differential intervention effects, generally favoring direct intervention.

Conclusions

In this chapter we presented a description of SSDP's approach to early intervention (as of 1978) and a summary of the evaluation studies conducted during those "toddler" years. The foundations for this approach are firmly entrenched both in prior work on early intervention and in research on the development of children's social skills. The evidence concerning the efficacy of this synthesis of early intervention strategies and a social competence model warrants continued efforts of this kind.

One does not need an empirical microscope to detect beneficial changes in the short run owing to SSDP direct intervention and consultation. Both nonexperimental and experimental analyses show some important changes justifiably attributed to major areas of program functioning (e.g., reactions and ratings by teachers; changes in observed behaviors and in social skills). Conversely, more neutral findings also appear in several of these analyses. Teachers did not report changes in problem behaviors, nor did they differentiate between directly served and consultation children in their ratings. Children who received direct intervention did not improve in some areas of social skills (e.g., interpersonal problem solving) compared to consultation children. Neither direct intervention nor consultation led to improvements in such important behaviors as "Appropriate Solitary" and "Peer Cooperation."

Such a mixture of findings suggests at least two things. First, methodologically, it is vitally important for large-scale intervention programs to employ a multimodal assessment strategy, preferably using published assessment devices. Without such a strategy in the present work, for example, we would have had much less data to assist us in comparing direct intervention and consultation effects. Also, the use of published assessment devices facilitates comparison across programs (e.g., Durlak, 1977; Kirschenbaum, Marsh, & DeVoge, 1977) and future replications.

Second, the less than perfectly consistent results suggest that the SSDP direct intervention is less than perfect. We believe that the program is a good one, but recognize its flaws. Programs like SSDP typically produce greatest gains for children who demonstrate a moderate level of social skillfulness prior to intervention (Durlak, 1980; Goodman, 1972; Lorion, Caldwell, & Cowen, 1976; Lorion, Cowen, & Caldwell, 1974). Some of the more relationship-based therapeutic interventions may need to become more behavioral in focus. The work of Fo and O'Donnell (1974), Patterson (1974), Durlak (1977, 1980), and Jason and Ferone (1978) is instructive in this regard. These investigators showed that intensive behaviorally oriented interventions produced improvements even with children evidencing rather extreme deficits in social and academic skills (see also Humphrey et al., 1978).

The "new frontier" in early intervention programs should build on these findings, with further analyses of the political and environmental milieu of early intervention programs (Allen et al., 1976; Moos, 1976; Saunders & Reppucci, 1978). Such integrative efforts should lead to truly effective and powerfully humanistic social skills "inoculations."

Notes

1 During the 1977–1978 school year three additional sources of money were obtained to expand the quality of services and to cover increasing costs. For the purpose of describing staffing, service, and cost variables, data from the 1976–1977 year are used. Evaluation data for the 1977–1978 year were not complete at this writing.

2 The title AML is not an acronym or abbreviation. If it were an acronym, the questionnaire might have been called "The Acting-out, Moody-withdrawn, and Learning Problem Scale."

3 The authors greatly appreciate the cooperation of Joey's team leader (Rita Leytze) in providing the information on this case.
4 Tables of mean teacher ratings may be obtained from the first author.
5 A correlation matrix for both teacher ratings and behavioral data is available from the first author.

References

Albee, G. W. *Mental health manpower trends*. New York: Basic Books, 1959.

Allen, G. J., Chinsky, J. M., Larcen, S. W., Lochman, J. E., & Selinger, H. V. *Community psychology in the schools*. Hillsdale, N.J.: Erlbaum, 1976.

Anderson, S., & Messick, S. Social competency in young children. *Developmental Psychology*, 1974, *10*(2), 282–293.

Anthony, W. A., Buell, G. J., Sharratt, S., & Althoff, M. E. Efficacy of psychiatric rehabilitation. *Psychological Bulletin*, 1972, *78*, 447–456.

Ashby, W. A., & Wilson, G. T. Behavior therapy for obesity: Booster sessions and long-term maintenance of weight loss. *Behavior Research and Therapy*, 1977, *15*, 451–464.

Blechman, E. A., & Olson, D. H. The family contract game: Description and effectiveness. In D. H. Olson (Ed.), *Treating relationships*. Lake Mills, Iowa: Graphic Publishing, 1975.

Borke, H. Interpersonal perception of young children: Egocentrism or empathy? *Developmental Psychology*, 1971, *5*(2), 263–269.

Bower, E. M. *Early identification of emotionally disturbed children in school*. Springfield, Ill.: Thomas, 1960.

Brownell, K., Colletti, G., Ersner-Herschfield, R., Herschfield, S. M., & Wilson, G. T. Self-control in school children: Stringency and leniency in self-determined and externally imposed performance standards. *Behavior Therapy*, 1977, *8*, 442–455.

Butler, A. C. The child health questionnaire: Preliminary data. *Psychology in the Schools*, 1975, *12*, 153–160.

Campbell, D. T., & Stanley, J. C. *Experimental and quasi-experimental designs for research*. Chicago: Rand McNally, 1963.

Chandler, M. Egocentrism and antisocial behavior: The assessment and training of social perspective – taking skills. *Developmental Psychology*, 1973, *9*, 326–332.

Clarfield, S. P. The development of a teacher referral form for identifying early school maladaptation. *American Journal of Community Psychology*, 1974, *2*, 199–210.

Cone, J. D., & Hawkins, R. P. (Eds.). *Behavioral assessments: New directions in clinical psychology*. New York: Brunner-Mazel, 1977.

Coopersmith, S. *The antecedents of self-esteem*. San Francisco: Freeman, 1967.

Cowen, E. L. Some problems in community program evaluation research. *Journal of Consulting and Clinical Psychology*, 1978, *46*(4), 792–806.

Cowen, E. L., Davidson, E. R., & Gesten, E. L. Program dissemination and the modification of delivery practices in school mental health. *Professional Psychology*, 1980, *11*, 36–47.

Cowen, E. L., Dorr, D., Clarfield, S. P., Kreling, B., McWilliams, S. A., Pokracki, F., Pratt, D. M., Terrell, D. L., & Wilson, A. B. The AML: A quick screening device for early detection of school maladaptation. *American Journal of Community Psychology*, 1973, *1*, 12–35.

Cowen, E. L., Dorr, D., & Pokracki, F. Selection of nonprofessional child-aides for a school mental health project. *Community Mental Health Journal*, 1972, *8*, 220–226.

Cowen, E. L., Pederson, A., Babigian H., Izzo, L. D., & Trost, M. A. Long-term follow-up of early detected vulnerable children. *Journal of Consulting and Clinical Psychology*, 1973, *41*, 438–446.

Cowen, E. L., Trost, M. A., Izzo, L. D., Lorion, R. P., Dorr, D., & Isaacson, R. V. *New ways in school mental health*. New York: Human Sciences Press, 1975.

Davidson, W. S. II, & Seidman, E. Studies of behavior modification and juvenile delinquency: A review, methodological critique, and social perspective. *Psychological Bulletin*, 1974, *81*, 998–1011.

Debus, R. L. Effects of brief observation of model behavior or conceptual tempo of impulsive children. *Developmental Psychology*, 1970, *2*, 22–32.

Denney, D. R. Modeling effects upon conceptual style and cognitive tempo. *Child Development*, 1972, *43*, 105–119.

Dorr, D. An ounce of prevention. *Mental Hygiene*, 1972, *56*, 25–27.

Dorr, D., & Cowen, E. L. Nonprofessional mental health workers' judgments of change in children. *Journal of Community Psychology*, 1973, *1*, 23–26.

Drabman, R. S., Spitalnik, R., & O'Leary, K. D. Teaching self-control to disruptive children. *Journal of Abnormal Psychology*, 1973, *82*, 10–16.

Durlak, J. A. Description and evaluation of a behaviorally oriented school-based preventive mental health program. *Journal of Consulting and Clinical Psychology*, 1977, *6*, 48–52.

Durlak, J. A. Comparative effectiveness of behavioral and relationship group treatment in the secondary prevention of school maladjustment. *American Journal of Community Psychology*, 1980, *8*, 327–340.

Durost, W. N., Bixler, H. H., Wrightstone, J. W., Prescott, G. A., & Balow, I. H. *Metropolitan achievement tests: Teacher's handbook*. New York: Harcourt Brace Jovanovich, 1971.

Eysenck, H. J. *The effects of psychotherapy*. New York: International Science Press, 1966.

Farina, A., Fisher, J. D., Getter, H., & Fischer, E. H. Some consequences of changing people's views regarding the nature of mental illness. *Journal of Abnormal Psychology*, 1978, *87*(2), 272–279.

Felner, R. O., Stolberg, A., & Cowen, E. L. Crisis events and school mental health referral patterns of young children. *Journal of Consulting and Clinical Psychology*, 1975, *43*(3), 305–311.

Finch, A. J., Jr., Wilkinson, M. D., Nelson, W. M. III, & Montgomery, L. E. Modification of an impulse cognitive tempo in emotionally disturbed boys. *Journal of Abnormal Child Psychology*, 1975, *3*, 47–51.

Fisher, J. D., & Farina, A. Consequences of beliefs about the nature of mental disorders. *Journal of Abnormal Psychology*, 1979, *88*, 320–327.

Fo, W. S. O., & O'Donnell, C. R. The buddy system: Relationship and contingency conditions in a community intervention program for youth with professionals as behavior change agents. *Journal of Consulting and Clinical Psychology*, 1974, *42*, 163–169.

Fry, C. L. Training children to communicate to listeners. *Child Development*, 1966, *37*, 675–685.

Fry, C. L. Training children to communicate to listeners who have varying listener requirements. *Journal of Genetic Psychology*, 1969, *114*, 153–166.

Garfield, S. L., & Bergin, A. E. *Handbook of psychotherapy and behavior change*. New York: Wiley, 1978.

Gesten, E. L. Health Resources Inventory: The development of a measure of the personal and social competency of primary-grade children. *Journal of Consulting and Clinical Psychology*, 1976, *44*(5), 775–786.

Gesten, E. L., Flores de Apodaca, R., Rains, M., Weissberg, R. P., & Cowen, E. L. Promoting peer related social competence in school. In M. W. Kent & J. E. Rolf (Eds.),

The primary prevention of psychopathology. Vol. 3: Promoting social competence and coping in children. Hanover, N.H.: University Press of New England, 1978.

Gilbert, L. A. Situational factors and the relationship between locus of control and psychological adjustment. *Journal of Counseling Psychology*, 1976, *23*, 302–309.

Glynn, E. L. Classroom applications of self-determined reinforcement. *Journal of Applied Behavior Analysis*, 1970, *3*, 123–132.

Goodman, G. *Companionship therapy*. San Francisco: Jossey-Bass, 1972.

Gottman, J., Gonso, J., & Rasmussen, B. Social interaction, social competence, and friendship in children. *Child Development*, 1975, *46*, 709–718.

Heider, E. R. Information processing and the modification of an "impulsive conceptual tempo." *Child Development*, 1971, *42*, 1276–1281.

Homme, L. *How to use contingency contracting in the classroom*. Champaign, Ill.: Research Press, 1970.

Humphrey, L. L., Karoly, P., & Kirschenbaum, D. Self-management in the classroom: Self-reward versus self-imposed response cost. *Behavior Therapy*, 1978, *9*, 592–601.

Jason, L. A., & Ferone, L. Behavioral versus process consultation interventions in school settings. *American Journal of Community Psychology*, 1978, *6*, 531–540.

Joe, V. C. Review of the internal–external construct as a personality variable. *Psychological Report*, 1971, *28*, 619–640.

Joint Commission on Mental Illness and Health. *Action for mental health*. New York: Basic Books, 1961.

Kagan, J., Pearson, L., & Welch, L. Modifiability of an impulsive tempo. *Journal of Educational Psychology*, 1966, *57*, 359–365.

Kanfer, F. H., & Saslow, G. Behavioral diagnosis. In C. M. Franks (Ed.), *Behavior therapy: Appraisal and status*. New York: McGraw-Hill, 1969.

Karoly, P. Behavioral self-management in children: Concepts, methods, issues, and directions. In M. Hersen, R. M. Eisler, & P. M. Miller (Eds.), *Progress in behavior modification* (Vol. 5). New York: Academic Press, 1977.

Kazdin, A. *The token economy*. New York: Plenum, 1977.

Kellam, S. G., Branch, J. D., Agrawal, K. C., & Ensminger, M. E. *Mental health and going to school: The Woodlawn program of assessment, early intervention, and evaluation*. Chicago: University of Chicago Press, 1975.

Kendall, P. C., & Finch, A. J., Jr. A cognitive-behavioral treatment for impulse control: A case study. *Journal of Consulting and Clinical Psychology*, 1976, *44*, 852–857.

Kendall, P. C., & Finch, A. J., Jr. A cognitive-behavioral treatment for impulsivity: A group comparison study. *Journal of Consulting and Clinical Psychology*, 1978, *46*, 110–118.

Kirschenbaum, D. S. *The Social Skills Development Program's method of mass screening: Is it effective*? (SSDP Research Report Number 1). Cincinnati: Cincinnati Health Department, November 1976.

Kirschenbaum, D. S. *Summary evaluation of the Social Skills Development Program: Report to the Citizen's Advisory Council of Community Development* (SSDP Research Report Number 5). Cincinnati: Cincinnati Health Department, November 1977.

Kirschenbaum, D. S. On observables and reliabilities: A reply to Ronnberg. *Behavioral Analysis and Modification*, 1978, *2*, 325–327.

Kirschenbaum, D. S. Social competence intervention and evaluation in the inner city: Cincinnati's Social Skills Development Program. *Journal of Consulting and Clinical Psychology*, 1979, *47*, 778–780.

Kirschenbaum, D. S., Bane, S., Fowler, R., Klei, B., Kuykendahl, K., Marsh, M. E., & Pedro, J. L. *Social Skills Development Program: Handbook for helping*. Cincinnati: Cincinnati Health Department, 1976.

Kirschenbaum, D. S., DeVoge, J. B., Marsh, M. E., & Steffen, J. J. Multimodal evaluation of therapy vs. consultation components in a large inner city early intervention program. *American Journal of Community Psychology*, 1980, *8*, 587–601.

Kirschenbaum, D. S., DeVoge, J. B., Pedro, J. L., & Marsh, M. E. *A description of the Social Skills Development Program's typical group therapy session* (SSDP Research Report Number 2). Cincinnati: Cincinnati Health Department, March 1977.

Kirschenbaum, D. S., & Karoly, P. When self-regulation fails: Tests of some preliminary hypotheses. *Journal of Consulting and Clinical Psychology*, 1977, *45*, 1116–1125.

Kirschenbaum, D. S., Klei, R. G., Brown, J. E. III, & DeVoge, J. B. A non-experimental, but useful, evaluation of a therapy/consultation early intervention program. In G. Landsberg, W. Neigher, R. Hammer, C. Windle, & R. Woy (Eds.), *Evaluation in practice: A sourcebook of program evaluation studies from mental health care systems in the United States*. Washington, D.C.: U.S. Government Printing Office, 1979.

Kirschenbaum, D. S., Marsh, M. E., & DeVoge, J. B. The effectiveness of a mass screening procedure in an early intervention program. *Psychology in the Schools*, 1977, *14*, 400–406.

Kirschenbaum, D. S., & Pedro-Carroll, J. L. Helping teachers utilize classroom behavioral observation data: A case study using the Teacher Feedback Form. *Behavioral Engineering*, 1979, *5*, 155–160.

Kirschenbaum, D. S., Pedro, J. L., & DeVoge, J. B. A questionnaire for the process analysis of social skills oriented group therapy with children. JSAS *Catalog of Selected Documents in Psychology*, 1977, *7*, 42 (Abstract). (Ms. No. 1474)

Kirschenbaum, D. S., Steffen, J. S., & D'Orta, C. The social competence classroom behavioral observation system. *Behavioral Analysis and Modification*, 1978, *2*, 314–322.

Kohn, M., & Clausen, J. Social isolation and schizophrenia. *American Sociological Review*, 1955, *20*, 265–273.

Lefcourt, H. M. *Locus of control: Current trends in theory and research*. Hillsdale, N.J.: Erlbaum, 1976.

Levitt, E. E. Research on psychotherapy with children. In A. E. Bergin & S. L. Garfield (Eds.), *Handbook for psychotherapy and behavior change: An empirical analysis*. New York: Wiley, 1971.

Lorion, R. P. Socioeconomic status and traditional treatment approaches reconsidered. *Psychological Bulletin*, 1973, *79*, 263–270.

Lorion, R. P., Caldwell, R. A., & Cowen, E. L. Effects of a school mental health project: A one year follow-up. *Journal of School Psychology*, 1976, *14*, 56–63.

Lorion, R. P., Cowen, E. L., & Caldwell, R. A. Problem types of children referred to a school-based mental health program: Identification and outcome. *Journal of Consulting and Clinical Psychology*, 1974, *42*, 491–496.

Lorion, R. P., Cowen, E. L., & Caldwell, R. A. Normative and parametric analyses of school maladjustment. *American Journal of Community Psychology*, 1975, *3*, 291–301.

McFall, R. M. Smoking-cessation research. *Journal of Consulting and Clinical Psychology*, 1978, *46*(4), 703–712.

Meichenbaum, D. H., & Goodman, J. Training impulsive children to talk to themselves: A means of developing self-control. *Journal of Abnormal Psychology*, 1971, *77*, 115–126.

Meyer, W. R. The politics of evaluation research: The Peace Corps. *Journal of Applied Behavioral Science*, 1975, *11*(3), 261–280.

Mischel, W., & Zeiss, A. Internal–external control and persistence: Validation and implications of the Stanford Preschool Internal–External Scale. *Journal of Personality and Social Psychology*, 1974, *29*, 265–278.

Moos, R. H. (Ed.). *Human adaptation: Coping with life crises*. Lexington, Mass.: Heath, 1976.

Nowicki, S., & Duke, M. P. A preschool and primary internal–external control scale. *Development Psychology*, 1974, *10*, 874–880.

Nowicki, S., & Strickland, B. R. A locus of control scale for children. *Journal of Consulting and Clinical Psychology*, 1973, *40*, 148–155.

O'Leary, K. D., & O'Leary, S. G. *Classroom management: The successful use of behavior modification*. New York: Pergamon Press, 1972.

Patterson, G. R. Changes in status of family members as controlling stimuli: A basis for describing treatment process. In L. A. Hammerlynck, L. C. Handy, & E. J. Mash (Eds.), *Behavior change: Methodology, concepts, and practice*. Champaign, Ill.: Research Press, 1973.

Patterson, G. R. Interventions for boys with conduct problems: Multiple settings, treatments, and criteria. *Journal of Consulting and Clinical Psychology*, 1974, *42*, 471–480.

Patterson, G. R. Multiple evaluations of a parent-training program. In T. Thompson & W. S. Dockens III (Eds.), *Applications of behavior modification*. New York: Academic Press, 1975.

Pekarik, E. G., Prinz, R. J., Liebert, D. E., Weintraub, S., & Neale, J. M. The pupil evaluation inventory: A sociometric technique for assessing children's social behavior. *Journal of Abnormal Child Psychology*, 1976, *4*, 83–97.

Phares, E. J. *Locus of control: A personality determinant of behavior*. Morristown, N.J.: General Learning Press, 1973.

President's Commission on Mental Health. *Report to the President* (Vol. I). Washington, D.C.: U.S. Government Printing Office, 1978.

Reppucci, N. D., & Saunders, J. T. The social psychology of behavior modification naturalistic settings. *American Psychologist*, 1974, *29*, 649–660.

Robin, A., Schneider, M., & Dolnick, M. The Turtle Technique: An extended case study of self-control in the classroom. *Psychology in the Schools*, 1976, *13*, 449–453.

Robins, L. *Deviant children grown up*. Baltimore: Williams & Wilkins, 1966.

Roff, M. Childhood social interactions and young adult bad conduct. *Journal of Abnormal and Social Psychology*, 1961, *63*, 333–337.

Roff, M., Sells, B., & Golden, M. M. *Social adjustment and personality development in children*. Minneapolis: University of Minnesota Press, 1972.

Rosenthal, R., & Jacobson, L. *Pygmalion in the classroom: Teacher expectation and pupils' intellectual development*. New York: Holt, Rinehart & Winston, 1968.

Rotter, J. B. The future of clinical psychology. *Journal of Consulting and Clinical Psychology*, 1973, *40*, 313–321.

Sandler, I. Characteristics of women working as child-aides in a school-based preventive mental health program. *Journal of Consulting and Clinical Psychology*, 1972, *39*, 56–61.

Sandler, I. N., Duricko, A., & Grande, L. Effectiveness of an early secondary prevention program in an inner-city elementary school. *American Journal of Community Psychology*, 1975, *3*(1), 23–32.

Saunders, J. T., & Reppucci, N. D. The social identity of behavior modification. In M. Hersen, R. Eisler, & P. Miller (Eds.), *Progress in behavior modification* (Vol. 6). New York: Academic Press, 1978.

Seiden, R. H. Campus tragedy: A study of student suicide. *Journal of Abnormal and Social Psychology*, 1966, *71*, 389–399.

Seymour, F. W., & Stokes, T. F. Self-recording in training girls to increase work and evoke staff praise in an institution for offenders. *Journal of Applied Behavior Analysis*, 1976, *9*, 41–54.

Shantz, C. U. *The development of social cognition*. Chicago: University of Chicago Press, 1975.

Shantz, C. U., & Wilson, K. Training communication skills in young children. *Child Development*, 1972, *43*, 118–122.

Shure, M. B., & Spivack, G. Means–end thinking adjustment, and social class among elementary school-aged children. *Journal of Consulting and Clinical Psychology*, 1972, *38*, 348–353.

Shure, M. B., & Spivack, G. *The PIPS test manual*. Philadelphia: Hahnemann Medical College and Hospital, 1974.

Shure, M. B., & Spivack, G. *Problem-solving techniques in childrearing*. San Francisco: Jossey-Bass, 1978.

Spivack, G., Platt, J. J., & Shure, M. B. *The problem solving approach to adjustment*. San Franciso: Jossey-Bass, 1976.

Spivack, G., & Shure, M. B. *Social adjustment of young children*. San Francisco: Jossey-Bass, 1974.

Staub, E. The use of role playing and induction in children's learning of helping and sharing behavior. *Child Development*, 1971, *42*, 805–816.

Stengel, E. *Suicide and attempted suicide*. Middlesex: Penguin, 1971.

Stokes, T. F., Fowler, S. A., & Baer, D. M. *Training preschool children to recruit natural communities of reinforcement*. Paper presented at the meeting of the American Psychological Association, San Francisco, August 1977.

Stringer, L. Academic progress as an index of mental health. *Journal of Social Issues*, 1959, *15*, 16–29.

Taplin, P. S., & Reid, J. B. Changes in parent consequences as a function of family intervention. *Journal of Consulting and Clinical Psychology*, 1977, *45*(6), 973–981.

Tolor, A., Tolor, B., & Blumin, S. S. Self-concept and locus of control in primary-grade children identified as requiring special educational programming. *Psychological Reports*, 1977, *40*, 43–49.

Urberg, K. A., & Docherty, E. M. Development of role-taking skills in young children. *Developmental Psychology*, 1976, *12*, 198–206.

Walker, H. M., & Hops, H. The use of group and individual reinforcement contingencies in the modification of social withdrawal. In L. A. Hammerlynck, L. C. Handy, & E. J. Mash (Eds.), *Behavior change, methodology, concepts, and practice: The fourth Banff international conference on behavior modification*. Champaign, Ill.: Research Press, 1973.

Watt, N. F., & Lubensky, A. W. Childhood roots of schizophrenia. *Journal of Consulting and Clinical Psychology*, 1976, *44*, 363–375.

Wilson, G. T. Methodological considerations in treatment outcome research on obesity. *Journal of Consulting and Clinical Psychology*, 1978, *46*(4), 687–702.

Wood, F. H. & Zabel, R. H. Making sense of reports on the incidence of behavioral disorders/emotional disturbance in school-aged populations. *Psychology in the Schools*, 1978, *15*, 45–51.

Zax, M., & Cowen, E. L. Research on early detection and prevention of emotional dysfunction in young school children. In C. D. Spielberger (Ed.), *Current topics in clinical and community psychology*. New York: Academic Press, 1967.

Zax, M., Cowen, E. L., Rappaport, J., Beach, D. R., & Laird, J. D. Follow-up study of children identified as emotionally disturbed. *Journal of Consulting and Clinical Psychology*, 1968, *32*, 369–374.

Conclusion: Life history research in the public arena

David F. Ricks

A major report on computer usage and citizen rights concluded with this comment:

> It is the custom of Americans to believe that no "lady-or-the-tiger" choice has to be made between science and liberty. For 200 years, in the tradition of Franklin and Jefferson, we have hammered out legal rules that allowed each successive wave of invention to realize its potential, but also required each to be brought under the rule of law. Sometimes it took a while for the principles of regulation to become clear, and we have come to realize that the awesome effects of contemporary technology give us less lead time for social learning and regulatory response than we had in earlier eras. But that is the challenge we face, and there are promising signs that our society understands how important it is to develop, soon, the standards by which we can pursue the benefits of both science and liberty in the field of health care. [Westin, 1976, p. 308]

This book was produced during a transitional period for life history research. Our work is visible. We are discussed. But this is also a time of questioning and doubt brought on by a growing fear of institutional invasion of privacy. A replication of the Judge Baker studies in schizophrenia (Ricks, 1974), for instance, was held up for more than a year by questions about legal and ethical issues involved in the use of children's psychiatric records without informed consent from the children and their parents for such secondary use of information about their private lives. This concern is shared by the public, by legislators, and increasingly by research workers. We have not always been so alert to patient rights. A decade ago we might have launched a new life history study with the conviction that our search was for truth, truth was good for all concerned, and we had no reason to worry that our data might be used in some way that could do harm to the people studied. My own innocence in this regard ended abruptly several years ago when a government intelligence agency requested all of our available information regarding a young man engaged in some political activities. We had his child guidance clinic records, summaries of his psychiatric records from the army, and his records from subsequent hospitalizations, together with current interviews. On the advice of counsel for the agency where the research was being conducted, I gave the intelligence service only the information on our "face sheet" for the young man – that is, that he had been seen, and when. I heard nothing more, but I spent some months wondering what the penalties might be for obstruction of justice, sequestering evidence, and my other crimes. My conclusion from this episode was that life history scientists have no choice but to learn about the laws that govern their activities, even when they find legal reasoning obscure or legal prose murky and imprecise.

The perils of trying to do research without considering the legal and ethical rights of the people we study are illustrated in extreme form in one of the few research projects that have been examined by the courts, *Merriken* v. *Cressman*. The case is summarized in a report of the National Commission for the Protection of Human Subjects of Biomedical and Behavioral Research:

> In Merriken, a suit brought by a junior high school student and his mother, a federal district court enjoined implementation of an experimental drug abuse prevention program. The program required students' responses to questionnaires that asked highly sensitive questions concerning their home life, an area protected by Supreme Court decisions, and also asked students to identify classmates whose behavior was unusual or inappropriate. On the basis of such information, compulsory remediation was to be instituted by teachers who lacked proper training in psychological therapy. Further, the results of the questionnaires were to be made available to individuals not involved in the program, such as athletic coaches, administrators, and members of the PTA and school board. When the suit was filed, the defendants had planned what the court called a "book-of-the-month-club" approach to obtaining parental consent, in which silence would be construed as acquiescence . . . The court found that the program infringed on the child's constitutional right of privacy, and further that "there probably is no more private a relationship, excepting marriage, which the constitution safeguards than that between parent and child." [1977, p. 83]

Currently, data-protection laws are either enacted or in preparation in Sweden, Austria, Germany, France, Belgium, Norway, Denmark, Great Britain, the Netherlands, Spain, Switzerland, Finland, Canada, Japan, and the United States (Müller, 1978). All of our future life history research will be done within the legal framework erected by those laws. We should be doing what we can to shape them in ways that will be responsive to research needs and patient rights. No amount of scientific worth could justify the kind of blatant disregard for personal rights apparent in *Merriken*. It is also important for us to learn, as Aronoff told us in Chapter 11, that unwitting dissemination of information, without special concern for the privacy of the individual concerned, is the most common danger to privacy. Our data is ours only on loan and by permission. It belongs to the person with whom it originated.

The Robins and Babigian chapters (9 and 10), and the lively discussion that followed, show that some research workers have protected the civil liberties of the people we study. Note that I did not write "our subjects." As Klein mentioned in his comments, we do better work if we think of the people we study as collaborators, co-investigators, and peers in our research endeavor, not "subjects."

Earlier Society for Life History books have dealt with the dilemmas created by the use in life history research of data originally designed to record pupil progress or patient care. Our concern at that time was with research use of clinical data. Current work on legal issues in our research has raised a reciprocal question: Might data gathered and used for research be leaked into the clinical or administrative system, and there be used for purposes anticipated by neither the patient nor the researcher? In the Multi-State Information System (MSIS), serving both administrative and research purposes for institutions housing about 400,000 mental patients, confidentiality of the sensitive psychiatric data stored is protected by a special state statute. Researchers planning studies with similar kinds of data will do well to check into current medical confidentiality laws in their states, and into medical research privilege statutes that may protect them and the people they study. Babigian offers useful guidelines for making such checks.

We work within hospitals, clinics, and schools whose own immediate needs may conflict with the long-term needs of research. In our work on outcomes, we sometimes have to deal with information protected by the therapist–patient relationship. The personal material communicated to a psychotherapist is often considered to have an even more privileged status than material in other doctor–patient records (Teichner, 1974). It is especially important that the relationships among researcher, community, and therapists be collaborative enough so that data are gathered with some sensitivity to the needs of the community and agencies, and that arrangements are made to communicate general research findings to everyone concerned in the study. We also should be receptive to discussions of the meaning, dangers, and the uses that others see in research results.

Informed consent raises special issues for life history research. When a longitudinal study begins with a high-risk population, the likely length of the study can be described and the risks and benefits of participation explained, and consent to participate can usually be considered both informed and voluntary. Even in these instances, however, there are some ambiguities. Suppose the study begins with children and obtains consent only from the parents? Have the children's rights been observed? Or suppose the group at risk is low in IQ, organically impaired, or demonstrated to have difficulty in learning. Courts are likely to take the position that in order for consent to be informed, the implications of that consent have to be understood.

There are further problems when existing records are used for research purposes. It would be prohibitively expensive to contact, for instance, all of the thousands of children who may have been at one time patients in a metropolitan child guidance clinic, if the aim were only to find the 2% or 3% who are likely to have had schizophrenic periods in adult life. The principle Westin (1976) recommends is this:

> While securing informed, voluntary consent should cover most situations in which medical research and program evaluation need to be conducted, through the use of identified data from health systems, there will be situations in which this is not feasible. In those cases, a health data system should have the purpose, procedures, and safeguards of the research reviewed by a special panel made up of representatives from the organization owning the data system, outside scholars of high reputation, and leaders of public-interest groups relevant to the research project (minority racial groups, womens' groups, civil liberties groups, etc.). Furthermore, securing a legal privilege against any compulsory disclosure of research records should generally be a prerequisite for a health data system's agreement to participate in a research study, disease register, or program evaluation involving highly sensitive personal information. [P. 300]

The data-storage capabilities of large-scale computers have made possible the systematic study of huge amounts of personal information. Their data-analysis capabilities, together with the development of cross-lagged panel analysis, path analysis, and other methods, have given us powerful new designs and tools for analyzing longitudinal data. These methods are illustrated here by Chapters 3, 7, and 8. This statistical development has accompanied a growth, within psychology and related disciplines, of an interactionist perspective on human development (Endler & Magnusson, 1976; Runyan, 1978). We are now prepared to deal conceptually and statistically with organism and environment interactions, and to do this in natural settings, over long time periods. This development should result in better understanding between clinicians, who have always thought in terms of interactions, and researchers, who can now deal with clinical data without the oversimplifications of past years.

Considering Aronoff's picture of the computer in the state capital storing thousands of bits of data on all of the citizens of a state (Chapter 11), one wonders about the social control function of the mere existence of these data. Like gossip in a rural village, which tends to prevent any behavior that might be talked about too much, the mere existence of all of that information may dampen extreme behavior. I once consulted with a group of Japanese scholars concerned with control of delinquency in their country. They were amazed that we, in this country, kept so few records, and that we had statutes governing destruction of juvenile records after set time periods. How, they asked, could we expect that these delinquents would not grow up to be criminals, if they knew that we would not be keeping records of their behavior?

In the middle ages the monk Theophrastus, reprimanding the quickness with which his fellow monks judged people, commented, "Thou knowest this man's fall. Thou knowest not his wrestling." Studies such as Erlenmeyer-Kimling's (Chapter 1), which describe a high-risk group as it is growing up, begin to give us a sense of what is going on during the wrestling before schizophrenia. Her studies are reminiscent of Shakow's (1962) demonstrations of segmental set, showing that high-risk children are more likely than controls to make errors in a sustained attention task, and that they are less able to resist distraction. On tests that have a component of visual integration, whether of human figure drawings or of abstract forms, they more frequently show developmental lag, a slowness to reach neuropsychological integration that fits well with similar results found by Bender (1953) and by Fish (1960). Because the children she reports on are still below the age of highest risk for schizophrenic episodes, she has only preliminary evidence about whether they will be schizophrenic. The clinical data on those who are now having psychiatric difficulties, however, suggest that her early tests are indeed predicting which children will "break down" in late adolescence. When their paths into disturbance have been traced thoroughly, these routes will suggest times and techniques for early intervention. Her collaboration with Norman Watt (1982) in the study of school records is a good example of the kind of teamwork the Society for Life History Research in Psychopathology was organized to promote.

Chapter 2 probably underestimates drug usage, because a number of the first graders it describes were dead by the teen years, and as both Robins (1966; 1968) and Groeschel (1974) have shown, drug users are at high risk for early death. It is also likely that a relatively high proportion of those boys and girls unavailable at the time of follow-up were involved in drugs. With that one reservation, I think this report could be studied by classes in life history research as exemplary of the best we can do at this point. The study combines a relevant sample, large enough to provide for multiple comparisons between sexes, life patterns, and outcomes. The temporal scope of the study is long and ambitious, so that the results have long-term significance. And although most good research results in new knowledge, the combination of research and clinical work, in a natural setting, takes this work beyond factual knowledge into an integration of knowledge and action that is the foundation of wisdom.

The children are considered in each of the natural fields in which they participate, home, school, and community. They are rated by "natural raters" in each, so that parents and teachers are participants in studying the growth of the children. A great deal of care has gone into systematic methods for observing social adaptational status and psychological well-being. Had the study focused only on the familiar kinds of symptoms, it would have been far less fruitful. The results merit a good deal of thought. What would most of us have predicted, prior to reading this chapter, about drug use by shy and by aggressive first graders as they grew and became adolescents? I do not suppose it is too surprising that shy children are not likely to use most drugs, other than opiates. But this finding does point to a research strategy advocated for some time by Joseph Zubin (1974), that of looking for social and community factors when we want to predict drug use, and of working with sociologists and epidemiologists if we want to describe routes into drug use. It also shows that what might be a social deficit in one sense, for example, in working as a salesmen, can be an asset in other ways, as shyness seems a protection from involvement in the ceremonials of adolescent drug abuse. It is not surprising that aggressive children – especially boys – are more likely to get into the drug culture than are their adjusted peers, because aggression in males is one way to achieve status with peers, and drugs are another. What is striking in this chapter's data is the positive association between both high IQ and learning readiness in first grade and later drug use. What does this finding imply for intervention? We cannot look to educational remediation of some kind of intellectual defect in these children, because they are already intellectually ahead of their peers. We might consider some kinds of behavior therapy to help them achieve self-control for aggression. But the results really point beyond the children. What kind of community have we created on the South Side of Chicago, where the ecology of the community presses the brightest children into the drug culture? Or should we reevaluate how dangerous "soft" drugs are? If bright kids are using them, they may be less dangerous than current law assumes they are.

Another value of this study is its attention to prediction for girls as well as for boys. Life history research has tended to focus mostly on men, probably because child guidance clinic records have more boys than girls represented in them. Boys also cause more trouble and generate more detailed records in schools. And because men do not change their names, they are easier to follow in public records. Kellam and his co-workers show, however, that the social and academic sorts of data that predict for boys do not predict well for girls. The characteristics that predicted adolescent difficulties in the sample of first-grade girls were "sad and worried, trouble with feelings, muscular tension, and speech problems," and the antecedents of these were found, in turn, in the feelings of the mother, and in the family emotional atmosphere. Combined with Knight and Roff's description of the long-range predictive power of emotions (Chapter 7), even in a male sample, these findings should lead to a new interest in the emotional life of children, and a new research directed to these feelings.

How are we to intervene in a troubled child's development? Should our focus be on the child, the family, or the larger social system? For some issues, such as lead poisoning, it is clear that legislation to get the lead out of paint and gasoline is far more efficient than remedial effort with each damaged child, an effort that is inevitably too little and too late. But for most difficulties it is hard to find where the main influences toward adult difficulties originate and become manifest. Chapter 3 poses two models: In the first, the authors look at the child's characteristics and ask how well these predict adult characteristics, and then add in the effects of environmental stress and check to see if their predictions are improved. In the second model, environmental influences are studied first, and the effects of the child's own characteristics are entered into the equation to see if they add predictive power. For this to be done adequately, both the environment and the early behavior have to be specified comprehensively and precisely, so that their relative weights can be compared numerically. The conclusions drawn are quite complex. If our concern is with the child's own symptoms and his or her degree of impairment, the best predictors are early symptoms and impairment. Not surprisingly, like predicts like. If we want to predict social events such as being arrested, however, we can do this more accurately from social data than from early knowledge of the child: Knowing the child's environment, or change in environment, can be more of a help in predicting the community outcomes than knowing the child's behavior or change in behavior. This suggests that prevention of undesirable community outcomes will require social changes, such as better housing, less crowding, and better job opportunities.

Earlier life history research put to rest the idea of the "schizophrenogenic mother" as the source of schizophrenic outcomes. The research presented in Chapter 2 and the comment that "previous analysis indicated that the more friends you have, the higher your risk of arrest," ought to show the limits to the equally pernicious "deficit model" of psychopathology. Some children end up in difficulty not because of early deficits, but because early assets are misused by those entrusted with their care. And it will do no good to blame parents – the peer group is a powerful influence, and behind that is the larger society, its patterns of growing up, its social and vocational opportunity structure, and its blindness and prejudice.

Chapter 5 proposes a very general "pathogenic triad": close proximity of serious illness or injury leading to exhaustion; extreme loss, that is, loss of a loved person; and disruption of usual sources of support. This triad seems to result in demoralization, a sense of helplessness in the face of events felt to be uncontrollable and beyond one's capacity to cope. For all of this there is a good deal of research evidence. This is the stress side of the familiar diathesis–stress model for disorder. The chapter then begins, speculatively, for the numbers are small, to answer some questions about vulnerability; that is, are there specific vulnerabilities based on specific early experiences at specific ages? The data suggest that loss, by death, of a mother during the preschool years, or of a father during the early school years, may result in lasting vulnerability to later losses, a vulnerability that results in measurably greater demoralization than occurs in people who have not experienced early loss. Other writers have suggested that the mechanism for such vulnerability might be very early damage to self-esteem. Current research in developmental psychology (Harter, 1978) has shown the importance of the child's own sense of competence, a set of feelings rather close to the "attitudes of mastery" that Dohrenwend and de Figueiredo believe might be damaged by early loss. Perhaps what early death of a parent does to a child is to damage that sense of efficacy, of being able to handle the world, that leads one to keep on trying in later stress situations. It may be, though, that the problem is how Americans handle loss. For poor rural children in Africa or Asia, loss of a parent during early childhood is probably about as frequent as growing to adolescence with both parents available. Yet these children do not show a helpless or demoralized stance to the world; they often have a quiet dignity and stoic persistence in the face of adversity that Americans might admire. It may be that in our highly compartmentalized society, with its specialists in illness and death, we have forgotten how to prepare children to cope with death as a natural event.

The pathogenic triad is strikingly represented in a flood: Death, loss, exhaustion, and disruption of one's usual community supports all occur together. Chapter 4 indicates that these stresses can be made worse by public responses that are poorly thought out. In the Buffalo Creek disaster there was more impact on the women than on the men. Is this evidence for feminine weakness? Not at all. The men were offered a chance to be active, to get out and clean up houses, to remove debris, and to construct shelters. Women were expected to sit and wait – and some suffered demoralization. Future programs for disaster relief ought to have as one goal helping people deal actively with their own situation, and this goal includes both men and women. Later, in a superficially reasonable first-come, first-served system of allocating housing that ignored the need of people under stress to maintain their usual sources of support, and in the building of a highway that further disrupted housing patterns, the world of neighbors and kinfolk was split apart just when it was needed most. Had social action been informed by what we know about stress, this need not have occurred. The children's response to the flood was what the authors would have predicted – a loss of interest in learning, a decrease in grades and interest in school – a loss syndrome that might help the child endure the original stress of the flood at the cost of vulnerability to later losses.

Childhood depression is of interest in its own right. A four-year-old child has described to me how she once, when her parents quarreled, went out and lay down in the road, hoping that a car would come and run over her. Another child told me, "I can't do anything right, so it doesn't matter what I do." We all want to prevent pain of that degree. But childhood depression is also, as Chapter 6 suggests, extremely important as a possible precursor of adult depression, and schizo-affective or schizophrenic disorders. If we can understand the origins and natural course of childhood depressions, and especially if we can move beyond description to sensitive measurement of the severity of depressive symptoms, we can begin to make precise studies of the spectrum of outcomes of depressed children.

Chapter 6 raises a problem that has occupied students of the origins of psychopathology for some time: Are we dealing with types of disorder or with one general syndrome that has separable stages? The question is important. If we are dealing with separate diseases we should expect different genetic, biochemical, and life history patterns to be characteristic of each. But if our work in child guidance clinics, schools, hospitals, and so on brings us in contact with people at different periods of their lives, perhaps we are all dealing with the same general disorder, but at different stages of its development. This possibility is laid out in the accompanying table, in which various titles that have been given to stages of a loss syndrome are compared.

In Table 6.2, Kovacs describes three sets of symptoms that occur in

Stages of response to loss or other painful, stressful, or overwhelmingly aversive events

Theories of loss	Stages in rough order of occurrence					
Physiological stress (Selye, 1976)		Alarm	Resistance		Exhaustion	Death
Loss of attachment (Bowlby, 1980)		Anxiety	Protest	Despair	Apathy	Death
Learned helplessness (Seligman, 1975)		Fear		Learned helplessness		Death
Stages of dying (Kübler-Ross, 1967)	Denial		Anger/bargaining	Depression	Acceptance	Death
Synthesis	Denial	Anxiety	Protest	Despair	Apathy	Death
"Usual diagnostic" label	Hysteria	Anxiety disorder "neurosis"	Character disorder	Depression	Schizophrenia	

children. One group shows antisocial behaviors, temper tantrums, running away, phobias, hyperactivity, truancy, and anxiety – a mixture of alarm and resistance. A second group shows unhappiness, social withdrawal, low self-esteem, and somatic complaints – the signs of despair and depression. The third group is irritable, apathetic, suicidal, and unable to cope with school. I would like to suggest that Kovacs, like Watt et al. (1980), in research reported to the Society for Life History Research earlier, may be dealing not with discrete types of disorder but with different steps in the development of a general loss syndrome, or of stages of disability (Ricks, 1980). I am not suggesting that the calm acceptance that Kübler-Ross (1969) described is the same thing as schizophrenia – only that they have in common a quality of turning away from the world, of giving up, of detachment. The neat listings in a table also give a false sense of discrete categories; the relationships between the stages are probably shifting and overlapping. But the fact that people working with physiological response to stress, with rats and dogs unable to escape from aversive stimuli, with dying patients, and with infants separated from their mothers all found much the same sequence suggests a loss response pattern of wide generality. We have all seen, in longitudinal records, a series of diagnoses that goes from "adjustment reaction of adolescence," through various kinds of anxiety and angry protests, and into depression and schizophrenia. In its early stages the process is readily reversed. As Bowlby (1980) has pointed out, protest that works leads to restoration of the original mother–child bond, and despair calls out mothering from others. It is only when protest fails, and despair fails to elicit a response, that apathy comes to dominate the affective and motivational life of the child. I am proposing that if we can begin to understand how anxiety and protest lead into depression, and depression into the sapping of motivation that produces apathy, we will be well on the way to understanding our most serious forms of psychological disorder. Kovacs moves us a good way in that direction. The cases provided in Chapter 13, Joey and Janie, provide vivid examples of protest and despair.

Chapters 7 and 8 are probably the most difficult in the book, but also among the most rewarding. One of the originators of life history research in psychopathology, Herbert Birch (1974) told us that we would make progress only when we got away from static "type" models for disorder and began to work out developmental models that took account of the origins and course of disorder, the organism's efforts at restitution, and the temporary or lasting characteristics of different disorders. Statistically, this translates into cross-lagged panel analysis, multiple regression, and path analysis models. These allow us to describe developmental paths into disorder, to differentiate which early characteristics predict, which later characteristics are predictable, and the complicated interactive ways in which the casual ties work.

The few studies of normal development that have included childhood, early adult, and middle adult data are justly famous. Those anonymous children who first participated in the genetic studies of genius, (Terman and Oden, 1959) the small groups in the Oakland and Berkeley studies (Block, 1971), and the Fels children (Kagan and Moss, 1962) have given us a great deal, often at some cost to themselves. Chapter 7 is one of the first life history studies in psychopathology to include comparable childhood, early adult, and middle adult data. The study is full of surprises, such as that middle adult outcomes are better predicted by childhood data than by the more proximate data of early adult life. The possible reason the authors advance, that behavior in the stressful situation of army life may not be typical of behavior in general, and so may not predict as well as situationally more typical childhood behavior, sounds sensible. If we follow this line of reasoning, however, we will have to look skeptically on the body of research that has attempted to make long-term predictions on the basis of hospital admitting data – surely not a situation that elicits typical behavior from the terrified or relieved people going through admission, or from their families.

The developmental model suggested in the "Stages of response" table, if applied to Knight and Roff's data, would predict that people whose disorders were dominated by anxiety (the Neurotic Type) and protest (the Unsocialized Aggression Type) would have had better outcomes than those who were more apathetic (the Schizoid Type), because their disorders had not progressed so far. This is in fact what happened. Even in early adult life, in an army situation where extraneous variables may reduce the predictive power of the person's own characteristics, being apathetic (flat affect, seclusion, poor peer relationships, apathy) is a predictor of later disorder. The old dichotomy of depression as an emotional disorder and schizophrenia as a thought disorder must be questioned on the basis of this chapter's data. Emotional apathy in young adult life predicts later thought disorder. Beck (1967) has argued forcefully for the idea that depression is a cognitive disorder. We might as well admit this, and suggest that on the basis of current evidence, schizophrenia is an emotional disorder. The best model will have to look at both cognitive and emotional elements in both schizophrenia and depression. Chapter 7, like Chapters 2 and 6, puts a new value on emotional and motivational variables as predictors of psychopathological outcomes. A few years ago, Kohlberg, LaCross, and Ricks (1972) concluded that measures of childhood competence and intelligence were the best predictors of adult psychopathology currently available. Their report promised little hope for emotional characteristics as predictors. It is pleasant to report having been wrong on such an important issue, and to say now that we can use emotional states, particularly anxiety, depression, and apathy, as powerful predictors of long-term outcomes. When we can measure emotional characteristics as well as we can measure IQ and achievement, they should become still more powerful predictors.

Knight and Roff, of course, do not allow us to overlook intelligence. Low IQ is a predictor of poor outcomes, particularly if the dull child is *not* aggressive, does not protest. And low competence involves the neurological factors life history researchers have often found to put the child at risk for later bad outcomes: birth complications, poor attention, speech problems, poor motor coordination, and developmental lags. Here Chapter 7 fits well with Chapter 1, and with a great deal of other work.

Because life history research works with people in natural settings, involved in complicated relationships, and capable of adjustment and reaction to environmental pressures, it lacks some of the simplicity and clarity of laboratory work. One way to try to come to terms with complexity is multivariate analysis of the sort that Knight and Roff did. Another is to use path analysis in large-scale, long-term studies of the type reported by Schooler (Chapter 8), who considers cognitive flexibility and work complexity and asks what kinds of effects link the two, both immediately and over a 10-year span. The effect of a complex job on intellectual flexibility is apparently immediate but relatively weak: A complicated job requires that a person in the job think abstractly and flexibly. More generally, this conclusion implies that situations influence behavior quickly but not very powerfully. In contrast, the effect of the person's own characteristics is slow but powerful: Over the course of the study the initially flexible people moved into complex jobs. It may have occurred to some readers that this chapter, no matter how elegant it is conceptually and statistically, may lack relevance to clinical work. But consider the following question: We want to influence a given clinical population, and we can use our resources either to change these people's life situations or to try to help them to change themselves – which way should we proceed? An implication of Schooler's work is that if we want quick change we had best alter the environment; but if we want long-term, powerful change we will do well to concentrate on changes in the people themselves.

Research in which multivariate methods are appropriate involves complex predictors, several dependent variables, and multiple ways in which the influences might combine. Path analysis requires that we make our models explicit and comprehensive. It repays us by allowing us to compare models, refine them, and choose the best. It does not free us from the need for replication and estimation of cross-population robustness of results (Karoly & Steffen, 1980). These methods generate controversy, but I think that future life history research in this age of instant computer output will increasingly turn to their use. Increasingly, our psychopathological classifications are multiaxial rather than typological, quantitative rather than qualitative. As we quantify predictive characteristics in individuals and in their environments (Bartko & Gulbinet, 1980), we move naturally into multivariate systems such as Schooler uses.

Knowing more about the origins and course of psychopathological development has intrinsic value. But funding agencies and the general public are more interested in practical applications. Chapter 13 suggests at least three uses for our work: (1) early identification of children at risk and design of prevention-oriented programs for them, (2) sensitive differentiation of those characteristics in the children and their environments that are open to change from those that are not likely to respond to intervention, (3) provision of baselines against which to judge the short- and long-term effects of interventions. Both practical and theoretic work can be seen as one endeavor, with early intervention programs the more applied side, life history research the more investigative side. For example, Kirschenbaum and his coauthors do not provide a rationale for having the children in their program selected in the schools, primarily by teachers; but life history research (Kohlberg et al., 1972) shows that teachers are better judges of childhood behavior than clinicians are. Other aspects of the program – multimodal assessment, use of standardized instruments, home visits, and emphasis on the strengths of the children – are all consistent with what life history research has found out about long-term prediction.

Chapter 13, like Chapters 2 and 3, links research in psychopathology to the institutions in our surrounding community – family and school – that give our work context and meaning. It also provides a bridge to the stimulating and provocative work of Cowen (1973), Albee (1981), and all of the others who are out in the schools trying to help children struggle through to adulthood. The focus on social skills, on the child's strengths, seems an eminently reasonable one; but its limits become apparent when we remember Chapter 2's report that the best and brightest were at *higher* risk than the less gifted for drug abuse in Chicago's South Side, and Chapter 3's statement that children with more friends were more likely to be arrested. If we are to have any effect on pathologies with a large social element, particularly crime and addiction, we must intervene in larger social systems than the individual school and family.

Chapter 12 reflects a lifetime of study, research, and treatment experience. Reading this chapter, I had a sense of Wynne as an anthropologist from a wider and more sophisticated culture than our own, looking over our notions of cause and blame, seeing their unrecognized historical components, and asking us to understand our still fairly primitive state of scientific and professional culture. But there is also in Wynne's wise and gentle reflections a sense that we are evolving and capable of doing better.

Wynne's chapter has special importance to the theme of this book, research and public policy. If responsibility for being schizophrenic is seen as residing in the individual, the identified patient, and if we are blind to the possibility that this is simply blaming the victim (Ryan, 1976) what implications does this point of view have for public policy? Attribution of responsibility to the schizophrenic patient for his or her own disorder led to the building of large hospitals, to individual psychotherapy with adults as the preferred method of treatment, and to public subsidies for training of large numbers of psychiatrists, nurses, social workers, and psychologists. If we believe that the focus of the disorder is in the individual, as we did in the 1940s and 1950s, then it also makes some sense to see all respectable therapy as either psychoanalytic or analytically oriented. Though Wynne does not say so, his was a major voice among those leading us to take a wider view.

If responsibility for schizophrenia is not to be attributed to adult perseveration on childhood traumata, but to genetic and biological disorder, we need early genetic counseling programs and early identification of vulnerable children. Early symptoms may be apparent in neurological examinations or in psychological testing for such capacities as visual integration or sustained attention. If we can identify vulnerable children early we can perhaps strengthen their ability to cope through early intervention programs (Mednick & Witkin-Lanoil, 1977; Rolf & Hasazi, 1977). Chapter 13 indicates many ways in which this strengthening can be carried out. The implications for public policy are fairly clear. We should intervene early, with all children who might be at risk; so we should work through the public schools, the institution likely to reach the largest and most representative group of children. We should reach out to children and offer early screening, not wait for clear and present problems to be brought to us. We should train early intervention workers, who may or may not have advanced degrees, but who surely must be familiar with children and able to communicate with them. We should try many possible interventions and study their effects carefully to see which work, and why.

But what if responsibility for disorder rests only partly on conflicts within the child, only partly on biologically determined vulnerabilities, and partly on family deviance and social stigmata? We have to consider ways to influence all of these sources of difficulty. We can strengthen children and "inoculate" them against future stress and loss; but we should also know how to intervene in a family that expels or binds or delegates a child (Stierlin, 1974) or in other ways forces him or her toward apathetic withdrawal. And if we know that poverty, racism, or sexism has some role in development of a disorder, we ought to be alert to ways in which we can try to change the larger society. "In the ultimate analysis, a therapy for some forms of depression may be money" (Levitt & Lubin, 1975). As experts in the development of psychopathology, we have special responsibility to try to prevent stereotyping and prejudice against people whose lives have contained one or more episodes of psychological disorder. We would do well to follow the examples of Sullivan and Fromm-Reichman, as Wynne describes them – to seek for more social acceptance of eccentricity, and to see a society as being enriched by having a lively interest in diversity of life-styles. We can also follow the example of people like Father Benedict Groeschel, who discovered through his research that young people coming out of Children's Village in New York often broke down because they lacked support systems – and proceeded to develop halfway houses that provided the needed support. And this again leads us into issues of training. We clearly need to develop alternatives to the traditional hospitals and jails, and we need to train people to work in these alternative living arrangements and use them for prevention of illness or rehabilitation for those who need it.

If a person who had a life history orientation were put into a position of great influence of public policy, what would that person do? Several members of this society were members of the President's Commission on Mental Health, and their influence was visible in the emphasis the commission's report gave to work with underserved populations and to prevention of disorder. The clearest example, though, is the work of Gerald Klerman as administrator of the Alcohol, Drug Abuse, and Mental Health Administration. The three traditional tasks of this federal body have been research, training, and clinical service. Klerman has worked to raise prevention to the level of these three, making prevention one of the four major goals of federal mental health programs.

When the Society for Life History Research in Psychopathology was formed, a number of us were worried that new ideas coming out of research were not finding their way into public policy and into practical applications. That concern is no longer justified. Now that policy makers and clinicians are getting our message, our concern need only be that we do our work well and do not mislead them.

References

Albee, G. W. Politics, power, prevention, and social change. In J. M. Joffe, and G. W. Albee (Eds.), *Prevention through political action and social change*. Hanover and London, University Press of New England, 1981.

Bartko, J. J., & Gulbinet, M. S. *Multivariate statistical methodologies used in the international pilot study of schizophrenia*. Washington, D.C.: NIMH, 1980.

Beck, A. T. *Depression*. New York: Hoeber, 1967.

Bender, L. and Helme, W. H. Quantitative test of theory and diagnostic indicators of childhood schizophrenia. *Archives of Neurology*, 1953, *70*, 413–427.

Birch, H. Methodological issues in the longitudinal study of malnutrition. In D. F. Ricks, A. Thomas, and M. Roff, *Life history research in psycopathology* (Vol. 3). Minneapolis: University of Minnesota Press, 1974.

Block, N. *Lives through time*. Berkeley: Bancroft Books, 1971.

Bowlby, J. *Attachment and Loss* (Vol. 3). London: Hogarth Press. New York: Basic Books, 1980.

Cowen, E. L. Social and community interventions. *Annual Review of Psychology*, 1973, *24*, 423–72.

Endler, N. S., & Magnusson, D. (Eds.). *Interactional psychology and personality* New York: Wiley, 1976.

Fish, B. Drug therapy in child psychiatry: psychological aspects. *Comprehensive Psychiatry*, 1960, *1*, 55–61.

Groeschel, B. J. Social adjustment after residential treatment. In D. F. Ricks, A. Thomas, and M. Roff (Eds.), *Life history research in psychopathology*, (Vol. 3). Minneapolis: University of Minnesota Press, 1974, 259–74.

Harter, S. Effective motivation reconsidered: Toward a developmental model. *Human Development*, 1978, *21*, 34–64.

Kagan, J., and Moss, H. A. *Birth to maturity*. New York: Wiley, 1962.

Karoly, P. & Steffen, J. J. (Eds.). *The long-range effects of psychotherapy: Models of durable outcome*. New York: Gardner Press, 1980.

Kohlberg, L., LaCross, J., & Ricks, D. F. The predictability of adult mental health from childhood behavior. In B. Wolman (Ed.) *Manual of child psychopathology*. New York: McGraw-Hill, 1972.

Kübler-Ross, E. *On death and dying*. New York: Macmillan, 1969.

Levitt, E. E. & Lubin, B. *Depression*. New York: Springer, 1975.

Magnusson, D. & Endler, N. S. (Eds.). *Personality at the crossroads*. New York: Wiley-Erlbaum, 1977.

Mednick, S. A. & Witkin-Lanoil, G. Intervention in children at high risk for schizophrenia. In G. Albee & J. M. Joffe (Eds.), *Primary prevention of psychopathology: The issues*. Hanover, N.H.: University Press of New England, 1977.

Müller, P. J. *Privacy legislation and research: emerging data protection and social science need for access to data*. Paper prepared for Cologne conference on data protection laws, 1978.

National Commission for the Protection of Human Subjects in Biomedical and Behavioral Research. *Report and recommendations: research involving children.* Bethesda, MD: DHEW Publication No. (OS) 77-0004, 1977.

Ricks, D. F. Supershrink: Methods of a therapist judged successful on the basis of adult outcomes of adolescent patients. In D. F. Ricks, A. Thomas, and M. Roff, (Eds.). *Life History Research in Psychopathology* (Vol. 3). Minneapolis: University of Minnesota Press, 1974.

Ricks, D. F. A model for promoting competence and coping in adolescents and young adults. In L. A. Bond & J. C. Rosen (Eds.), *Competence and coping during adulthood.* Hanover, N. H.: University Press of New England, 1980.

Robins, L. N. *Deviant children grown up: A psychiatric and sociological study of deviant personality.* Baltimore: Willams & Wilkins, 1966.

Robins, L. N. Negro homicide victims – who will they be? *Transaction,* 1968, *5,* 15–19.

Rolf, J. & Hasazi, J. E. Identification of preschool children at risk and some guidelines for primary prevention. In G. Albee & J. M. Joffe (Eds.), *Primary prevention of psychopathology: the issues.* Hanover, N. H.: University Press of New England, 1977.

Runyan, W. M. The life course as a theological orientation: Sequences of person–situation interaction. *Journal of Personality,* 1978, *46,* 569–593.

Ryan, K. J. *Report and recommendations: Research involving children.* Bethesda, Md.: National Commission for the Protection of Human Subjects in Biomedical and Behavioral Research, 1977.

Ryan, W. *Blaming the victim.* New York: Vintage (rev. ed.), 1976.

Shakow, D. Segmental set. *Archives of General Psychiatry,* 1962, *6,* 1–17.

Stierlin, H. *Separating parents and adolescents.* New York: Quadrangle, 1974.

Teichner, V. J. *Working Paper for A.P.A. Conference on Confidentiality of Health Records,* November 1974.

Terman, L. M., and Oden, M. H. *The gifted group at mid-life.* Stanford: Stanford University Press, 1959.

Watt, N. F., Grubb, T. W., and Erlenmeyer-Kimling, L. Social, emotional, and intellectual behavior at school among children at high risk for schizophrenia. *Journal of Consulting and Clinical Psychology,* 1982, *50* (No. 2), 171–81.

Watt, N. F., Prentky, R. A., Levine, R. R. J., & Fryer, J. H. Prediction of outcome from childhood behavior and clinical picture at first hospital admission. In S. B. Sells, R. Crandall, J. S. Strauss, & W. Pollin (Eds.), *Human functioning in longitudinal perspective.* Baltimore: Williams & Wilkins, 1980.

Westin, A. F. *Computers, health records, and citizen rights.* Washington, D. C.: National Bureau of Standards, 1976.

Zubin, J. Comments on Schuckit, M. A., Holikas, J. A., Schuckit, J. J, McClure, J., and Rimmer, J. Drug use and psychiatric problems on the campus: I. Methods and drug use at outset. In D. F. Ricks, A. Thomas, and M. Roff, (Eds.), *Life History Research in Psychopathology* (Vol. 3). Minneapolis: University of Minnesota Press, 1974, 163–76.

Subject index

Name index